ACKNOWLEDGEMENTS

There are many people I have to thank for encouraging me to write this book over the years but my biggest encouragement has been my upstairs neighbour, Sharon Rodgers. She has on numerous occasions told me to 'just get it published'.

A huge thank you goes to her for just being there. I want to thank Val Basson, my neighbour in Clarens, for spending hours poring over my writing and giving feedback, thank you so much for your gracious ways of telling me to do another re-write. I need to also thank Arnie Bellini, a channel swimmer I crewed for, he insisted it was time to put this book into publication, thank you Arnie for the time we spent together in long conversations that got me going again.

Last but not least I wish to thank my husband Geoff for helping me to proof read the manuscript and encouraged me with loving words, thank you my darling for being there when I needed you most of all. I would also like to thank those people from the body of Christ who helped me through the tough times shortly after Peter's death. The Lee family who put up with me for months on end without so much as asking for anything in return. Ray Lowe and his wife Sue, and Pam and Peter Williams who came to my rescue when I was in dire need. To the Dihlabeng church in Clarens for standing with me through the most horrendous year of my life, when I had not a farthing to my name and without whom I would never of had the time to put pen to paper to write this book. Thank you all from the bottom of my heart, may God bless you all. There are so many pec  l be impossible to single th ows who they are and will ure.

GU00505620

First published in the UK by Gibson Publishing

Printed and bound by CMP (uk) Limited

In At The Deep End
Text copyright 2014 by Loretta Cox
Image copyright 2014 Loretta Cox

ISBN 9-780992-71-185-6

IN AT THE DEEP END

LORETTA COX

Gibson Publishing

This book is dedicated to the memory of my late husband
Peter Dickerson.

This is how I will always remember Peter. . .

CHAPTER ONE
The early years

I was born into a large family of seven children, I think Mum must have been drunk when she named us all, not that she drank, but the names she gave most of us where pretty unusual in those days. Today you get some pretty weird names, such as Death and Mischief, as I found out while out in Africa but by the standard of the day they were pretty way out. Starting with the eldest, my brother is a pretty plain Kenneth Frank. Not too bad you're thinking, then my elder sister who is Yvette Brenda, that's pretty so-so. Next is my elder sister Linda, who has the unfortunate middle, names of Naomi, Alberta, poor thing! She is followed by my Brother, Peter Brian, which is fine. Then it's my turn, Mum was heavily into film stars so I was named after Loretta Young and Ingrid Bergman, although it wasn't until my fifties that I found out I have all my life been spelling my name wrong. I remember my Mother telling me she had spelt it, I thought with one r and two t's when in fact it's the other way around, never mind as my Mum would say, worse things happen at sea! After me there was Theresa Louise, there is a seven year gap between myself and Theresa. Last but not least is my little sister, Elissa, Jaunita, pronounced Wanita, Mirriam, with a family name of Marchant that's an awful lot?

My Father was a Docker or Lighter-man, which meant he

unloaded and loaded barges and boats at the busy docks at Tilbury in Erith where we lived. We were a poor family, I remember all the hand me downs and sharing a bedroom with my two other sisters. The house we lived in was I assume once a grand Victorian house, with a below stairs and above stairs situation. The house was now split into three families, the Abbott's a couple in their 50's had the lower floor as you came in from the front door, their rooms where on either side of the hallway. We had the middle floor, which was huge by today's standards, having two massive bedrooms and a box room, a colossal kitchen and dining/living room; we shared a toilet on the middle floor with the family upstairs the Kenworthies. The Kenworthies were I thought an unruly family, especially the son Billy. Billy would hang around with my brother Ken; they would shoot pigeons and sparrows from the flat roof of the toilet and put them down in the basement or under the back step. Billy got a good beating for making Old man Abbott slip over one cold morning. He had put buckets and buckets of water over the back path ready to make an ice slide for him and my brother to skate on, but old man Abbott got there first and went head over heels, they really copped it when my Dad came home. My brother was no better, I remember clearly one day he was doing target practice down on the marshes with Linda, Peter and I. He owned an air rifle and commonly shot targets but in this instance he asked Linda to hold up a small piece of metal with the guarantee that if he hit her he would give everything that he had in his pocket to her. She knew he had just been paid, so she agreed. Ken hit the target but because of the position Linda was holding the piece of metal at the bullet ricocheted off and hit her on the cheek, Dad went ballistic.

My Mother and Father sent us to Sunday school ever since I could recall which I wasn't too enthusiastic about. It wasn't so much the going to church that was a dilemma, as much as the people that were there. Looking around the church one day during one of the laborious hymns, I looked at the swath of faces, they were like small Gold fish opening and closing their mouths. "Hypocrites" I thought. I knew many of them didn't live Godly lives throughout the week, did they if truth be told think about what they were singing? Were they just here to be seen I wondered. It wasn't long before I found another channel for Sunday mornings.

At first I skived off church and told my brothers and sisters not to say anything to my parents about not attending church but after a while I didn't worry if they found out the truth. I was having a ball, in my element, doing just the thing that really inspired me, not like those dreary hymns and sermons, where the Reverend spoke down at you. You sinner he would say; even now it makes me cower. Instead I went to Erith Athletic club every Sunday without fail. There didn't appear to be a coach but everyone was really helpful. My first pair of spikes was given to me by one of the athletes. The older members coached the younger and newer members. It was a place of experimentation and I find out that I enjoyed sport and was good in most areas. I tried everything but in particular was good at javelin, shot putt and longer endurance running events.

At school I was deliriously happy, during my first second and third years at school there were enormous amounts of physical education, hours in fact and the better sports person you were the more you were esteemed by your peers. When it came to homework I never did any, as my mother did not agree children should do more work at home. She was of the opinion that if there wasn't enough time during school hours then that was tuff. It was lovely for me, after school my time was my own. I never had a school uniform, with seven children in the family there was never enough money to manage to buy uniform. It was Mrs Ward my favourite teacher who provided my blue woollen dress which I wore every day due to the fact I didn't have a change of uniform. During my forth year at secondary school the dress became a problem and the lack of uniform, the headmistress called me into her office and told me "unless I had a uniform I could not compete in any teams or events for the school". I was devastated, as not only was I in the athletic team but the rounders, hockey and netball teams as well... Gee! I thought it's so unfair and what would my team mates think. I soon found a way around that, my friend Tina Harrison was in mainstream although she had a gammy leg, I had taught her to swim and dive so I guessed she owed me big time and asked if I could use her P.E. kit when we were competing against other schools. I was a bit of a rebel during my school years; I smoked JPS, walked on walls and swore, well when my parents were not around.

Linda Peter and I were always in trouble; well it seemed that way to me. One Saturday morning it was customary to go to the pictures, I had gone ahead of my brother who was to catch me up, he was going scrumping. He had spied a peach tree at the back of the jewellers shop and together with a friend was in the process of emptying the tree when the owner came out. I don't know how many of them there where but it was my brother Peter who got caught. Eventually the owner after keeping him in a back room at the jewellers and reading him the riot act let him go. I met him outside where he was sobbing his heart out and in a flat panic in case our parents found out what he had been up to.

On another occasion we were all together, my sister. brother and I and getting up to no good. We had climbed through a window of the Catholic Church toilet; let ourselves into the main hall which was under repairs. At the end of the hall a huge scaffold was erected, Peter and I climbed all over it like preverbal monkeys. We chased each other playing tag while my sister who was not in the least bit athletic watched from below. The door opened and one of the monks entered, I assume he had heard all the commotion. As it happened it was the same monk that walked to school with us most days as we often past the convent on the way to school. He just told us not to touch anything and leave when we were finished the same way as we had gotten in. We thought we had got away with it. We went back into the loo, where we had come in and my brother climbed back through the window first, Linda was second and got stuck halfway through. My brother was on the outside pulling and I was on the inside pushing. My Mother and Father were just passing at that precise moment on a bus and saw us coming out. Unfortunately for me my brother had spotted them and after getting Linda through the opening had run off. Because I came out feet first I didn't see the huge hand landing squarely on my backside and shouted an expletive to my very red faced parents waiting the other side. I had never before seen my Dad so angry. My feet hit the ground running when I realized who it was;

as usual it was bed with no tea.

I couldn't wait for my thirteenth birthday, as I could join my brother doing a paper round. I had one of the longer paper rounds, it paid more money than most and I just loved it, it would put me in good stead later when I worked for Royal Mail as a post lady. One day in the shop while preparing my round my brother told me he would distract the shop owner if I would take some sweets when he wasn't looking. It was almost a dare and I was always up for a dare, so when he wasn't looking I took some chocolate off the counter and put it in my paper sack. Outside we shared out the booty which kept us going through our rounds. At the end of the week the money I got I spent on cigarettes, a whole packet of JPS which lasted me all week. My Father found out I smoked and told me he didn't want me smoking in the streets but didn't mind at home. It was one of the few memories I have of my dad sitting late into the night smoking with him and watching football on TV.

During that year I was introduced to a bible group which consisted of mainly teenagers. They had a summer camp for girls which only cost thirteen pounds for three whole weeks. I thought even my parents can afford that; I was delighted when they said I could go. The furthest I had ever gone was the Isle of Sheppey during my parents annual holiday, it mainly consisted of beach and bingo and the club house. Not that I minded those things, but I was looking forward to camping and going to Dorset. How far away was Dorset? It seemed a million miles away and so intriguing. It was to be some of the happiest times of my life. Each night we would go into the marquee for songs and listen to stories about Jesus. It was my first encounter with God, awesome! On around the 4th day I gave my life to Jesus, at that time I didn't know what baptism was and I was never baptized. The camp left a real impression on me and I went home a changed person. So much so my brother Peter ribbed me all the time. "Little miss goody two shoes" he would say, "whose mummies pet then" and a whole lot more, it wasn't long before I fell back into my old ways. Whenever good occurs for the kingdom the devil isn't far away trying to steal our joy and sometimes he uses our family and friends to do his bidding. My brother was used in this exact way and it would rob me of my joy for many years to come. I turned my back on God just as the Jews did during their escape across the desert from Egypt and roamed the dessert for forty years because of their lack of faith. My faith hadn't time to grow; it was blown away at the first hurdle. The Jews didn't enter the land that was promised to them because they too had turned their back on their God and made false idols, I had my own idol, and it was sports.

At fifteen I was a string bean, all arms and legs and straight up and down. My breasts were non-existent and I felt happier in trousers and climbing trees, my brother Peter went on about my fried eggs, meaning my non-existent breasts, it wasn't very flattering. My sister Linda was so good looking, with her long hair as opposed to my tight cropped hair, her miniskirts as opposed to my tight trousers, which looped under my feet. Even the next door neighbour thought I was a son and not a daughter, until my mother put her right.

At fifteen I was able to leave school but wanted to stay on and study to become a PE teacher. My father would have none of it. I didn't know my father could be so cruel. He said "I've kept you for all these years, now it's your turn to go out and bring in some money. I'm not an endless pit". My mother took me to the labour exchange to get my first job. We entered a small office at the back of the building next to the public library, just down from the town hall. The lady across from us had curly hair and beady eyes. She turned and opened up the filing cabinet behind her after my mother explained it was my first job. As she lifted the card out of the file my mother said "She will take it". I was aghast, mum hadn't even heard what it was and already I was going to take it Beck & Politzer it said on the heading, what was that I thought? It turned out to be a packing company, who packed mainly brown sugar for Tesco's but sometimes did cherries in season.

I didn't mind the work and soon made friends with the girls there. It was on a good day, a mad house with Elvis Presley blaring out, but on a bad day it was a frenzy of activity. We were paid according to our output, peace work they called it and most weeks I cleared thirteen pounds, it was at the time a really good wage. My mother took a third for housekeeping and the rest was mine.

I had money and felt really grown up. My friend Mary who was a traveller decided during my first week how I would spend my new income. She said we should go to London and get some new clothes, which sounded very grown up and I agreed. I bought my very first dress there. On the way home in the rush hour of the tube I had my purse lifted. A man bumped me and as I looked into my open basket that was all the rage in those days, my purse had gone. I just saw the back of him going into the carriage to my left. The platform was heaving and we had a struggle to even get on the train. Mary was disgusted and shouted down the carriage, "whoever stole my friend's purse, I hope you rot in hell". I was mortified and cried most of the way home, my very first wage packet had gone and I hadn't even paid my mum yet, what would she say?

My time at Beck and Politzer was short lived and I was made redundant, I hadn't a clue what that meant but it was explained to me that it was last in first out and I had to go.

My next job was at Braziers, a small company out on the mashes, it made soldering irons and was full of young mechanical engineers. "Yippee" I thought, all those lads. It wasn't long before I felt eyes boring into me as I worked one day. Jake was seven years my senior, handsome and exciting all at the same time. I would catch him watching me most of the time, it made me go weak and hot, and before I knew it he was taking me out for a date. I was 15 going on 16 and it felt wonderful. We spent alternate nights between his parent's house and my parent's house as we didn't have any money after putting it all away in savings. Jake wanted us to buy a house and for that we had to save for a deposit.

We found a small end terrace house in Sidcup with two bedrooms and the largest kitchen I have ever seen. The garden was over ninety feet long and it had a garden shed which was massive. We bought the house and began getting the furniture on the run up to our wedding.

I remember his mother Mandy, she was so house-proud. One day I came down stairs and Mandy was standing at the foot of the stairs waiting to pass. I stood on the wooden flooring peeping between the runners. "What do you think you are doing standing on my floor"? I thought she was joking, so promptly stood on the carpet and then on the polished floor again laughing, she wasn't amused and I ended up doing penance with her ironing.

His Mother Mandy McKinnon was so house-proud, I should have realized like mother like son, forget the father, he was mild and meek compared to Mandy. I should have taken the heed that was given just days before I got married, a colleague at work told me "If you marry a man and don't change the letter you're married for worse and not for better". My maiden name was Marchant and his McKinnon and yes he was as house proud as his mother, if not worse. Jake sat opposite me and my sister across from me, perched on the edge of our cottage suite. We had just finished a cup of coffee and woe is me! I placed my cup on top of the fire and not on a place mat and shouldn't I have taken it out to the kitchen and washed it up and heaven forbid if I told a rude joke, that was for men only and I shouldn't be so crude it wasn't becoming.

Our sex life was mediocre too, just to add insult to injury. We didn't have a sexual relationship before we got married and it just felt gross to me, wham bam thank you mam. I wasn't mature enough at the time to speak to Jake about how I felt but kept it inside. The other thing that really annoyed me was his lists. He would list all the chores that needed doing; a Saturday morning would go something like this

Do washing at the launderette.

Do shopping

Lunch

Wash floor in kitchen

Wash windows

Mow lawn

Dinner

Jake wouldn't do any of this himself, he just dropped me off at the launderette and picked me up when I had finished, accompany me while I shopped, and I made lunch and washed and mowed. All this time he tinkered with cars of his friends on the front drive and then never even charged them for all the hours of labour he had put in. I just didn't get it at all, where was the love and companionship I longed for. In Ephesians 5v25 it says: Husbands, love your wives, just as Christ loves the church and gave himself up for her. The lack of love and Godly direction from my husband made me feel more like a maid than a wife.

It was during a holiday that I think I reached the final straw. We had gone away with Jake's Brother and his wife to a caravan; I don't remember the name of the place but just remember the weather was terrible. It was so bad that during that week Ted Heath, the prime minister at that time was almost grounded during a storm in his yacht just off the beach where we were staying. The rain lashed down and the wind was something else.

We amused ourselves the best we could but soon got bored. We decided to go out for the day, even though it was raining and went to Christ church, during the visit Jake bought a game of scrabble using up most of the meagre money we had left. On the way home he looked at me scowling and asked "was I going to say thank you or not?" I hadn't intended to thank him as I thought the game was for everyone and just looked at him blankly. With that he just lashed out with his left arm, his fist hitting me in the face, his brother Simon was too dumb struck to say anything in my defence and his wife Sue just sat with her mouth open. Jake opened the window and threw the scrabble out, he stopped the car about a mile down the road and pushed me out shouting "If you don't find it, don't come back". I promised myself while walking back for the scrabble that no man would ever hit me again.

It was about that time I met a guy at work, his name was Mark, he was a sales rep and in charge of the exhibition of cookers and fires that now stood in the centre of the shopping mall I had been sent to. My job at that time was for British Gas and I normally worked out of Orpington the headquarters for British Gas in the area. I had started there when Jake's mum Mandy had started, she worked in the canteen doing lunches. My first job was on the switch board answering customer queries which I did for about nine months and then switched to the operations side of things. One day my area manager wanted me to go and help out the sales team at an exhibition. My job was to sign up people for service contracts on their water heaters and central heating. I first set eyes on Mark when he came to talk to one of the representatives, Norman Toply, I thought he was wonderful, he paid me attention and complimented me on my appearance, said I had wonderful hair. It wasn't long before I started to compare Mark to Jake. Mark was tall and dark and very intellectual, Jake was short, broad and good with his hands. Mark paid me compliments while Jake barked orders. Every day Mark would ask me out and every day I would say no, until eventually I gave in and had lunch with him. I hadn't done anything wrong and we enjoyed each other's company so I thought it all right but never mentioned it to my husband mainly because I knew I had feelings that were not altogether right for Mark.

One morning I sat up in bed and just told Jake flat "I want to leave you, please take me home". He cried, I cried but it made no difference, I had just had enough and wanted to be on my own. I guess looking back I was naïve, looking for something that Jake couldn't be and I must have driven him up the wall. Not that I was untidy, I liked a home to be lived in and not a show house. He gave me a lift to my parent's house in silence, dropping me outside, he even came inside and told my parents what I had decided and then drove away. I didn't feel anything but numb as I climbed the stairs to go to bed that night, I just knew it had ended and it was final.

It wasn't long before Mark got wind that I had left Jake; we started to go out together. We got a rented house together in Barnhurst just behind the ambulance station. Time went quickly and we moved house using Mark's connections to a new estate in Swanley. Swanley was an up and coming town and the house was in a small cul-de-sac, very quiet and better than I had ever dreamed of. We were married in 1980 at a registry office in Sidcup. I continued to work for British Gas until they nationalized it in 1982. I counted myself very fortunate as I had been offered a redundancy payment while being pregnant. I was at the time the youngest showroom manager at 24 years old and had been manager for two years. Two years which had flown past, I was very successful and enjoyed my job and colleagues very much.

The showroom was in the high street in Sidcup, situated on the corner of the High Street and another street. It was a small shop, with a store room at the back and a staff rest room upstairs. Everything I had learnt about the shop was from an elderly man in his late 60's called Jack. When I first started work there being much younger than Jack he could have given me such a hard time, but instead he was a real gentleman. He helping where ever he could and soon we were the best of friends. After I was made redundant I gave birth to Emma our first child. Those were fun years of building home, marriage and children.

The house was a constant joy and I was very content there. We had wonderful neighbours, who I got to know before Emma came on the scene as my redundancy came through in the May of 1982 and Emma was born in the September. At the back of the house the garden overlapped the side of a house owned by Joanna and her husband John, I was to become really good friends with Jo, we spent hours chatting over the back fence and passing never ending cups of coffee over the fence.

It was during a party for Emma's second birthday that I went into labour with our second child Phillip. The house had been ringing to the shouts and laughter of over a dozen children when I felt the first pangs of labour and by the time all the children had gone home and I had put Emma to bed the contractions had gone from mild to moderate. I thought I'm not going to rush to the hospital and be left for hours as had happened with Emma, no I would wait until the contractions were at least three minutes apart and then I would pick up my bag, now neatly packed and ready and find my way to the hospital. So I needed a distraction and my friend over the road would be the very thing. Picking up keys in between contractions we found ourselves outside her front door. She was very surprised to see me and soon realized I was in labour, a very exciting time. We sat in her kitchen having tea as if nothing at all were happening, only the watch now in her hands reading off the contractions gave it away, we were going to have a baby. By the time they were three minutes apart my husband couldn't wait to get on the road. I find men are nervous and cannot wait to hand over responsibility, they fear that mums will just pop out their babies as soon as the car gets rolling. I wish! It was to take 23 hours of labour before Phillip made an entrance, on the evening of the 30th of September 1984

By now my husband had risen from Rep to Sales manager and eventually made Area Manager. Things at home were a constant round of nappies and feeding but Phillip was a good baby and fell into a routine quickly. After two years plus at home I was ready to go back to work but could only manage night shifts as the children were full on during the day. I found a job at Asda supermarket where my friend Ann from around the corner worked filling shelves over night while the store was closed. It worked quite well, I would work through the night over the weekend and then while I slept for a few hours my husband would look after the children until I woke up. I had noticed now that my husband Mark was transferred to the Surrey Area he was getting home later and later.

CHAPTER TWO
Matthew 11:28
Come to me, all you who are weary and burdened,
And I will give you rest.

Marriage collapse

By the time Phillip was two we had moved to another cul-de-sac on the same estate only to a detached house with three large bedrooms and a landscaped garden. I was extremely happy and thought everything was just peachy. Mark came home from work one evening and told me we were going on holiday with my old friend from British Gas to Portugal. We had become friends as we were both managers of showrooms together and Tina often asked me for advice about running her showroom which was at Orpington High Street. We would often call in there and have a cup of tea while shopping, she had at one time been a manager under my husband and I had become close to her and her husband.

During the run up to the holiday, which we planned to share with another two other couples, who were God parents to our children, we were having dinner at Tina's house and discussing plans for the upcoming holiday. My napkin fell to the floor as we were just sat chatting, we had finally finished eating but I had forgotten about my napkin. As I bent down under the table I almost bumped my head, I glanced at my husbands hand up Tina's dress opposite. I sat bolt upright not daring to breath as my mind took in the immensity of what I had just witnessed. Had I been dreaming, I wasn't sure, so I dropped my napkin again and repeated everything just as before. Now I was positive, He really did have his hand up her skirt. I demanded we leave, only to be rebuked by Tina who said it was too early to go and we hadn't had coffee.

When we stepped out of the front door with the two children, one in Mark's arms and one in mine, I just couldn't wait to get to the car and ask Mark what the hell he thought he was doing. I think if I had been a volcano I would have erupted at that point but all he could say was he must have had too much to drink and didn't know what he was doing. We drove home in silence and I put the children to bed and climbed into bed myself giving Mark the cold shoulder.

The holiday to Portugal arrived; we were sharing a villa in the Algarve with Sue and Alan, long time friends from Greenwich. Alan had worked with Mark when he was a rep in London and he and his wife were Godparents to Emma and Phillip. Sues Uncle Ron was also with us along with another couple who we both knew from our days in British Gas. The couple had travelled down and arrived before us and were sat beside the pool soaking up the sun. As the car pulled in finally reaching our sunshine destination we hopped out of the car and hugged David and his wife eagerly. After all the introductions had been made the unpacking began only to be interrupted by screams from outside. Emma had snuck away while I was unpacking and just jumped in at the deep end of the pool fully clothed and unable to swim. Luckily David was still sat at the pool and was busy fishing Emma out who seemed none the worse for wear. That made up my mind I was going to teach Emma during that holiday to swim.

The next morning as I was walking around the outside of the villa to the car I almost was knocked over by Tina's husband coming the other way. Catching his breath he exclaimed "I would have knocked your husband's head off last night if it hadn't been for the fact you were here". He didn't say anymore or explain his motives but rushed off again. I had a good idea what he was getting at but chose to ignore the remark. Soon it was evident to everyone what was going on, every time I got up to see to the children Tina would immediately sit in my place. She was all dewy eyed at my husband. At one point we were altogether sat at a beach café and the children wanted me to play sand castles with them. I got up to leave and was replaced by the ever present Tina. I just sat on the beach with tears rolling down my cheeks unable to react. Alan came and found me and told me not to leave them alone and he would play with the children while I went back to the table.

If it hadn't been for the fact that the children were on my passport I would have cheerfully left him to it and gone home again. It was torture watching his affair before my very eyes and with her husband there also. I was glad to get back home and put it all behind me. By September I had discovered condoms in his jacket. Ann had come over for our daily ritual of coffee and discovered me crying. She phoned Jo who also came over and together we went through all Mark's belongings. It was Ann who came up trumps with the condoms, which I knew were not mine as we didn't use that form of contraceptive. When Mark came home I confronted him with the evidence but he made an excuse, which I can't for the life of me remember now but not wanting to face up to things I put it behind me.

It was several months later that things became clearer, not that they needed to be any clearer but I just didn't know what to do about it all. Having Emma and Phillip put a whole new spin on things, I just couldn't up and leave. Ann had asked me over for dinner with her and her new boyfriend as she had divorced the previous year, she was now going out with a rep from British Gas who she had met through her work as an estate manager. Her boyfriend's name was Ron and over dinner the conversation had got onto my problem. Ron knew my husband and told me he was having a fling with another showroom manager called Tina and I could find them any night of the week in a pub in St Mary Cray. I was shocked to say the least but a plan formed in my mind to catch the two of them red handed. I knew my husband well and knew he wouldn't be able to keep his hands off of Tina even in public.

About a month had gone by since the conversation with Ann's boyfriend and my opportunity came one evening while I was preparing dinner. Mark's Mother Daisy was staying with us and sharing a room with my children. She had the bottom bunk bed while Emma and Phillip shared the top bunk bed. Daisy had a drink problem and would far sooner drink than eat. She had been unwell for some time and had had her breasts removed having had cancer. Because she was so frail she often came to stay with us for months at a time. This was such an occasion but that evening she was running low on alcohol and asked me would I be a dear and go buy her some more. I saw my opportunity and went out in the car. I intended instead to spy on my husband and Tina.

I got to the pub around 6.30 when I knew they should have been there for some time, but my timing was off and I had arrived early or had been spotted, I wasn't sure which. Now I was in a flat spin, worried about the time I had taken to get back with the spirits for his mum and the suspicion it would arouse. Just as I was going down sandy lane in the dark I must have hit a brick in the road and got a puncture, as if I wasn't late enough already. Thinking what to do next I saw a house just down a bit from where I was parked and knocked to get help. The man there was sympathetic to my plight and helped me get the tire changed. It had begun raining and just as we got the tire back on I saw my husband's car hurtling towards me down the lane. I huddled over the car hoping he wouldn't see me. Getting in the car I made my way to an off license where I bought a bottle of gin and sped off for home. It wasn't until I got to the underpass that I realized I had been spotted, my husband was parked up under the bridge and saw the car go by.

The game was up and I could no longer put off what was to come. The house rang with voices arguing including his mother who defended her son and said he would never do any such thing and how would I ever find anyone like him again. He was a good husband and father. Little did she know what had been going on all those years while I was at home? On one occasion I had phoned his work and asked to be put through to my husband Mr Mark Riscombe-Burton, the operator asked how I enjoyed the party the evening before and as I was by now separated I asked her what she meant. She said you are a gas showroom manager and I said I had been a showroom manager. It appeared that Mark had introduced Tina as Mrs Riscombe-Burton. I was dumbfounded and furious and hurt all at the same time.

It was around this time that I changed jobs; I began working for the post office as a post lady which worked well as I could be home in the afternoons before the children got home from school. I received three times what I had previously earned working at Asda and was keeping fit too. My round was one of the longest and was at least a mile away from the office which I cycled there and back twice a day. I loved being a post lady, working outside and meeting loads of people. I liked my boss whose name was Hue Richards and shortly after joining Royal Mail it was apparent he liked me too. He would help me sort the mail when I worked overtime and would come out onto my round and check I was ok. It wasn't long before we were dating although we kept it a secret from the rest of the office.

Hue was married and living in Aylesford with his wife. You possibly know how the story goes, he wasn't getting on with his wife and he was about to split up with her but it never quite happened. I would meet Hue once a week down in his home town. I was heavily into running at that time and already one of the up and coming stars of the county. I had done the London Marathon three times and was Sevenoaks district triathlon champion for three years on the trot. I would alternate my training nights with two nights at club and one night running with Hue near his home.

Eventually Hue did get a divorce and moved to a single's house on a new estate close to where I lived. He would never make the move to come and live with me but instead came to the house maybe four nights out of the seven and stayed. Our lives evolved around work, running and later football refereeing. Hue belonged to Dartford referees association and after watching all his matches for a season he said I should at least learn the laws of the game so I understood what it was I was watching. After taking classes at the association I found I truly enjoyed it and wanted to referee myself.

I didn't want to do school children's football, although I did do some matches for them on a Sunday and I didn't want to do Ladies matches, as they were at the time technically inferior, although today the girls play a great game. At that time ladies football was in its infancy. Instead I set my sights on men's football. I refereed at district level and lined on the league above which was county level. I was regarded as an oddity by the men until they realized I knew what I was doing and in the process sent a couple of the men off who wanted to make their point. I travelled long distances to get to games going down to Dover and Hythe and other places in between, watching Hue scale the ladder of refereeing. It was mad but happy times. After watching Hue's match I would wait long periods while he got changed and then we had after match drinks and I was always invited into the board room which was exciting.

As Hue moved up the scale he was lining on the football league which meant we went to all the London clubs, Spurs, Arsenal and QPR. When we went to Arsenal we took my son Phillip with us as he was a huge Arsenal fan. He got to meet all the players and had signed balls and things. I remember watching Phillip with his nose pressed up against the trophy cabinet in the halls of Arsenal he just loved going to the matches with us.

Hue had always wanted to run a marathon and we decided that his first marathon would be the London marathon as that is the highlight of all marathon running, that's of course assuming we got an entry into the race. One morning while I was sorting the mail I came across the envelope which I knew contained the rejection or acceptance into the race and took it directly to Hue who was in his office with his head in paperwork. Hue gingerly opened the envelope and all at once was beaming from ear to ear, he had been accepted. It was to be another two full days before I got my acceptance. Now the training started in earnest with half marathons booked whenever possible to help build us for the marathon.

The big day arrived and I was quite nervous for him as we entered Greenwich Royal Park. There were thousands of people and the air was thick with camphor oil which the competitors rubbed onto their legs to warm them up before running. Everywhere you looked there were people in funny costumes which ranged from the sublime to the ridiculous. We made all the pre-race rituals and stood together with the thousands in each pen waiting for the off. Although sunny it was still chilly and we had brought black bin bags to wear over our kits to ward off the cold.

I was that year supposed to run with the elite women but such was my love for Hue I wanted to show my support for him and be there to encourage him when he no doubt would go through tough times during the race. We decided to wear our referee's kits which were black and would keep us warm during the race as they would absorb the sun. My heart was pumping and the adrenaline was coursing round my body, I knew Hue must have been feeling the same as we anxiously waited for the gun to go off and the mass of human bodies to move as one.

The crowds surged forward in anticipation of the gun and then we were off. Slow at first but soon got in our stride. I always find the first five or six miles hard and try to get in a rhythm and get my breathing right. I told Hue to move to the outside of the pack, almost in the gutter as fewer people ran in this area. At the drinks stations we were alert to the fact that runners in their haste to get rehydrated would often cross in front of you and there was always the danger they may trip us up, so I told Hue to be alert at those times.

We were running well until around the fourteen mile mark when Hue suffered stomach cramps. So we walked for a bit, I guess for a first timer he was doing well and a race of this calibre isn't without its difficulties. Eventually Hue found his pace again and we continued to make progress.

Just as we were about to cross Tower Bridge I spotted one of the commentators at the side of the road who just happened to be a sports commentator, a former footballer. Seeing the connection with our refereeing garb I approached him and said we were scoring one for referees by wearing our kits. I don't know if it ever went on air. We also passed some boys standing on a traffic island in the middle of the isle of dogs. I recognized some of them from a match I had refereed the week prior which was a miracle in the midst of thousands upon thousands of people. We waved as we passed and they recognized me as well and started to clap hard.

The route of the London marathon is like no other, steeped in history with many places of interest which is why so many tourists' runners want to do the London. It takes in the museums in Greenwich and passes the Cuttysark as it makes its way onto the south bank of London. Then it crosses Tower Bridge before winding through docklands and onto the embankment. It passes up the Mall to Buckingham Palace before turning onto Westminster Bridge and passing Big Ben where it concludes. Running down the Mall we knew we were not far from finishing and put all our efforts in the last bid to gain some precious time but the elation I felt at seeing the finishing line was just awesome. Hue and I crossed the line hand in hand, jubilant at our achievement. We filed down the tunnels at the finish to receive our well-earned medals.

It wasn't until I got to one of the tents with our clothes that we had collected from the busses now parked along the embankment that I realized how stiff I was becoming. I had slid down the side of a tent to sit on the floor to put on my trousers and realized I was unable to get up again. Hue played the gentleman and reached out for my hand guiding me to my feet once more. We walked to the rail station in silence still trying to grasp the magnitude of the day's events before returning home again.

There were many attributes to Hue that I really liked, he was spontaneous and romantic, the things we did together were exciting such as the cruise we went on to Greece. I had been struggling with my divorce, Mark and I shared the custody of Emma and Phillip although they lived with me they saw their dad frequently. He had given me the house in Dahlia Drive which should have fetched enough money once it was sold to allow me to buy a small house for me and the children and the au pair. Having an au pair was a blessing and a curse, firstly they were good company and gave the children an insight to other cultures, and they did light house work which gave me more time when I came home for the children. They were also a curse as at least one third of my income went to pay for them but on the whole I had been blessed with really good au-pair's who truly loved the children. It also meant Emma and Phillip had to share a bedroom together which for the moment wasn't an issue. At ten the law said they needed their own rooms which I agree with and by then they would be much older and things I hoped would be better. For the moment we just ticked over. I had agreed to sell the house as soon as the divorce went through but I hadn't realized that the Channel Tunnel would be coming out of the ground not more than two hundred yards from my front door and the impact that would have on the price.

When I first put the house up for sale there had been no mention of the plans to build the Channel tunnel rail link into London, but now it was a real thorn in my side. I watched as the house prices plummeted and realized I would have no equity when at last I found a buyer. I even went back to the courts and asked if I could remain in the property and not sell it. The court said I had made an agreement with my husband and I would have to honour it. Eventually just as I had predicted the house was sold with zero equity and the children and I moved into a council house in Westerham.

When I first set eyes on the property I wept, it was so different from what I had been used to. I was looking at a 1960's house with three bedrooms that were tiny and a small kitchen and living room. There was no dining room and the grass in the back and front gardens came up to my shoulders. At the back of the house the garden went down to a car park where often old cars were burnt out and dumped. Well this was my bed and I had to lie in it I thought! I moved into the house in January 1990, it had been a particularly cold winter and the house seemed bleak but it was in one of the more pleasant area's looking at the up side, although it was nearly thirty kilometres from work and would be a really early morning start for me as I still worked for Royal mail six days a week. I would need to get up at three in the morning if I was to make the five o clock start on time.

Emma and Phillip started school in a little village school which was a real blessing. For the most part they had taken the changes well, although Emma didn't get on too well with Hue, they would often ague. Phillip on the other hand treated Hue as if he were his own dad and would play with him when he got home from school. We had a huge bonfire party in the back garden that October. I had gotten to know a family who lived across the road through Emma and Phillip who played with their children.

They were a lovely family and I am still friends with them today, I found them to be both loyal and compassionate. Pat and Paul Holroyd had three children. The eldest child was James followed by Laura and Sam the youngest. They were a mad family but so kind, you couldn't help but like them. I would often go across the road to Pat and we would talk about the world and his wife for hours, when I was down I knew I could rely on Pat for a shoulder to cry on. We started a business together working for Amway but that soon folded. It was about this time when my Mother passed away.

My Father had died from emphysema following an accident he had while at work. He was with a group of young lads mixing chemicals in one of those tanks that you put your hands into gloves and mixed the chemicals inside. What he didn't know was the tank had not been maintained and during the time they had spent in the room the tank had leaked toxic waste into the room. All the guys were taken to hospital but my dad being the eldest took the brunt of it. He was in hospital for nearly ten days. At first it was touch and go if he would make it all right but they allowed him home as he improved. It left him with emphysema which is a degenerating debilitating illness leading eventually to death.

My mother on the other hand had always suffered from diabetes which is also a debilitating illness which affects all parts of the body especially the heart. She had suffered with heart problems for years and told my brothers and sisters and I that now dad had passed away she was realizing new freedoms. One of her new found freedoms was that she enjoyed traveling and had just received an invitation to go to Germany to see some old friends and really wanted to go but her doctor had told her she should have a triple bye pass before that could happen. So she told us that was the reason she was going for surgery. It wasn't until after her death that we found a letter explaining to my Aunt Bee that if she didn't have the surgery she would die anyway.

Mum was taken into hospital and they operated on her doing the bye pass surgery that she so evidently needed. I am one of seven children; at times the hospital waiting room resembled a sardine can. Mum was sat up in bed when I saw her after her operation; she was talking to my sisters. She was in ICU for the moment until they could move her to a ward when she was more stable. I gave her a huge hug, well the best I could give her at that time as she was still very sore after the hours of surgery. During the operation they had spread her ribs and she had an incision from her belly button to the top of her breast bone. She was laughing and making jokes, it was so good to see her making progress, and I could not have imagined what was to come.

Later that week we were called in to the surgeons office where he said he was about to wean mum off the equipment that was keeping her alive. Her lungs, heart and kidneys were all being supported but she was doing so well they thought it was time to take away her life support systems. Two days later in that same office the news was grim, circulation to her legs was not sufficient and they were thinking of amputating her legs. For my mother this would have been devastating news, her own mother had gone through amputation and was never the same again after her operation and now my mum was facing the same dilemma. Mum was very depressed; somehow she had lost all the previous days bounce. Two days later I received the phone call I most dreaded, Mum had not responded to the machines being turned off that were sustaining her life. They had taken them off and now had to put them all back on until the family decided what to do. It was explained that Mum would either live as a vegetable or we could switch off the life support. My brothers and sisters and I all sat in the waiting room. Each one had taken turns in saying goodbye to my mother, it was a horrendous choice to make but it could not be put off. We deliberated and realized that Mum would not want to live life in the way that had been described and we decided to turn off the life support. It was the hardest decision I have ever had to make in my life but deep down I knew it was the right choice.

I quietly crept into the ICU and sat next to my Mum, her head was swathed in a towel and tin foil to keep the heat in her frail body. Gone was the laughter of just days before. I sat in silence holding her hand as they switched off the machine. My best friend had died and I thought the earth would fold in around me; I was totally and utterly numb.

We buried Mum in a cemetery in Northumberland heath not far from the family home. It was a wet day and that's just how I felt inside, dark and foreboding. Mum was buried just next to my Father who had died just the year before; it was as if an old wound had just been opened up again.

In the February of that year I was diagnosed as having cancer in the tissue behind the womb. I still had private medical cover through Royal Mail and was able to go to their hospital which was near Lamberhurst in the heart of Kent. The hospital was more like a five star hotel. It had silver service dinners in a dining room when I first went there for some tests. After getting the confirmation from Harley Street in London that the diagnosis was correct I was again admitted to the hospital. I underwent surgery to remove my womb and the tissue that surrounded it. The stay was to be ten days but after just five I felt like a million dollars. It was Easter time and the wards had emptied due to the holidays and I practically had the ward to myself. As soon as they took out the stitches and I was able to get out of bed and walk I decided to sign myself out. The doctors agreed with me I was making really good progress and as long as I didn't lift anything I could go home.

I had just had a new au pair arrive she was Spanish, she had arrived a few weeks prior to my operation and now it would fall to her to look after the house while I was making a full recovery. I think in all honesty she should never have come to the UK under the conditions that she had left her family. Her Father, just before she came over had fallen from a tractor and severed his leg. Her thoughts and mind were understandably not on the job at hand. During a visit from Sue and Alan, long-time friends, it was clear things were not right with her. We had been out for the day and I had just got coffee for Sue and Alan and shouted up the stairs to see if she would like a cup as well. The reply was slamming of doors and thumping around in her room. It was totally uncalled for and out of character for her. It was also crystal clear by the end of the day that she wanted to go home to be with her family, which is exactly what did happen later that week. So I was left to get on with it even though I wasn't supposed to lift anything for at least six weeks. I just carried on as normal and I felt really good. About a week later after seeing my doctor I was allowed to drive, even though it was weeks before I should have been able to, a further week saw me back at work. It was quite a miraculous recovery by any standard of the imagination. Those eighteen months were the worst I think anyone could have endured, I had lost my husband, my home, my Father and Mother and had cancer myself just for good measure. It was a miracle I got through everything with my sanity intact, looking back I know God was there too, walking right beside me and I'm now positive that was the reason for my speedy recovery.

From when I first made a commitment to God, when I was thirteen at a summer camp, even though I had turned my back on God he hadn't left my side. He was there through all my bad decisions, he was there and held me through my divorce and my parent's deaths and he was there during my episode with cancer.

CHAPTER THREE
The tour of the UK and Scotland

I was out doing my rounds as a post lady one Friday morning and had just come to the end and was heading back to the office a mile away. It was a hard cycle back to the office, mainly up hill and I was running later than normal. The coats they issued were made for men and on my slim frame came to well below my bottom. As I came to the T junction and had my foot almost to the ground the bike was still in forward motion and I put on the brakes to adjust my speed, the coat caught behind the saddle and slammed the saddle into my spine. It must have caught me in the most delicate part of my spine and the impact left me unable to walk properly. I hobbled back to the office in server pain and was sent home, before long it was obvious that I had done a lot of damage. It took ten days in traction and an operation under aesthetic before I could walk normally again. After about a month I started work again, the doctor told me I would never run again as the impact of constantly pounding as I ran would leave me an invalid if I were to resume.

This was a major blow to me; running was such a great part of my life, it made me feel free from the routine of life. I had once been a size sixteen but over the years running I had gone from a sixteen to a size twelve and had lots of confidence in my new size.

It was as if I had rediscovered myself and now it would disappear. For over a year I battled with the lack of exercise and the feeling of failure and gloom which now pervaded my whole attitude, I was getting fatter and becoming depressed.

One morning, feeling sorry for myself and having my very own pity party I decided to go visit the Doctors and ask if it was as bad as the previous doctor had made it out to be. The doctor's surgery was up in the High Street, I had been off work sick and just dropped Emma and Phillip at school. I decided to walk through to his surgery and pose the questions to him. If only I could run again it would make all the difference to how I was now feeling. The doctor was very gracious and listened as I whined on about my condition and was it possible I might be able to run once more. He examined me and looked at the x-rays of my injury and sat for a while deliberating. The answer was just as before but he did say I could swim. Swimming he said was really good for me and it was weight bearing and would put no pressure on my back. I left feeling very depressed but as I walked home thinking about my situation and putting my running career behind me I was forced to think about what he had suggested.

At first I remembered seeing a figure of a boy not much older than sixteen stood on a beach at Dover covered in grease. He was a Channel swimmer and at the time I thought how wonderful it would be to swim the English Channel. My mind raced as I walked along. I didn't know what would be involved if I did decide to attempt the swim or even if it was possible but I knew I had a good foundation with the triathlons and marathon background I had. Most of my sporting achievements had been set against an endurance background so I knew I would be in with a fighting chance. By the time I got home I had made up my mind I would give Channel swimming the best shot I had. The thought was daring and almost preposterous at the time, I considered what my family and Hue would say but the idea was just growing and growing in my mind.

The first order of the day was to see if there was such a thing as a Channel Swimming Association at least that would be a place to start from. When I arrived home I got to work on the phone, fishing for a lead on how I should start. I rang Hue to tell him my bright idea, I didn't think he would pour oil on my thoughts, I found him to be supportive even though he was a little bit doubtful I would ever get started. The operator connected me to the Chairman of the Channel Swimming Association, his name was Mike Oram, he lived at Folkstone, and he was later to be my pilot during my swim. Mike was polite and listened as I poured over my background, I didn't wish to be put off at the first hurdle. He asked where I lived geographically, I suppose to see if it was feasible for me to get in the necessary practice, when I said I lived in Westerham he sounded surprised and exclaimed that Alison Streeter the current world record holder lived in the next village, I should contact her for directions for my training.

I was delighted with my phone effort, and the results from the phone calls. By the time Hue came to the house that night I was bursting with news and couldn't wait to tell him all that had happened since our conversation earlier that morning. Not only had I found the Chairman and spoken to him but I had also got a complete training schedule from Alison and what's more it was all feasible.

The following week when Hue had time to think, he thought perhaps Royal Mail might sponsor my swim and started phoning around on my behalf. The director asked Hue outright if he thought I had a realistic shot at completing the swim and Hue was emphatic that I had just the background to achieve the objective. With that the Director agreed and said he would make sure I got all the support I needed.

The next week I had secured a pool to swim in at a local school for disabled children. It wasn't the ideal place to train for Channel swimming as it was only sixteen meters long and was really hot for the disabled children who normally would use it. But it was free and I was given a key which enabled me to could come and go as I pleased.

The sensation of swimming in an empty pool has always inspired me, when the sun streamed through the windows of the pool it was impossible to keep me away. Alison had given me the task of swimming sixteen sets of six repeated lengths. I must admit the first set I ever did was painful and I struggled to get my breath after even the first two. So for all you budding swimmers out there it's not impossible to dream or to achieve, it just takes the first step and you quickly build on that. After the first month I felt much better and already could see the progress I was making. Alison suggested that I joined the swimming club at Reigate where she and other Channel Swimmers trained on Tuesday and Thursday nights. It was from eight thirty till ten and wouldn't interfere with the children as they would be going to bed and the au pair was there to watch over them. So I began training at the swimming club, fortunately all the fees were covered by royal mail which was a huge blessing to me

Royal Mail was just gearing up to be the sole sponsor of both the Para Olympians and the Olympic athletes and I was to become a part of that as well. The director who had agreed to back me was heading up the project and had hand chosen people from around the regions to work with the Olympic association in raising money and awareness of the coalition between Royal Mail and the athletes and Olympic Association. It was my dream job. I was co-opted into the project to work alongside Julie who was later to become my first aider during the majority of my swims but for the moment was my boss. Soon Julie was taken off the project to head up the first aid department in competitions nationally. She would look in from time to time to see if things were going well but I was mainly on my own.

I had been given a blank canvas and had a meagre budget to achieve my goals but God had given me a huge imagination which I used with vigour. My designated role was also to include Postman Pat visits to schools and fetes etc. along with all recycling projects within my region as well as raising awareness and money for the Olympics. The latter was what kept me up late into the night dreaming of what could be done and how I would go about such a task.

The main money raised would come from my channel swim and the sponsorship but I wasn't swimming until August and it was only December, how was I to continue training and fit in all the work. The idea came to me one afternoon. I thought to help with training I had to push myself as I had done when I was a runner. When I had been running I would do smaller events which helped reach the overall objective and acted as a build up to the larger event. With this in mind I was thinking where I could swim in the UK which would involve the media and prick the imagination of the nation, part of my awareness I had to achieve for Royal Mail. I was thinking about this very question when a P.C. from the local police station had an appointment with me. He wanted to hire our Postman Pat outfit and train for his fete later in the season. I posed the question to him, if he was a long distance swimmer where would he go to get media attention and it couldn't be the Thames as I had already looked into that possibility and it had turned out to be a dead end, they were doing railway tunnelling which had caused them to half the traffic flow down the Thames. That and the vials decease caused by rats excrement was enough to put me off.

He had a quick think about it and told me he would swim across from Scotland to the Isle of Skye, at that time all the locals were up in arms about paying the bridge toll each time they wanted to cross over to the mainland. When he left I sat and thought on what had been said. It seemed feasible, but it also appeared to be a long way to go for just one swim, there had to be more to it than that.

My preparation for the Channel was coming along nicely, I was now able to swim an hour non-stop and I looked forward to my daily trips to the pool. Sometimes I would go to the pool on my way home from work and still return later in the day when the children where in bed. It was a place that was quiet and as each stroke through the clear water broke the surface I was transported to another world. A world that I could blank out all the hustle and bustle of work and children and all the other things that went into making up my busy life.

The idea of going up to Scotland really appealed to me as I had never been there but it held a romantic association of hills and heather and huge fir trees, I didn't really know what to expect but I was very excited by the idea.

Over the next few weeks as we drifted into February the idea grew in its complexity. Royal mail would be the key to achieving my objective and minor goals on the way to my larger Channel swim. I decided that I would put together a road trip around the UK to include lots of swimming and talks to highlight the sponsorship of royal mail and collect as much money as I could. With all that had to be completed the road trip had to start in early April, as towards the middle and end of the year I was fully committed. I hadn't taken into consideration that in April the water off of Scotland's shores would be freezing but sure enough as April approached everything was ready; Hue was to accompany me as an aid. It was his help that had made my Channel swim possible. I thought it proper that he should also enjoy the fruits of his labour.

The first stop on our journey was Lake Windermere, being one of the most well-known of all the lakes. In early spring it was buzzing with tourists and I was sure to have an audience for my talk on Channel swimming the following day. First we had to find the town hall and set everything up for the following day. Royal mail had made posters and given me a professional tape to show, we had all the projectors and equipment with us and where self-sufficient. The rooms we had been given to speak in where above the town hall in the centre of town on a road traffic Island. The road outside was small and there wasn't a huge number of cars passing but throngs of tourists, which I was pleased about.

Hue and I stayed in a small B & B overlooking Lake Windermere and pulled up in the car park at the rear of the B&B, the works car making a loud noise as its tires penetrated the gravel. We parked the car and unloaded the remainder of our things, mainly personal things as we had off loaded a huge amount at the town hall. The B&B's front door was directly onto a small winding country road, mainly walled in local stone. It was a lovely warm day and the light enveloped the room as it streamed through the lace curtains and fell onto the bed. The land lady left us to unpack and headed back down stairs. It was late afternoon when we headed off to find something to eat. There were lots of places to eat from grand hotels to slick restaurants to the ever present chip shop and we decided on a small family run bistro. The food was plain but wholesome and reasonably priced. I was more sleepy than hungry due to all the days' activities and after a stroll along the lake we retired to bed.

The talk at the town hall went down well and we raised some money, I was glad of the materials that Royal Mail had given us; it gave my talk a professional touch, it was the first time I had talked in public but I was on safe ground talking about Channel swimming and was surprised at how many people had come to such a talk. The video I was showing from Royal mail highlighted the fact that Royal mail was sponsoring both the elite athletes and the Paralympic athletes as well. It's much more difficult for the Paralympic athletes not only to raise money but also to compete on the international stage. They go from being relatively unknowns to competing at international level, and because most of them don't work, finances are a big issue. I had arranged at each venue to have a Paralympic athlete there to take questions and it also helped with the fund raising as they personally got involved.

After a wonderful breakfast the following day we strolled through Bowness looking at all the shops, it was again sunny and warm unusually so for the time of year and we made our way to the pier and hopped on a cruise boat going up and down the lake. After paying for our stay we took our bags and belongings to the car and headed off for Derwent Waters. I didn't know it at the time but later I was to return to Windermere to swim it but not with Hue at my side. Not knowing Derwent water, which was to be our next stop where I would swim, I couldn't help but wonder if I shouldn't have swum Windermere instead. The venue was chosen by one of the local Royal Mail P.R. Personnel, I didn't get any choice in the matter but I was sure it would be lovely anyway. I also had the task of showing off the new Olympic first day covers to the press and TV who would be there. It was to be my first TV appearance but not my last. After dinner we settled in for the night as the following day was to be a busy day. We got up around eight and went for breakfast, I hadn't slept that well as thoughts of my pending swim and subsequent TV appearance played on my mind. The next venue was Derwent Water.

Derwent Water wasn't too far away and as we entered the park there was a small building in front of where we parked the car and off to the right I could just see the water peeking through the trees. We walked over to the stairs leading down to the beach area, looking out over the jetties laying side by side along the banks of the lake the water glistened as the sun shone on its surface, there was hardly a ripple and in places you were able to see the reflection of the trees on the water. I had projected the path my swim would take and looked down the length of the lake taking in the islands we would have to pass as we travelled down the other end which was out of my view. We had a little time before the press and TV arrived to look around and sum up what we needed for the swim.

The PR lady arrived with outsized stamps for me to hold in front of the cameras. They thought it best I get changed into my costume as that made a better point of what I was doing there and I stood on the end of one of the protruding jetties smiling and holding up the huge stamp. The PR lady was to give all the details for the media so I was left to get on with the task at hand to swim Derwent Water.

Hue set off in the boat just ahead of me; the water was chilly but not too cold. I had already had my first swim at Dover and this water was like bath water in comparison, I soon settled into my stride. The water was quite clear and I could see the small pebbles and stones which made up the bed of the river as I swam over the top of them until the darkness of the depths stole them from me. I had to swim a little harder than I had anticipated; there was a current as I entered the middle of the lake. I caught up with Hue who had the engine on idle waiting for me in the main current and together we began the long swim to the end of the lake. We passed a few small islands and later a slightly larger island with people peering over a decked area surrounded by a balustrade. They waved to us as I swam past it lifted my spirits a little. The swim was quite short by Channel swimming standards and I always find the first four to five hours of swimming hard and this swim wasn't as easy as I had at first thought.

As we turned around on the return leg the swimming became easier, I was now swimming with the current and not against it much to the amusement of Hue. He was watching the reactions of a jogger out for his daily constitutional, jogging on the banks beside us about 20 meters away and to my right. He had been fascinated and kept his eye on us as we glided back down the lake, we were keeping pace with each other, it was really a weird sensation. At one point when the current picked up we were actually going faster than him, which is why Hue couldn't help but grin. Stroking away I could see the jetties coming into view again, at each stroke I could now see the pebbles once more as the water began to get shallower and soon we were on the beach. I felt quite exhilarated now that the second challenge was over. We stayed for the night at the northern end of Windermere in a town called Ambleside and for the first time since leaving home I fell into a deep sleep, waking refreshed in the morning.

Hue and I set out again, heading for a sorting office on our way to Glasgow. I don't rightly remember the name of the town or the sorting office but that doesn't matter now. The sorting office was a huge affair and stood in the centre of an industrial estate. I had checked with the PR department in Brighton that all the details were in place for our visit and the Paralympic athlete was waiting for us as we turned up. The management gathered together the workers and we introduced ourselves and gave an account of what we had been doing and what was to come, we then made an appeal on behalf of the Olympic Association and gathered up all the monies the staff had collected on our behalf. The manager there was really nice; he was in his mid forties a huge guy with brown hair and glasses. On our way out and while we were saying our farewells he gave us a lunch pack, our next stop wouldn't be until Glasgow which was a good way off. We hoped to reach Glasgow around five p.m. and settle into our guest house before our visit to their sorting office the following morning.

The guest house was in the heart of Glasgow on a one way street, we had several attempts at getting there. We could see where we needed to be but just couldn't get there. The one way street we were trying to cross to get to our B&B was manic! We eventually managed it and parked just outside of a tall greying Victorian house. Glasgow isn't one of my favourite places, I could picture the grey buildings during a downpour and all I could conjure up in my mind was grey and dismal. I think in part because the area we had chosen to stay was devoid of trees or any greenery come to think of it.

In the morning we packed all of our belongings, we were going to head onto the Isle of Skye that evening to stay before my swim there. We headed off to the sorting office and repeated the previous day's work. It had been really nice meeting all the athletes and hearing their stories of how they had got into the Olympics and all the adverse obstacles and things they had to overcome to get to their objectives. They are truly brave people and I admire them all greatly. Again the sorting office manager gave us some food for the journey and we left the office heading for the outskirts of Glasgow.

About ten minutes outside of Glasgow the scenery changes dramatically. It goes from austere, grey and dowdy to wonderful breath-taking countryside. Every place you look there are awesome rolling hills and valleys with winding streams and huge boulders. It is amongst some of the most beautiful countryside I have ever laid eyes upon. I don't know if it was the rhythms of the car or the events of the past days but around lunch time I fell into a deep sleep. When I woke up it was still light and I asked Hue where we were and he said we were about two hours away from Skye and perhaps we should look for somewhere to eat as it was getting late. I hadn't realized that in Scotland it didn't get dark until around eleven at night which was very odd but the further north you travel the lighter it gets later.

We pulled off at a deserted restaurant in the middle of nowhere, except to say it was breathtakingly beautiful. Hue and I ate in silence, each thinking of tomorrow and what lay ahead. I have never been to the Isle of Skye and didn't know quite what to expect but I had been in touch with the harbour master who was arranging a boat for back up and a place to shower after I had finished. He said that in his memory nobody had ever swum across to the island and he was sure the media would be gagging for the story. Just the right reaction I was hoping for. When we finally reached our destination it was almost eleven at night and we went straight to bed. We had inadvertently taken lodgings at the home of the old ferry operator and when we told him of our plans to do an alternative crossing he was ecstatic.

We crossed back over the bridge we had crossed the night

before and made our way to the harbour masters office to meet the harbour master and let him know we had arrived. He was almost as I had imagined, a bit like Captain Birdseye, complete with beard, except that his beard which was red not grey. He wanted us to wait until the afternoon so that he could make sure all the things were in place ready for the swim. I planned to do a two way swim starting from Scotland going over to Skye and then returning. The plan was that I would take some of the first day covers or stamps depicting the Olympic athletes in a waterproof bum bag. When I reached the ferry ramp on the Skye side of the water, I would meet the post master who was bringing the stamp to stamp the envelope to show I had been there. So the envelope would be stamped in Scotland, then stamped in Skye and then stamped in Scotland for a second time, to show the two way journey. The envelope would then to be auctioned later in the year; it was a very unique item and would fetch a good price. The stamp on the Isle of Skye had to be brought to the ramp from the Islands museum it had ceased to be used on Skye for many years.

Later that afternoon I stood with Hue looking at the opposite ramp from where we stood, taking in the view of the waters in-between. As I looked into the water which was ice cold but crystal clear, I could see all the jelly fish, hundreds of them. What had I got myself into I thought as I stood there. Well it was too late to back out now and I had come so far to swim this small stretch of water. The harbour master had told me the water here flowed at between three to seven knots depending on what was happening out to sea, I just prayed that today it would be reasonably calm. It looked calm but what lay just beneath the surface was quite another matter.

I went off to the local toilets just around the corner to get changed and met Hue back at the ramp. Bye now there were a number of onlookers as it was the drop down area for all the tourist coaches and the boat that was to accompany us had just appeared and was pulling a crowd, it was a RNLI boat. It was a massive boat and had a full crew to man her. Just behind the life boat was a Hearst and I wondered who had died but was shocked to find out the Hearst was for me. The area didn't have an ambulance but used a

Hearst for emergencies. I couldn't envisage using a Hearst as an ambulance and I didn't need an ambulance in any case so I sent it away.

The time had come for me to get in and make a start, inside my heart was thumping against my chest and my legs felt like jelly but that was normal just before an event. Taking courage I went down to the water's edge, all eyes were firmly fixed on me as I entered the water. At first the chill of the water took my breath away but it was now or never, I ploughed through my first strokes at break neck speed hoping the workout would keep me from freezing. In fact it didn't bother me at all; the thing I worried about more was the jelly fish. At about 150 yards out my worst nightmare occurred, I came face to face with a huge Lions Mane jelly fish. They are about the size of a dustbin lid and the long thick brown mane of tentacles hangs two and a half feet under the water line. Shear panic doesn't come even close to how I felt; I was paralyzed and for a moment my natural reaction of dread cut in. It must have looked pretty peculiar to the life boat crew who were off to my left as my arms went in full reverse at break neck speed, pushing me away from the monstrosity that I had just encountered. How I didn't get stung is any ones guess but I came out without a scratch, phew!

I made steady progress towards the opposite bank and could easily see the ramp ahead. Because of the current pushing me down stream and left of the ramp I swam as close to the banks as possible. It was too shallow for the life boat so they lay off about 20 yards astern of my position. On the bank I could see the remains of a turret or tower which had over the years succumb to the wind and weather and now lay half in a heap. Ten minutes later I had made no progress and the turret still lay off to my left, so I put everything I had into the strokes but my progress was zero, I was just staying in the same spot. The crew of the boat was getting a bit anxious at my lack of progress and afterwards Hue told me they asked him if I was all right, not really knowing if I was or I wasn't his reply had been an affirmative. Thinking to myself, I knew I would never make it to the ramp if I didn't do something quickly, so I changed direction and headed back out into the main current, within ten minutes I was walking up the ramp to a waiting crowd of people.

The post master identified himself and placing a wooden box on the wall opened it to reveal the ink pad and stamp which had come from the museum. Looking around at all the people I could only say that in that part of the world nothing much happens and so I had become the main attraction of the day, Well that and the fact that the old ferry skipper must have told everyone he came across that I was attempting a coup by swimming across and not paying the toll. The press and TV had also got wind of what I was doing and my swim was live on Scottish TV.

Hue urged me to get back into the water again, I had begun to shiver, the air temperature wasn't kind that day and although it was sunny there was a distinct chill in the air. Having already traversed the water once the return journey was a piece of cake and by the time I stepped out on the other bank there were hundreds of onlookers. They assumed it was either a rescue, as the life boat was there or a stunt and were glued to every stroke I took. Walking up the ramp I felt like a super star, I was mobbed by people wanting my autograph, something that I will never get used to but it's flattering at the time.

By now I was getting cold and went to change as Hue spoke to the now numerous media personnel. It had been a glorious day but I was thankful to be warm once more as we got into our car and headed for home. We stopped once on the way home for the night and I was soon in my office in Gravesend again writing a full report to the publicity department of Royal Mail.

The tour had been just one step in the plans running up to the Olympics but one of the most exciting for me. I was moved from my office in Gravesend to an office in Orpington which was a lot nicer and nearer to home. The journey each morning to Gravesend had been a nightmare and I was glad it was over.

While at Orpington and during the course of my normal routine I was approached by Hue to join a cycle to France. One of the Office managers had a boy who was ill and needed some specialist treatment and Royal Mail had agreed to help by utilizing its equipment. In reality that meant they would give back up to the cyclists with support vans and we were able to use post bikes which was novel. I readily agreed as I was always up to help and the challenge would benefit my fitness.

We started just outside of Westminster Abbey, as we parked and started to off load the bikes a policeman came over to tell us we couldn't offload there, the minister of sport was just coming out of Westminster with a TV crew in tow. Accident or not it was a golden opportunity, we were allowed to stay put and we were all filmed turning around in the area just in front of the Abby with the Minister for sport looking on as if it had all been pre-arranged, which it hadn't.

I don't know who had done the planning for the ride but by the time we got to Folkstone docks to catch the ferry to France most of the boys on Post Office bikes had no lights with them which is illegal, shame!

We made the ferry and were glad of a break from cycling, it would take quite a time before we landed in France and we took the opportunity to tank up on food. It was around nine o clock when we finally arrived, one of the drivers knew of a camp site where we were supposed to camp for the night, we were unable to find the camp site and after two tries decided it was getting too late. We found a lay bye with enough grass to pitch the two tents and settled down for the night. One of the tents was for the interpreter which I shared as the interpreter was a female and the larger of the two tents was for the remainder of the team, all being men. The two vans pulled up, one in front and one behind.

I woke in the morning to the smell of bacon wafting through the tent flap. The leader of the cycle venture was busy in the back of one of the vans cooking breakfast for the hungry rabble. I was busting to go to the loo but there were no toilets in sight, I took myself off further up the field out of sight of the team, hopped over the fence into a corn field and did what came naturally. Breakfast was ready when I got back and we all tucked into what seemed like a banquet before setting out for Paris.

It was later that day, riding alongside Hue that we passed three of our guys in a lay bye supping a cold beer. I don't know how they sweet talked the people they were with into parting with their cold beers but they had. I thought to myself, post men will be post men and we cycled on after exchanging a brief conversation. The towns we passed through were stunning and I was by now really enjoying the tour and the company of the rest of the team.

That night we did find a camp site, complete with showers and toilets, I don't think I have ever been so grateful. During the day I had begun to feel terribly saddle sore, on closer inspection of my private parts I found an ear of corn in my cycling shorts. It must have been from my earlier trip to the corn field to relieve myself; I was so so relieved to remove it and a whole lot more comfortable.

We all went into town to find a restaurant where we could eat having worked up an extraordinary appetite after all the days cycling. We found a small bistro serving Italian food, it was a really good find, and we all sat down to a hearty meal, just the job too.

Hue when I saw him the next morning looked terrible; he hadn't had a wink of sleep. He had slept in what was the cooking area of the tent and gone to bed early, during the night the other cyclists returned and being a little worse for wear just collapsed in a heap snoring, one of them was even sick. He had been caught unaware and chose to throw up by putting his head outside the tent. The only problem was he didn't get up to go to the flap he just lifted the side of the tent which was very close to Hue and threw up. Hue said the smell was awful and it made his stomach wrench.

We all climbed back onto our bikes after breakfast and got into the routine we had now adopted whereby we cycled for a hundred kilometres and then stopped for lunch on whatever safe place we could find. I remarked to Hue that we had come all this way and not even had a puncture. It wasn't long before those words came back to haunt me, just on the outskirts of Paris, low and behold I had a puncture. We pulled up and a number of my team mates went drifting by but some of the tail Enders stopped and gave a hand.

Cycling into Paris was wonderful as we were nearing our objective but hazardous as well. The Arc de Triomphe was such a place, negotiating the roundabouts was quite something else. We made it all in one piece and stood facing the Eiffel Tower, legs sore and hugely sun burnt but happy. The fountains in front of us were just too much and I left Hue holding my bike. Nearing the fountain I could see all the tourists and Parisians sitting dangling their feet, I just jumped in fully clothed not caring what people thought. Before long the fountain was alive with a sea of humanity, it was hysterical. On the ferry during our crossing home, Hue purchased a broach for me. It was a rhinestone bicycle and at the time very precious to me as a reminder of the tour we had just completed.

Later that year we did another ride from Dover to Plymouth to raise money for a new wheel chair for a motor cycle accident victim. It was all done through Royal Mail, who again loaned us the backup vans and cycles. This time I chose to ride my own racer rather than a post office bike. We gathered the team together for the obligatory photo with Dover Castle in the back ground and set off. I had licenses to do collections along the way but on post office bikes the going was slow for the majority of the team. I had been blessed with our accommodation, all of which was free. We stayed at varying types of accommodation, ranging from the post office floor in Eastbourne, to bed and breakfasts, a youth hostel in Brighton and a holiday park in Lyme Regis. We finished on Plymouth Hoe as the sun went down over another busy team event.

The whole year was one event after another, it was crazy but wonderful. I hadn't enjoyed a job so much in all my life and was having a blast. In June of that year at a meeting for the customer relations team of which I was one, it was decided that from every region Royal Mail would choose a person who had excelled at raising awareness and money for the Olympic effort, they would go on an all-expenses paid trip to the paralympic games in July the following year. As an athlete it had always been my dream to go to the Olympics but I had never been that good an athlete to have ever gone under my own ability. Here was a golden opportunity to go with all expenses paid and it only fuelled my work all the more.

A while later I heard that I had been chosen to go, along with around another ten people from all over England, the trip included spending money, accommodation and trips out to the sporting venues as well as the opening ceremony. I was speechless, which if you know me is something that doesn't happen often. It would be a trip of a life time and I had been chosen, it was awesome and felt like I was dreaming. Training was still on schedule and the crossing was getting ever closer.

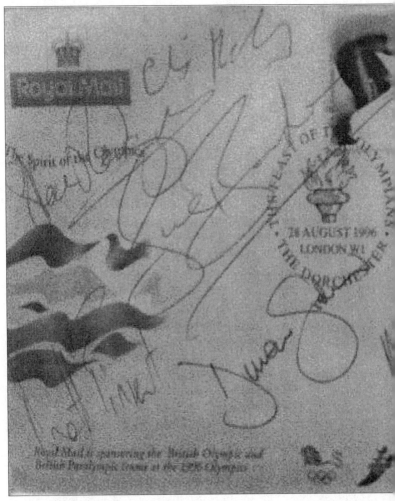

1st day covers I carried in a dry bum bag on my 2way swim of Scotland- Skye-Sco

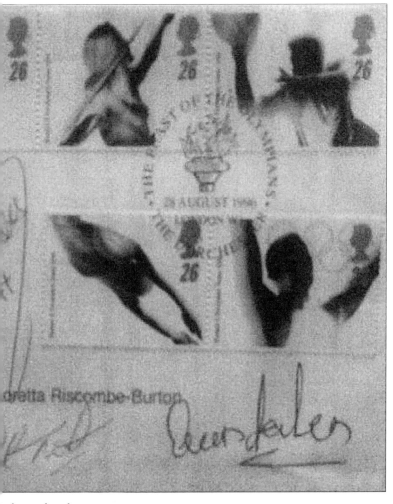

o be auctioned.

The Royal Mail cycling team approaching the Arc de Triomphe in Paris on our Westminster to Paris charity cycle.

CHAPTER FOUR
Channel Swimming Training

I am no wonder woman, and the training for the Channel swim was really tuff. As said in a previous chapter I had begun by swimming in a school pool which was too short and too hot but was a wonderful blessing to me as it enabled me to swim whenever I wanted to having been given the keys to let myself in and out. I had also joined Redhill and Reigate swimming club and swum there twice a week in the evenings. As April arrived and the Easter weekend along with it I was very apprehensive. I had pictured in my mind the bulging biceps of tuned and honed athletes standing on Dover beach head, waiting in eager anticipation to train together and the thought sent shivers down my spine. The truth was far from what I had imagined.

The training at Dover, Alison told me, was to begin on the Friday of the Easter holiday and I was to meet up with the other swimmers on the beach just in front of a miner's statue that stands in the gardens along the beach front at Dover. Because it was a bank holiday I had the time off and was able to go down to Dover for the long weekend. The swimmers were swimming all through the weekend and so had three whole days to get us settled into what was to be a routine until our swims were scheduled.

I found the statue just at the end of the buildings that lined the sea front and parked my car. I thought swimming would be cheap as it only; I thought involved a costume goggles and hat. The petrol was being covered by Royal Mail but I hadn't thought about the parking. Having to park at Dover all day Saturday and Sunday would be costly and something I hadn't bargained for. The other thing I hadn't taken into account was the food I would consume after each swim, the hunger created by swimming for hours on end soon mounted up but it was a price I was willing to pay.

Crossing the road I spied Alison and her mother Freda who was the trainer of the Channel swimmers. I went over to her to let her know I had arrived and to meet some of my fellow swimmers. The first order of the day was a photo call in front of the two statues of Channel swimmers that had just been erected after which we all went back down to the beach. There were about thirty swimmers in all and as Freda explained things, we were told to get changed. Now this was late April and the weather although sunny was chilly and it wasn't pleasant getting undressed. First of all you had to balance yourself on the stones as undressing under towelling robe isn't easy. Freda applied Vaseline to my armpits, groin and neck, in fact everywhere the costume had openings as while you swim the salt in the water collects at the openings of your costume and if the body part there moves you end up with friction burns, hence the Vaseline.

Freda told us it would be around eight degrees in the water and we had to keep moving or we would get hyperthermia. The task was to swim for fifteen minutes, seven out and seven back roughly, I was glad I had brought a waterproof watch as it was to prove invaluable. It was impossible to walk on the stones and Alison had warned me to bring flip flops to wear, donning my flip flops whilst putting on my sorbrathane swimming hat and a pair of goggles I marched with the other swimmers down the beach to the water's edge. There we lots of people who had stopped to watch the spectacle and stood by the railings above the beach head starring at this Looney group of people about to get in the sea when it was freezing outside and while they had on winter coats.

I knew I was more than capable of swimming fifteen minutes and felt my confidence building as I looked around at the other swimmers. Instead of muscled athletes they were ordinary people just like me. They came from all walks of life, newspaper reps, teachers, administrators etc. None of them had appeared elitist and we were all in the same boat, just wanting to achieve a life's ambition, it was far better than I had imagined.

I kicked off my shoes and the stones were unbearably painful on the underside of my feet and made me hobble and groan as I approached the last couple of feet to the water's edge, even then the pain was intense as I slid into the icy water which took away my breath. Stroking out with swimmers all around and ahead of me I had to stop as my lungs felt like they had imploded and all the air had been sucked out. The cold was consuming my very being, but I knew I had to keep going and remembered what Freda had said about hyperthermia. It may have been only fifteen minutes but it was going to be an agonizing fifteen minutes, no matter what Freda had told me nothing could prepare me for the extreme cold that I now felt with every fibre of my being. Long distance swimming is very much about rhythm and breathing and here I was floundering like a proverbial fish. After the first five minutes my body grew accustomed to the intense cold and my breathing became easier, my strokes longer. I could see the people walking along the promenade watching which filled me with pride and kept me going. Our objective given the time allowance was to reach the first stone jetty protruding into the bay and turn at that point and head for home. Just as well it was only fifteen minutes as by now I was unable to feel my feet, they had gone completely numb. I turned just in front of the jetty and could just make out Alison climbing out of the water, she had achieved the objective with ease and now watched us all bringing up the rear.

My pace slowed as my body temperature began to drop and I was glad to finally pull myself clumsily out onto the beach once more and put on my shoes. The stones hurt even more on my now frozen feet and I was shivering all over, my skin was orange and in some places blue, literally. However I was elated to have completed my first swim or that is what I thought. As it turned out it was the first of two swims, the second being after our bodies temperature had raised to normal once again after a three hour break.

The break enabled us all to get something to eat to replace the energy we had used. I would never have guessed I would have been so hungry after such a short time. Everyone got a take away from the chippie and followed Alison and Freda back to Alison's flat in the centre of town. Freda put the kettle on for tea and we gathered in the living room with several conversations going at once. Freda is an amazing trainer and team builder and this was all part of the strategy to build team. All too soon it was time to go back to the beach for the second swim and I realized I would have to put on my wet costume as I hadn't come prepared for two swims.

When we arrived at the beach head Freda was coaxing us all to get on with it as she didn't want us all to go in at different times but as a body of people, that way she was able to keep a sharp eye on us. I reluctantly put on my bathers along with others who hadn't realized they were in for two swims. The cold was immediate and now I just wanted to get the swim over with. The wind had picked up and made my costume feel cold next to my body. As we entered the water I was pleasantly surprised, it didn't seem as cold as the first time and I was able to keep up with the bulk of the swimmers. We reached the pier in no time and I checked my watch, seven minutes exactly, knowing I had a minute to spare I trod water and just took in everything around me. I was now about thirty meters from shore, there were straggles which hadn't yet got too the pier which I was relieved about not wishing to be the last person. The sun broke through the clouds and fell on the water which was unusually clear, I had seen the bottom as I swam which was to be the last time I would ever see the bottom. As the season goes on and there are more boats and swimmers the storms come in etc. the bottom isn't visible.

This pattern of training continued throughout the Easter weekend. We started on the Friday with two swims of fifteen minutes; on the Saturday we begun with fifteen minutes and on the second swim increased that to twenty minutes. On the Sunday we started with twenty minutes and the second swim was twenty five minutes.

The following week I was working doing my round early in the morning as by now I had returned to doing a postal round. I had to be at Dover by ten o'clock and so literally ran my round to get it finished by nine as it would take an hour from Swanley to Dover down the M20. I had packed the car the night before and as soon as I put my delivery bag into the office I was immediately on my way. The au pair was looking after Emma and Phillip so the day was off to a good start. Arriving at Dover just before ten, I found a spot to park the car and joined the others on the beach. Freda greased us up as usual but told us we were to swim in pairs but go in different directions. Today we were to swim two half hours and we were to keep an eye on the time as late or early swimmers at the beach would be given extra time in the water which was the last thing we wanted.

I teamed up with Jacque a French breast stroke swimmer who was on his first attempt at the Channel like me. He had a running background as well, so we had something in common. He was a chef at the French embassy in London, amazing the people you meet. Jacque and I went out to our right as we had previously swum out left and wanted a change. We headed to the pier at the end of the beach, you were unable to go any further, checking our watches we had turned around exactly on the fifteen minutes and knowing as we got colder we would slow down we began to pick up the pace to keep ourselves warm. The timing was perfect and we arrived back just on the half hour. Some of the other swimmers had cut their swim short and arrived back early and Freda true to her word had made them swim an extra five minutes. On this occasion there were no late swimmers because it was so cold.

The following day we did exactly the same swim as the day before as the waves were shall we say challenging? Even the ferries were having a job getting into harbour. Freda had told us all to swim off to the right so we would be in the lea of the pier for a short while? Going out to the left would mean we would be exposed to the elements for too long. When the swim was over and we were dressed Freda gave us all sips of coffee from a hot flask but I was so cold I couldn't even hold the cup without shivering and spilling it everywhere.

The following week Hue and the au pair and children all came with me as it was such a sunny day and beginning to get warmer. The water temperature had started to rise slightly as the swims became longer and we acclimatized to the conditions. Emma and Phillip played on the beach as we broke the first water of the morning. Today we were swimming two one hour sessions with a three hour warm up at Alison's flat in between. When I finished my hour and I was sure I wasn't early and all the other swimmers were approaching the beach I went in too. Hue was there with my flip flops and a towel which was lovely. As I dressed under my bath robe the shakes started as they always did but my au pair watching thought I was going to die and was really upset. It wasn't long before she realized that everyone was just the same as I was.

At the flat Alison put on a video of previous swimming years, some of the footage was hysterical. A few years prior there had been a Lord who was training, his hat was straight out of Woolworths complete with dimples. He was standing on the beach drinking what I imagined was soup and slopping it ever where. Then he began to dress himself and was sat in his towelling robe rocking backwards and forwards and writhing all over the place with his head inside the robe which looked hilarious. When he eventually got to putting on his socks his feet were just a smidgen out of reach as by now he was as cold as a fish finger and stiff to boot. His wife came to the rescue and as she did we heard him say in a very posh and proper voice "what it is to have a wife". I bet his wife could have killed him at that instant. Alison's flat was like a shrine to Channel swimming with loads of pictures of different swims and a picture of her receiving her M.B.E. from the queen. It was a place where we really got to know each other and a place filled with laughter and sometimes tears as we shared together our triumphs and woes.

So the weeks went by, the training had gone from two separate hours to one swim of two hours. Freda was now adding whole hours onto a single swim. At the end of each circuit of an hour all the swimmers would gather at the beach still standing in the water and was given a cup of hot juice. The mixture was a powder called maxim which has the same value as eating a jacket potato and replaces all the energy used. This was mixed together with hot water and blackcurrant which takes the taste of salt away. So the pattern was repeated every hour. It was now late June and the first relays would be about to take place. Our average training was by now five hours each day.

The relay teams were always the first to take place as they were much quicker and less likely to fail than the solos. Relays in their nature were able to take rougher weather as each swimmer had only an hour to swim before it was passed to another swimmer to take over. Alison one Saturday approached me and asked me if I was willing to join her and a team of swimmers in such a relay. It would be time for me to experience what it was like out at sea and being on a little boat but not as challenging as doing my own solo swim. I was really pleased to have been asked as there were only six places in a team and it was a real privilege to be asked. It was to be an Annual World friendship relay and was to be held on the 2nd of July which wasn't too far away.

As it was to be part of my training Royal mail gave me two days off to enable me to take part and we all met at the dump on the 2nd very early in the morning. The dump is a harbour where boats can Moore up for the night but not for long stays. If a boat was going to stay in Dover for any length of time they were directed to an inner harbour.

I was introduced to my fellow swimmers some I knew but others I didn't. Nick Adams was training with us and hoped to do a two way Channel swim, to be the youngest two way swimmer on record. Karen Howard was completely unknown to me along with John Wyndham from South Africa. He was the instigator of the swim and ran a friendship relay every year. Karen was the Irish champion. There was also Alison and Kathy Batts who was something to do with the Channel Swimming Association and myself. I was the novice of the group and just watched what unfolded with growing curiosity. We loaded our swim bags onto the boat stowing them safely in case of rough weather and headed to Shakespeare beach about twenty minutes sailing away.

As we went through the gates of the harbour the water was very rough but soon calmed down. Alison was the first to swim as the order normally goes with the strongest swimmer first and then works backwards to the weakest. This means that with the rotation of the swimmers, the strongest swim more often and the tail Enders have to swim less. Because there are six swimmers each swimmer has five hours off and then swims their turn and then has another five hours off. The rotation of the swimmers is decided before the swim starts and if any one of us gives up the team is finished, so the order of swim is very important.

The five hours on the boat were murderous and we hadn't gone more than an hour before I felt sea sick. The boat we used was flat bottomed and was ideal for Channel swimming as its flat draft slowed the boat down but for those on board it was a night mare. It made the boat rock on every wave. Not being used to the sea swells and being it was my first time at sea the rest of the swimmers and crew were good to me, encouraging and caring. It's possibly the worst sickness I have ever had before and hope never to have again. Alison said you were far better off getting in and swimming than being on the boat which turned out to be true and it wasn't long before I ached to get in and swim.

The hours flew by and by nine in the evening we could see we were just off of the French coast, another hour and we would be on our way home. I was taken aback by the sight of the French coast; firstly it wasn't white like Dover's cliffs but a muddy brown. Secondly there were no lights to be seen and it appeared to be desolate. From the boat in the water you couldn't see a thing but on board the cliffs were easily discernible. I was in the water as we approached and Alison said I could finish the swim for the team but I didn't believe her that we were so close in and so got out at the end of my hour. She then had to get in and it was now clear to me that she had indeed been telling the truth and I had made her get in again. I was truly sorry I had not believed her and thought she was kidding me and apologized emphatically. The next relay I was part of wasn't until after my solo swim.

For the most part, I drove down to Dover after my round at work had finished but on bank holidays when we had three consecutive days to swim I chose to stay at a bed and breakfast. I had been told of a bed and breakfast called the Victoria owned by a couple who had an empathy with Channel swimmers. On the wall of their dining room hung copies of many of the Channel swimmers certificates and newspaper cuttings now hung in frames. They gave Channel swimmers huge breakfasts to keep them going through the morning's swims. I stayed there on many occasions and they made me feel right at home.

Swimming five hours can be tedious but swimming for ten is horrid. Freda as part of her training schedule had by Channel swimming regulations to put us all in for a six hour swim to ensure we were capable of at least doing a reasonable effort when it came time for our crossing. Freda being Freda knew that the Channel is as much a battle in the mind as a battle of strength and endurance. So it was one Saturday morning when we arrived we were informed that today was to be a continuous ten hour swim. Every one of the swimmers without exception groaned. Freda explained that once this swim was under our belts we would taper down the swims before our own swim was to take place. The actual thought of swimming ten hours was sufficient for most of us to hang it out before getting undressed.

Freda was right it would be a battle for the mind during this swim as each of us paired off and entered the water. We had to come back to the beach head each hour for the first four hours to be fed and then every half an hour so Freda could check we were all ok. The first three hours flew by; there was quite a lot to keep us occupied. My favourite haunt was to swim up and down the length of the pier to the right as that is where most of the tourists walked and I could watch them watching me swim which gave me a buzz. The other thing I liked to do was a little game I had made up during training. I would swim out to my left and go to the far pier, have a little chat while treading water with some of the swimmers. Often Freda would spot us slacking and tell us off for talking and sometimes give us extra time in the water as a punishment. After our chat I would head off up to the other pier at the far end and along the way engage my brain with songs or the alphabet, thinking of girls names to each letter. Sometimes when I approached a buoy in the water I would use it as a marker and swim as fast as I could to the next buoy, where I would slow my pace and repeat this over and over. It took away the tedium.

It's very hard to keep a straight line when you are swimming and the best way of achieving this is to pick out something on the horizon which is high up and easily seen and head for that. I often did just that, other times I would swim breathing on one side and watched the people on the promenade or the scenery or clouds. Dover castle stands high above the harbour and just beyond the castle high up in the cliffs are openings from underground workings cut out during the war. Sir Winston Churchill's war cabinet was dug below the castle and from his position he was able to see across the Channel to France. On a clear day you are able to see the coast line of France clearly. Just above the cliffs to the right there is an observation deck and on occasions I could pick out tourists standing high above the cliffs looking out towards France.

The ten hours seemed like a week but it must have been the same for all the swimmers. I was hungry even with the maxim and tired but I pushed on. Six hours came and went, by now we were feeding every half an hour. Every time I went in for a feed Freda was there to encourage us and get us all going again. Sometimes she would be found talking in hushed voices to a swimmer who was crying and obviously struggling but much to Freda's credit she managed to get all of us through the ten hours. It was with much relief that I finished and slowly climbed out of the water. My legs were like jelly and my head was still going up and down with the motion of the sea, someone helped me stand still long enough to get my flip flops back on and at the promenade wall Freda had hung black bags of water to heat in the sun which gave us all a shower, although just a trickle it was enough to warm us up.

I was jubilant and feeling like I had conquered the world now that my mind had unfazed and I realized what I had just done. It was almost what was required of an average swimmer to cross the Channel and it boosted everyone's confidence.

As the months of training had gone on Freda who also trained me at Redhill and Reigate swimming club told me I should cut out some of the other swims I did throughout the week. I had been swimming every day and on the evenings I would train at the club I would swim twice that day. There wasn't a day without swimming and she was right it was quality not quantity that was required and so I dropped three of my normal training sessions.

I had become great friends with many of the swimmers as we had spent so much time together and I was sorry the training was going to come to an end. Jacque had invited some of the swimmers to his flat at the embassy for dinner which was to be a grand affair. He was going to cook for Prince Charles at an embassy dinner and wanted to put the dessert he was making past us. The whole dinner was just perfection and I was amazed at his talent. We enjoyed a wonderful afternoon and I remember it with fondness. I think Jacque had a crush on me at the time.

There was always media around when we went to the beach at Dover, sometimes covering individual swimmers and other times doing pieces on Channel swimming in general. At one time we did an insert for a magazine as part of their advertising campaign. I had a little bit of coverage on the sports night news section, I was interviewed and I told the media about why I was doing my swim and how the training was going. The interviewer asked what if I didn't make it and I told her it didn't even come into my thinking, all I could think about was stepping out after the swim and that was what I was visualizing most of the time. It was true, that's what I pictured all the time. I went to bed dreaming about it and woke up having dreamt it. It surely is a battle for the mind; there are thousands of reasons to stop swimming and only one to keep you going so I just focused on that one thing.

It was from my home in Westerham I had an interview with Meridian TV. I was given a very brightly coloured track suit to wear by the Royal Mail PR section, it was the track suits the Olympic team was sporting and I was very proud to have one for myself. The interview was very casual and took place while the children were at school; I had been given the day off to do the interview on the run up to the swim. They showed it that night and I was introduced as being a mum of two that was going to France by an unusual method. After the interview I asked for a copy of it to keep and they said they would do their best to get one for me, which they very kindly did.

Swimming for long periods of time in the open has its hazards one of which is the wicked cap marks that I had. My skin had become well-tanned even though I didn't put any sun screen on I never got burnt but you could clearly see the mark left where my cap and goggles had been. It was a standing joke amongst the swimmers and we would compare our cap marks. One of the swimmers was very high profile in the American air force and often had meetings with top brass. It was on such an occasion I saw he was sporting a very pronounced cap mark right in the middle of his forehead. It looked for the entire world as if he had two hair lines. I knew he was going the following day to one of his high flying meetings and had to stand in front of all these dignitaries looking so stupid with this mark across his head. I pulled him to one side and pointed out the cap mark and suggested he wore make up on it to cover it up. He said he was proud of his cap mark and it had taken hours and a whole heap of swimming to produce it and he was blowed if he would cover it up. I thought it was sound advice anyway but I think it fell on deaf ears.

I was booked to swim on the first tides of August but had to wait my turn in the queue. The tides only last for a short while each month according to the lunar cycle and because we have many people who come from overseas to swim the first part of any tide is given over to those from overseas. They have to carefully plan for their swims allowing for weather delays and booking flights to cover their time in the UK. My turn was fast approaching and every weekend that I went to Dover to train might be my last. The pilot, Mike Oram, was the person who decided when the time would be right for me to make the attempt.

CHAPTER FIVE
My first channel swimming attempt

It was on a Saturday training session that my first call would come. I had been swimming for about three hours of the five I was to swim and had just come to the beach to get my cup of Maxim, when Freda came down to the water's edge to speak to me.

Freda said she had just got a call from Mike to say my swim was a go for the next morning and I was to go back to the flat after first having something to eat and get my head down. Freda would call me when it was time to get up. I was a little shocked at first as I had not expected that at all. As I dressed thoughts of my now imminent swim raced round my mind. What would it be like swimming during the night on my own? And I know I need to buy some Channel swimming grease and I had not bought any maxim down today so I will have to get some more of that. Are my goggles up to a long swim or will they leak, should I get another pair as a spare? All these things crossed my mind as I prepared for what was to be my biggest challenge yet.

Leaving the beach and all the swimmers was a strange feeling, while I was about to go shopping they were still ploughing up and down and hadn't a clue that I had been called for my swim, they would find out soon enough. It was a very hot day and now I had got dressed and was walking up the High Street I shed my track suit top and tied it around my waist. The bag hanging from my right shoulder weighed a ton with all my swimming paraphernalia and I would be glad to sit down for a while as my shoulders where feeling tight and sore, I think it was all in the mind but it seemed real enough.

I managed to buy the Channel grease in Boots, one of only two shops in the UK which make it especially for the Channel swimmers. Years ago the swimmers would ply their bodies from head to toe in the stuff but nowadays we realize it's only beneficial to put it on the costume openings. I knew I would be able to buy Maxim from Freda as she always kept a supply at the flat so I didn't have to worry about that. The next thing I should do is to find somewhere to eat but before doing that I phoned Hue to tell him my swim was tomorrow. I knew pasta was good for endurance events and so I walked down to the small Italian restaurant near to the fountain in the centre of town.

Whilst eating a huge plate of pasta at a table outside one of the people on my postal round passed me and recognized me. He obviously realized I was in Dover for the training and asked how it was all going as he and his wife were coming to the auction and knew it must be soon that I was due to go. As I told him I was in the process of getting ready my pulse and heart rate doubled. The adrenaline unfortunately hit my stomach and I really needed the loo. Have you ever felt like that? I know whenever I am about to do an event it always hits my stomach. As soon as he had gone I left my meal and hunted out the restaurants loo, just in time....

Back at the flat, Freda had told me what bedroom to use and I got into bed not feeling sleepy at all but I had to give it a go. My head was racing with what ifs and going over my strokes and thinking generally of a plan of action for tomorrow. Around four o clock Freda and Alison came back and Freda woke me up. I was a little surprised as it wasn't morning, in fact I had not been fully asleep just resting my eyes. Mike had phoned her to say the weather forecast predicted high winds and it was best to postpone the swim.

I was disappointed but at least now I was ready whenever they should ring me. Mike had my mobile, work and home number just in case. The next day was Sunday and as usual I went down to Dover and joined the rest of the swimmers training. The call didn't come that day either. Every day as I got ready for work I thought is today the day? Then by the time I came home from work I would be disappointed, eventually I rang Mike and asked what the holdup was. He explained that an off shore wind was gusting at 30 miles an hour and that translated meant rough seas. Mike said to check the shipping weather forecast on TV every night which was around six if I remember correctly. All the waiting was starting to get on my nerves and I had begun not to sleep well or eat a great deal as my stomach was in knots.

The time spent waiting and knowing now that my swim was immanent allowed the PR of Royal mail to arrange another TV interview. This time it was to be at Dover and they wanted shots of me swimming and overlaid shots of me on my postal round and part of the interview that had taken place at my home. At least I was able to do something positive and keep myself busy; it was hell on earth waiting to swim. Every day would be the same thing, it was fantastically sunny but there was an off shore wind. First it was on the English side then on the French side but I had to admit the water was rough.

One evening just as Hue and I were settling down to listen to the forecast the phone went. My heart slipped a beat and I wondered could it possibly be? Sure enough it was Mike the pilot phoning. He had been listening on the radio and gave me the all clear to come down to Dover; it was to be the following day. I was possessed and jumped and screamed all around the living room. It was actually going to happen nearly two weeks after I had received the first call to swim.

There were so many things going around my head, elation, fear, trepidation thoughts of, have I got everything ready?. My stomach reacted immediately and I couldn't eat dinner at all, which wasn't a good sign. I didn't want to go to bed but knew I should and I did go, but really didn't get any sleep at all. I had set the alarm for one thirty as that would give me lots of time to prepare and make sure I didn't forget anything.

One thirty soon came around, I didn't want to wake Hue but I just had to and give him a hug before setting out on this amazing adventure. Moving quietly so as not to disturb the au pair or the children, I got all my things together, reluctantly had a piece of toast which felt like boulders going down my throat and slipped out to the car, loaded up and was on my way to who knows what! Even as I am writing this paragraph it makes my stomach churn over, remembering so vividly how I felt at the time.

By the time I got to Maidstone and was coming up for the motorway services I knew I would have to do a toilet stop and I pulled off the motorway and made a quick dash for the toilets. I often stopped at these services; it had become a ritual before swimming to have a cappuccino and a croissant before traveling on. That morning the croissant was definitely out of the question and time was an issue as I wanted to arrive with lots of time to think things through before all hell broke loose and there would be no turning back.

Just before getting to Dover I went over the instructions Freda had given me regarding parking for my swim. She said that I was to take the right hand turn at the second roundabout and then turn onto the gates to the dump. There someone would come to the gate and I was to tell them I was going out in Aegean Blue, Mike's boat for the day and needed to park up on the docks so my car would be safe while I was gone. Following the instructions I found myself in front of the gates waiting for someone to come out and speak to me. The gates were on surveillance camera and I just hoped the gate keeper was alert to my arrival. As I got out of the car the air was crisp and still. I couldn't hear anyone at first but just as I was about to give up and park my car at a meter a man came out from behind one of the buildings and approached the gate. I didn't have to say anything and he willingly opened the gates for me. Aegean Blue was moored right next to the harbour wall and I found it easily but looking at my watch it was just gone four a.m. and the crew would all be asleep, I decided to go off for a walk and come back at the appointed time of six a.m.

There was not a soul around that I could see and I didn't feel in any danger as I walked down to the beach where I had spent so many hour training. The beach was like a second home to me and

I stood with the clock tower just to my right and thought about all the times I had swum to this end of the pier and glanced at this very clock to see if I was swimming to my allotted time or how long I had left to swim. The sun was just coming up over the horizon, reflecting on the water as the waves lapped the beach, my thoughts once again went to the challenge I was about to undertake and I said a prayer in my mind. I hadn't spoken to God for years but stood on the beach with this enormous task ahead, like most people when the chips are down they call to God and I am no different.

Now many years on, I know that God heard my prayer, even though it was said tongue in cheek, I prayed "God help me". How many of us at different times have prayed that or just said those words aloud. At this particular time I really meant it as I would need all the help I could get. I was thirty nine years old and here I was about to swim the Channel, what was I thinking? I sat for a long time just watching the waves and remembering the fun times that I had on the beach with all the swimmers and Freda and Alison, I realized I would miss so much when this swim was finally over and especially all my new found friends.

Glancing at my watch it was almost time to go back to the boat and see if anyone stirred. On reaching Aegean Blue Mike was busy with maps and he saw me approaching and came to give me a hand with the bags. He introduced Graham Pique the observer and Barry Darling his crew and Nick the two way Channel swimmer was just arriving. Nick had agreed to accompany me during my swim, under Channel swimming Association rules once I was three hours out of port a swimmer could get in with me and keep me company. They were not allowed to pace me or touch me but could swim just behind me which would be comforting to know someone else was in there with me.

The observer was also one of the Channel swimming Associations rules. Each swim had to have an observer who would take a count of my stroke rate once an hour and the water conditions and wave height etc. Graham would also write anything of interest that was happening at the time along with plotting each hour where my position was. His first order of the day was to ask me some questions about my feeding pattern and what I had to wear during the swim and what pain killers I would use if any. There are strict rules regarding drugs and it is within Graham's right to ask for a drugs test if he thought it necessary. The regulations regarding swim wear were one cap, one pair of goggles and an approved costume, all of which I had. The use of wet suits was strictly forbidden as they act as a floatation device and therefore enabled you to swim at a faster rate.

With the formalities over Mike sat down with me in the cabin and told me we would be starting from France and not England. The wind was still blowing off the English side of the Channel but Mike had been watching the weather for the past two weeks and it settled in a pattern. Each afternoon the wind would move away from the English coast and begin to blow off of the French coast. If we started in France by the evening it would have past right over us and would be calm for the latter half of the swim.

I had never imagined starting in France but always pictured myself standing on Shakespeare beach so it threw me a bit but I settled in for the ride. It would take three hours to motor to Cap griz nez in France our starting point.

I sat on the back of the boat on the open deck in a plastic chair as Nick came and sat next to me offering a sandwich for me to eat. Typical boy I thought always ready to eat no matter what the time of day but for me it was a no no and I turned the offer down flat. I told Nick it actually made me want to vomit even thinking about it and really struggled with him sitting in such close proximity chomping away with not a care in the world. Later during my swim my stomach would once again prove to be disastrous.

Entering the cabin to get out of nicks way while he stuffed numerous sandwiches into his mouth Mike and Graham were pouring over the course the computer had given them according to my stroke rate. It reminded me, I had a chart of the English Channel which I wanted Graham to fill in as we went to record my course and speed which I would eventually hang in my living room as a record of the swim. Delving into my bags I gave Graham the chart and asked if he would be so kind as to fill in the details for me. The chart does now hang on my living room wall and is a constant reminder of that swim.

I went out into the fresh air which I needed more than life at that time, I felt like a condemned prisoner about to go to execution sat there. The time seemed to pass so slowly and as we sailed over the waters I would have to come back over it was inevitable that my thoughts would soon settle on the enormity of the task I had set myself. All Channel swimmers know that the English Channels weather can turn on a sixpence; it can in the space of half an hour go from being flat calm to ten foot waves. It is like putting all your eggs in one basket and hoping none of them crack, I had one shot at this and I had to give it my best. There would be no second chances and you take what nature gives you and try to do your best with it. A whole year of training now hung in the balance and soon I would know if I matched up to the task.

We were approaching Cap griz Nez and it was time for me to prepare. I had already put on my costume before leaving the house, not knowing what the facilities were like on the boat. So I stripped off and put on my cap and goggles as I didn't want to get grease on the lenses as that would have been disastrous. Nick came to the rescue and greased me up with the channel grease I had brought with me. I gave instructions again about my feeding pattern to Nick who would make sure that on the hour I would have hot Maxim from my supplies, now all that was left was to get in the water and begin.

The boat steadied and slowed enabling me to climb down the ladder at the rear of the boat and get in. The boat now laid about three hundred yards from the shore as they didn't want to go aground or foul their prop in fishing pot lines. The beach was empty all except for a man walking his dog and he stopped to watch as I swam to shore. I had swum right over the top of a kelp bed which is one of my phobias. My imagination runs riot and I feel as though the kelp will grab me around the legs and pull me down so I wasn't a happy bunny. Standing on the shore I wondered what came next; did I just get in and swim back or what? Just as my thoughts were about to take off once more the horn on the boat sounded and Nick waved me in.

The water wasn't cold as I got back in, in fact it was warm which was a blessing as it takes numerous hours to swim the Channel, it's a long haul back to England and there is no duty frees. Someone jokingly had asked if I would get them some duty fee items and swim it back. The rules on non-port of entry are strict and the French authorities only allow us ten minutes on the beach before we have to leave again. Obtaining all the correct documents is part of the pilot's job and he is constantly in touch with the coast guard throughout the swim, keeping them informed that they have a swimmer in the water and the course they are taking.

When you are at sea sail takes precedence over motor but when you have a swimmer in the water that can change. The pilot will radio oncoming shipping and alert them to the fact they have a swimmer in the water so they can alter their course by a degree and avoid a collision. The Dover straights are one of the busiest shipping lanes in the world and hundreds of ships and tankers ply its waters every day. That doesn't even take into account the numerous ferries and catamarans that have a schedule to adhere to. During the swim I would cross two ferry shipping lanes twice and the odds of a collision were fierce. It's only due to the skipper's vigilance and the coast guard that we had a chance of crossing either.

We had started the swim at nine sixteen a.m. and it would take me over fifteen hours before I finished. It was on the eleventh of August 1995 and it wouldn't be until the twelfth that I would make it safe to the shores of Dover, it all seemed impossible but that's where I found myself in what appeared to be an impossible situation. The water was unusually warm for the time of year and normally it would be an average of 16 degrees but today it was reaching nineteen degrees, I was truly blessed and the water was flat calm, it was like swimming in a swimming pool but with the salt content there was a lot more buoyancy.

We were fast approaching the first hour and it was time for my first feed of the day. I didn't realize it but while I was treading water and getting ready for the cup that Nick was handing to me the motion of the boat going up and down was different to me. It was enough to make me nauseous and I threw up even before the food got to me. I tried to take in the Maxim but with every sip I felt worse. Mike indicated for me to continue swimming, he would try again in another hour. I was feeling hungry as I had not eaten for some time and my energy levels were low but I kept swimming. The next hour saw the same pattern, whenever I looked at the boat I vomited and again I set off swimming. Mike was getting concerned as its crystal clear I couldn't go on for ever without food. I could see the anxiety written on his face while he consulted with Graham and Nick. Mike phoned ship to shore to Freda and she gave him some instructions. Mike pulled me over around the fourth hour and gave me half a ginger biscuit which I managed to get down much to the relief of Mike. Thirty minutes later he was able to give me a whole biscuit and that also stayed down. He was gradually winning the battle and soon I was able to take a cup of maxim and completely drink it.

It's not easy drinking anything a sea while treading water, an art in itself. Sometimes a freak wave would swamp the cup, filling it with sea water; other times I would miss judge the waves and my cup would go under so it was in my own interest to gulp it down as soon as I had it in my hand, hot or not. The swim made slow progress and I was encouraged by Graham who came out on deck and called me over to say we had just entered the neutral zone. This is an area which isn't used by shipping going up and down the Channel only those going across the Channel would enter the neutral zone. Wow! I was out of the French shipping lane. Graham again came out when we had crossed into the English shipping lane and left the neutral zone behind, it was a real boost to my confidence levels; he also said that my stroke rate was faster now than when I had set out earlier that morning.

It was impossible from my view point to see a great deal or have any understanding of where we were except that I knew being in English waters had a wonderful ring to it. The sun was beginning to set and the boat swung behind me and they took a photo of the sun setting with me in the foreground which I thought was really nice of them. As soon as the sun had gone darkness closed in, I was surprised that I could see the plankton in the water; it had an aluminous glow and looked like stars shining in the water. The crew could easily know my position as before getting in at the start of the swim, Nick pinned a night stick to the back of my costume to enable the crew to see where I am at night. There was no wind chill on my back as I had expected instead I felt really warm, Nick had been in with me a few times and true to form had messed about. He was at one point doing synchronized swimming, pointing his toes in the air and spinning around, but I did find it amusing.

It had been a blessing that we had chosen to swim from France to England as now I could see Dover castle lit up high above the ferry terminal. We were still a long way off but it was very clear even from my position in the water and made me feel I had made progress. I felt even if I was unable to do crawl at the last minute I would doggy paddle my way in to shore, that's how I felt.

Mike came out on deck and called me over to have a word. He said he needed an hour of my best swimming if we were to make Shakespeare beach as we were on a flood tide and moving fast. It was now or never and I dug deeper than I knew possible. My arms had gone beyond sore and it was only sheer determination that kept me going and now Mike had said he would put me on the beach in an hour if I gave it everything.

I had drawn on reserves I didn't know I had in me and an hour later Mike came out again and said he was sorry but he needed another hour, I didn't have time to chew over what he said and in blind obedience continued giving my all. By now Dover castle loomed large and again I was encouraged by the thought of finally finishing. Mike came out on deck again and called me over to tell me I had missed Shakespeare beach by ten feet and was now on the outer wall of the harbour. Freda, Alison and Hue had all been watching me from the roundabout pull in at the top of the hill just outside of Dover and now were going onto St Mary's bay and did I want to swim onto St Mary's bay and put in there or did I want to go in under Jubilee way which was on the far side of the ferry terminal? I didn't even give it a second thought but just asked Mike to put me in as soon as possible.

Mike phoned Freda to tell her we were headed into Fan bay just below Jubilee Way and to meet us back at the dump. The water around the two gates was very turbulent and I admit it was difficult crossing them but after that it was a breeze as the finish was now in sight. Mike came out again to tell me to ease off and tread water as a large ferry was about to cross in front of us going into the ferry docks. It wasn't easy treading water and instead I had to swim slowly in the opposite direction as I was on a flood tide going in the wrong direction straight into the path of the oncoming vessel.

The ferry passed us and I safely navigated the opening and entered Fan bay. Graham came out and told me to follow the flash lights beam into shore as it was pitch black and I couldn't see anything without it. Following the beam of light I swam on cautiously not wishing to hit any rocks or obstacles. The beam of light started to sway first to the right and then the left, I didn't find it at all funny as I was exhausted and shouted for Mike to keep the beam still and in one direction. I found myself at the base of the white cliffs of Dover, scrambling to get out as I had been told that you must clear the water completely which I soon found was impossible. The horn on the boat sounded and the crew started shouting for me to return to the boat and I was then told that a new ruling had just come into force where when you finish at a cliff face and could go no further all you needed to do was touch it and the swim is over, no one had told me and I must have looked a real idiot trying to scramble out. Swimming back to the boat was like adding insult to injury after spending fifteen hours plus getting here only to find I still had further to go. Eventually I made it to the steps at the back of the boat and the helping hands of my district manager came down to haul me on board as we started motoring back to the dump and home.

I went inside and was immediately hugged by everyone; I was so exhausted and just about everything hurt. Back at the dump I had no idea but my sisters had been waiting for hours for me to come in. Theresa had been taken short and as there was no toilet facilities had gone to a dark spot away from the others and done her business only to discover much to her horror that she was on a security camera. It gave everyone a good laugh after wards. I got back into my track suit while on the boat; it took nearly half an hour to get back to where we had set out from all those hours ago. Hue and the children along with my sisters were all lined up on the key side clapping when we came to a stop and I got off along with my district manager and Nick.

I had made arrangements for us all to have a reception buffet at the local Royal Mail offices at Dover as I knew I would be famished. They gave me a wonderful reception at the office those staff that were on duty came to congratulate me and it was wonderful to have my family around me. Elissa came up and gave me a huge bear hug not realizing my shoulders were caning and I winced as she squeezed me, she said I looked as if I had gone ten rounds with Mike Tyson as my eyes where all puffy due to my goggles and the cap mark, well I don't think we should even go there!

I got home to Westerham at about four in the morning and just collapsed into bed and didn't wake up until ten the following morning. It was a Sunday and I knew all the swimmers waiting to swim would be on the beach, not that I had to hurry as I had done my swim, but I wanted to do my lap of honour around the bay which was customary. So we had breakfast and together with the au pair and Emma and Phillip set off one more time to Dover and to celebrate again but with all the swimmers.

A couple of days later I received the largest bunch of flowers I have ever seen, they came from no other than Sir Geoffrey Pratt, the chairman of Royal mail, congratulating me on my achievement and telling me I had the following week off to recover. It had been a dream come true and I hope it inspires you to dream big and to achieve those big dreams.

Arriving in France to commence swim.

Sea Satin with pilot Mike Oram leaving Dover to commence swim in France.

From left to right, Malvern Pantern, Freda Streeter and myself after Malvern and I successfully completed the Channel.

Certification.

CHAPTER SIX
The centenial paralympic games

During my weeks leave I was told to report to Orpington Office to take over from Julie to be the customer relations officer in my own right. Before going back to work I first had to deal with both of my shoulders which were frozen and very painful. Very slowly I drove to the doctors, it isn't easy with frozen shoulders and I was glad there were not too many corners to negotiate. The doctor took one look at me and decided to give me quarter zone injections into both shoulders. I knew it would be painful but I really wasn't prepared and as the injection went into the joints I screamed at the top of my lungs, You could have scraped me off the ceiling. To top it all I had to drive back home where I nursed my poor shoulders for the rest of the week.

Orpington was a whole lot nearer to my home at Westerham and I was thankful not to have to get up at the crack of dawn to do a postal round. I had already decided while at the Gravesend Office working under Julie that there would be an auction after my swim. I was to share the money raised with the Olympic Association and the school where I trained as they had a natural connection. The school was used by disabled children and I was working to raise awareness for the Paralympians. There was still a vast quantity of goods required for the auction and all I had so far was the first day covers I had carried on my two way swim of the Isle of Skye.

Once back at work in the Orpington Office, work on the auction began in earnest. I sent off numerous letters to every different venue for tourists I could think of asking for family tickets, loads of places sent tickets back to me and I was astounded by the generosity. I visited all the shops in Orpington as well as Westerham and Swanley, asking for products to auction, it was truly amazing the things shop owners gave. They ranged from dinners for two at some of the restaurants to meat vouchers from butchers and free cut and blow dries and a whole heap more.

The auction was scheduled for November and I would be able to have an athlete from the Olympic Association attend to give away some of the prizes and Sir Geoffrey Pratt the chairman of Royal Mail would also attend. There was to be a disco and a bar as well as a full sit down dinner beforehand, I was sure it would be a great success.

One evening at home I had a phone call from Alison, they were one lady down in a relay swim, The Gilbert girls relay team it was called. I phoned my boss as I hadn't been back at work for more than a couple of days and he assured me it would be fine. The crossing took place on the 26th of August 1995 and would prove to be the roughest crossing to date.

I met up with Alison and the other swimmers at the dump at six o clock in the morning, there was another boat moored up next to Aegean Blue with a mixed team from Jersey and we all had our photos taken before setting out. The Jersey swimmers threw down a gauntlet and challenged us. The last team to finish would buy the drinks, a challenge Alison could not refuse. We coasted round to Shakespeare beach and the two boats were side by side when the horn for Alison went off and she leapt into the water.

Alison made a lot of distance on the Jersey team and the second swimmer I thought could take it easy but the Jersey team soon overtook us. It was on about the fifth hour we saw the mast of the jersey boat dwarfed against the bulk of an oil tanker up ahead and I was sure they would have to lay up for a while as the tanker ploughed past them. The weather had started to get rougher as I took my first swim of the day. By the eighth hour we past the

Jersey team heading back home, they had decided it was too rough to make the attempt but we continued on.

Alison was a good captain and she asked each of us if we wanted to continue, which of course we did. I don't know any swimmer who would be courageous enough to tell the world champion they wanted to give up and so we continued. By my second swim it was difficult for the previous swimmer to even get out of the water let alone for me to get in. The wave pattern had to be calculated with precision as I jump over board to start my second swim. It was not unlike a roller coaster as I swam up the face of the wave and down the other side. Sometimes the waves were so high all I could see of the boat was the tip of the mast head as I was in a trough on one side of the wave and the boat in the trough on the opposite side. I found it increasingly difficult to keep my body from flipping over as I came down the wave but it was uncanny how it became a game of keeping the correct swim line and not tumbling head over heels down the wave face. Eventually the storm blew itself out and the waves became small once more.

We finished at just after six in the evening and motored for home. That night we stayed at Alison's flat and after eating a takeaway slept out on the floor in sleeping bags. Freda came into the room and told us to be diplomatic with the Jersey team if we saw them that morning on the beach as they were licking their wounds. After Freda had left us to get up, lee who is the smallest girl I have ever seen jump up and said "no way am I gonna keep quiet, it was their challenge after all" and we had to agree with her, they had been a bit in your face with the challenge. We never did get our free drinks from the team but we did do the fastest crossing of the year for an all-female relay team, even though it was a force eight blowing.

In December the auction went ahead and was a great success in all I had raised over sixteen thousand pounds for the school and Olympic Association. Hue was the auction master and even Emma and Phillip got in on the act, holding up the items to be auctioned off and giving out the tickets etc. I even managed to get a few outings for the family which we went on the following year. The timing of the auction had been a huge success as it was just before

Christmas and I believe people were buying things for Christmas presents.

July the following year just before my England/ France swim I went off to the Paralympic games in Atlanta. What a thrill! We met at Heathrow which was the first time I had ever flown from there before and the terminals were huge, bright and with loads of shopping outlets. We flew directly to Atlanta which was a blessing. I had always wanted to go to the States and here I was embarking on an adventure of a life time, the pinnacle of what an athlete could only begin to visualize or even dream about and it was all happening to me. I felt very privileged to have this opportunity.

When we were coming into land all that could be seen were trees as far as the eye could see with sky scrapers coming from the centre. It was a very green place with a bustling city at its core. Gathering our baggage we met one of the Olympic gold medallists in the arrivals, he had been a former Hammer Thrower and had five gold medals attributed to him although I had never heard of him which seems an awful shame that our media mainly cover the Olympics and not the Paralympics. The athletes work extraordinarily hard, even more so than the Olympic athletes as they have to overcome many adversities even before they begin to train.

We climbed into the largest MPV I had ever seen, almost a coach but not quite, with numerous wheels and very modern. If this was the beginning of the trip what would the remainder be like, I was awe struck. The hotel was a Holiday Inn on the outskirts of Atlanta city but accessible by the rail network. It had been chosen because of its immediate central location to most of the sporting venues and a little surprise we would have later in the week. The lobby was enormous, I had heard people say that the States is bigger and better, they were not far wrong. Inside the lobby all the bedrooms were facing into the lobby and towered above us with a sky light at the very top. Just in front of us was a life-sized statue of horses jumping through a hole in the crumbling Berlin wall.

Beyond was the reception and further on was an area for the residents to dine.

The reception gave us all cards which were in fact entry keys to our rooms which you swiped through a device at the door and it opened the room and switched on the lights. The bed was the largest I had ever seen in my entire life and as soon as the bellhop had disappeared I couldn't help but take a run and jump onto the bed. I was finally in the USA and at an Olympic games to boot and everything was just miraculous. Later that day we were given an orientation talk about the layout of Atlanta and the rail system and given free passes for the rail network which is laid out in a North, South, East and West configuration and very easy to navigate. We were then given a book of vouchers for the Paralympics which enabled us to enter any sports venue and to watch the athletes perform. We were also told the itinerary for the ten days which was to include the opening ceremony as well as four trips. The first was to the opening ceremony. The second visit to a Southern cotton plantation mansion, the third visit was to the site of the civil war battle fields. The fourth was for a dinner one evening at one of the top restaurants in the area and lastly a tour of Atlanta.

In between these tours we were free to go and see Atlanta for ourselves and just have a fun packed stay. I was sad that Hue wasn't with me and I missed him terribly. Every evening as late as I could because of the seven hours' time difference I would phone him and give him an update of what had occurred throughout the day.

The opening ceremony was on the evening of our first day and I had been out with some of the guys on the train to the downtown area of Atlanta and had already put my passport and money and tickets in the hotel safe. When it came time for us to go to the opening ceremony we took out some money and the tickets from the lobby safe and jumped onto the train for the short journey to the stadium. Joining the throngs of people that were making their way to the stadium we walked excitedly, there were thousands and thousands of people all going in the same direction it wasn't unlike moving water, a sea of humanity. Everyone was talking in excited tones and we exchanged conversations with anyone who was walking along side of us as everyone had a common goal and we were united together even though cultures and language should have been obvious barriers it had all fallen away at that time.

As we queued together in the surging mass we checked our tickets were safe in our pockets. I was mortified to discover my ticket wasn't there in my pocket and racked my brains trying to remember the sequence of events leading up to us being there. Then just as I was giving up all hope I remembered getting the tickets out of the safe and wondered if they had fallen onto the floor, the chances of finding them were slim but I just had to try as this was too important to miss. My heart was in my mouth and beating hard as I raced against the onslaught of the people all moving in the opposite direction that I wanted to go in. The train was not a problem and I had the carriage all to myself, I kept going over and over the moments when I had got my ticket out of the safe and the more I thought about it the more convinced I was that I had dropped it at the reception and could only pray to God that it was still there. When you pray to God, it is powerful stuff and never to be under estimated as I was to find out. Anyone who found the ticket could easily have sold it at astronomical prices to the black market even if they didn't want them themselves.

I entered the lobby as fast as my legs would carry me and rushed to the reception desk, looking all around at the ground but not seeing my ticket anywhere. I asked the receptionist and she gave me a blank stare as if I was a Looney and obviously hadn't got the ticket. I was just about to despair when the doorman, a huge hulk of a black man came over and asked if I was indeed looking for something and I explained with tears rolling down my cheeks that I had lost my ticket to the opening ceremony and I had been sure I had dropped it at reception but there was no sign of it anywhere. He put his hand in his pocket and said is this what you are looking for. I reached up and flung my arms around his neck giving him the biggest smacker ever. I was speechless and crying with relief, disbelieving that anyone would have saved them just in case the owner came looking for them, it was indeed a miracle and I thank God for that man who was so honest, wow!

Getting back to the stadium was a doodle, I was floating on air, knowing how lucky I had been but I didn't appreciate just how God had indeed answered my prayers that day and on many other occasions but today I am only just getting to grips with Gods miracles we see every day but just take for granted. I joined the others of Royal Mail now seated halfway up one of the stands and gazed down as the athletes began to file into the stadium grouped with their nation's team. Every person in the stadium was on their feet shouting for their own nation, flags waved frantically, voices shouting and lungs at bursting point trying to be heard above the roar of the crowd. Looking around there wasn't a seat spare and I counted myself very fortunate to be amongst them.

When all the nations had gathered on the centre field the spectacle began with a stage rising up from amongst the athletes. Numerous performers came on stage including Mohammed Ali although now very shaky with Parkinson's decease. The star that played Bat man also appeared in a wheel chair as he had been victim to a riding accident some years before and now was the voice of the Paralympics. Fireworks rose into the sky high above Atlanta, parachutists landed on the field carrying the Paralympic flag which was hoisted in front of the flame which was yet to be lit. Lastly the athlete entered the stadium carrying the Olympic flame on a lap of honour. We had seen the torch just outside our hotel that morning as it made its way through to the stadium. The torch was handed to Mohammed Ali who gave it to a disabled mountaineer who in turn scaled a rope and dropped the torch into the flame pit high above the stadium. We were all on our feet again shouting and clapping as hard as we could, fireworks exploded by the hundreds in a fantasy backdrop to what we were witnessing, it was stunning, and magical.

Everything about those ten days was out of this world and I was very privileged to be there. There were many things that stood out on that trip. John, who I had met on the trip, was one of the other recipients of the tour and went everywhere together, on one such trip we had gone to downtown Atlanta shopping. The weather was fantastic and the shopping mall was beyond belief with its cartoon characters in the mall and a full sized train just outside. Opposite was the Coca-Cola museum complete with oversized coke bottles holding up a stand. Just across from the museum was a freeze over a hundred foot long of whales, everything was bigger than I had imagined. Fountains were everywhere and we visited the centennial park where just before the Olympics, terrorists had bombed, with catastrophic effect but it had partially been reopened to the public. We visited a toy store as I had to get some presents for Emma and Phillip; we stood awe struck at the grandness of the shop, it was as though we had stepped into a jungle complete with trees.

I had made a few athlete friends that I had met during my tour of the UK and wanted to catch up with them and just maybe get to see them compete if the timing was right. John and I hopped on a train and headed for the swimming venue. It was open to the air which surprised me but a wonderful venue all the same. The competitors were sat on the opposite side of the pool and the spectators on the side we had entered; I spotted one of my friends sitting with the British athletes and waved in her direction but had no luck. John said we should try to get nearer so ended up above the dive area on a balcony connecting the athletes with the spectators and we did manage to get her attention and she came over. I had already missed her event which was a shame as she got a bronze medal. We watched for a few hours and then made our way out of the pool. Outside it was blazing hot and we were glad of the sprays dotted around. I had never seen anything like them, they were a very fine spray mist which you walked under and it was very pleasant.

The following day John and I headed off to the velodrome which was situated in boulder mountain national park. First we took the train and then a bus which stopped in a small town where Christmas is perpetual. In all the house windows were Christmas figures as the town was famous for their manufacture and each house displayed a different variety of ornaments.

While waiting for our bus a couple court my eye, they looked very distressed and I approached them and asked if I might help them. Their son was competing at the velodrome and was in the finals that afternoon. They thought they would be late and were in a panic. Nearby a bus was parked up and the crew were having a tea break, after explaining the situation and informing them that the couple had indeed come all the way from Australia, they agreed to drive them out there. I just couldn't believe how kind the people of Atlanta are and how friendly. John and I went along for the ride as we knew the bus would drive to the central car park, right in front of the cable car and we thought that would be a cool place to begin our day.

We had passed lots of cyclists competing as we came through the park which is vast; it houses a museum, a zoo, a hotel, boating pond, full sized train as well as a cable car which takes you to the top of Boulder Mountain. As we stepped into the cable car a commentary began all about the mountain. The mountain is the largest single boulder in the world and on its face is carved the civil war generals. The carving takes up the space of three football fields and took a very long time to complete. Just under the carving looking down is a huge pond and in front of it stands a copy of the statue that stands in our lobby at the hotel. We finally reached the top where there is a small restaurant and stepped out into the bright sunlight. The views were just breath-taking; we were able to see for miles out over the park.

After the mountain John expressed a desire to explore the park, we started at the museum and then took a stroll around the zoo. It was very lovely. We saw elk and mountain lion as well as some smaller animals. John went into a small shop nearby which looked for the entire world as if it had come straight out of a western movie. It had rocking chairs out on the veranda. On the way home we looked at the local shops just outside the station, John was fascinated by one in particular which had the old salon leather chairs and they did cut throat shaving, so John went in and had a shave while I took photos, the hairdresser must have thought we had gone crazy. I was fascinated by all the life sized bronze statues everywhere we went in every day poses.

There was so much to see it was like a fairy tale. Visiting Kennesaw we stopped at the National Battlefield Park, which commemorates the Civil War Battle fought there in 1864 during the Atlanta campaign. On the 27th of June major General William T. Sherman with 100,1000 men of the Union army fought a battle with General Joseph Johnston, who had just 65,000 Confederates. I think you can guess the outcome. The battlefield now held actors, who played their roles perfectly, dressed in Confederate uniforms complete with cannon, which made an almighty noise as they fired the cannon.

The main party was going to see where they filmed Gone with the wind and Martin Luther King's grave. I decided I had to do some training in the pool of the hotel as when I got home I wouldn't have long before my Channel attempt and having time off during training wasn't the best idea. I just had to come out to Atlanta and see the Olympics for myself but still had to keep up my training. The pool was very hot but that didn't matter, as I swam I thought over all the things that I had seen and what were still to come. That evening I spoke to Emma and Phillip and Hue, there was so much to tell it was all too exciting but it was sad not to have them here in person.

After breakfast the next day we were all taken by bus to a southern plantation house. Actors re-enacting the family which used to live at the house stood on the porch pretending they were waiting for their son who was due back from the battle front. The black maid who had died at over ninety had passed on all that she knew about the family and the trip was fascinating in its detail. After the tour of the house we went out into the back yard where tables where laid up with red checked table clothes. The staff had cooked a real southern BBQ. While we ate busily talking in loud voices full of excitement I noticed a dog flap in the barn to my left was moving. I was very surprised as a raccoon came through the flap, I was expecting a cat or a small dog but a raccoon was something I hadn't bargained for. I think that is what has enthralled me, you never quite know what to expect around the next corner.

In the evening a few of us went downtown to the cinema, I can't for the life of me remember what we saw but I do remember being approached outside as we sat on a bench by a local sheriff. He came over and chatted to us and soon realized we were Brits here for the Olympics. He shared a coffee with us right there in the middle of the street, I do like the way the southerners speak and was captivated by him in his uniform.

Our trip was coming to an end sadly, we had so enjoyed all the sights and sounds, the athletics and other sports I had attended will stay with me for many years, all that was left was to say goodbye to our hosts. They had arranged for us all to have breakfast with some of the athletes which were not competing that day and we met up at the house the Public Relations team had rented in Lower Atlanta. The team all went outside for one final photo opportunity before we set off home once more.

The trip had been a trip of a life time, meeting athletes and going to all the venues was beyond words. I had made some very good friends during my stay and seen things I will never forget, truly magical!

A couple of days after arriving back in the UK I had an invitation to the RAC club in London. It was the formal reception for all the athletes and Prince Phillip was the guest speaker. Each table was filled with Olympic athletes from both the present and the past people like Pincent and Redgrave the Olympic rowers and my hero Duncan Goodhew a gold medal swimmer from previous years. In fact I sat next to Duncan which I am sure was pre-arranged and on my opposite side was a former equestrian medal winner All around the dining room were actors sprayed to look like statues from Greek times and occasionally they would move and make people jump at the time it was a new concept but today I often see men dressed as statues in shopping malls.

August came at me in a rush and I knew I hadn't done enough training but it was my own fault and now it was time to again battle the elements in the English Channel. Julie came with me along with one of the swimmers from the training group. I just wasn't motivated in the same way that I had been for my first Channel attempt and as I stood with the team at the dump waiting to step on board I had a feeling of unease. It was definitely founded and my second attempt at the Channel failed. I had swum sixteen hours and been up and down the coast of France more than once that night. I just wasn't making any headway and I just gave up, sad but true, it just wasn't going to be my day that day. Looking back my heart just wasn't in it.

Gathering of Paralympic Athletes, Royal Mail personnel, British High Commission personnel and Royal Mail prize winners.

The lobby of our Atlanta hotel showing the statue depicting the fall of the Berlin Wall.

Downtown Atlanta, everything was over the top.

standing in the Centennial Park fountain.

Paralympics celebration dinner. I sat next to Duncan Goodhew former swimming gold medalist.

CHAPTER SEVEN
State side again

As the end of 1996 drew to a close, I was honoured by Royal Mail; they invited me to a dinner for the South East awards for employee of the year at Brighton along with others from around the region. Although I didn't win the Employee of the year, the panel highly commended me for the work I had done with the Paralympics. I was given a crystal rose bowl which had been engraved.

It had been a wonderful two years with the public relations department of Royal Mail but now it was all over I had been sent back to my role of post lady back in Swanley. The journey was crippling and after having got used to getting up and arriving at work for nine o clock it was difficult to get to work for five in the morning. My wages had dropped as well and I knew it was time for a change.

I found a job in Westerham working for a local paper, Biggin Hill News. I just loved the work and it had a car with the job. It gave me a certain amount of freedom; my days Wednesday to Friday were pretty mundane, Monday and Tuesdays were much busier as we worked towards our deadline. The paper had several issues each with local news according to the area it served and the people were friendly. My boss allowed me quite a lot of freedom with my swimming which would prove invaluable later during my next adventure.

Because I now worked in Westerham I didn't see Hue quite as much but he came over in the evenings and spent most nights staying at my house, except if we had a disagreement and then he would go to his own house in Swanley. I thought typical man, get out when the heat is rising and go to his little warren. We had been engaged for several years and I was left wondering if we would ever get married. Hue didn't seem in any rush and loved the idea of having his cake and eating it too. In fact he didn't have any real reason to get married; he liked things just as they were. I loved him dearly and carried on as if it didn't bother me, which it did, all the time.

I had heard the Channel swimmers talking about a race in Manhattan and asked Alison for the details so I could apply to swim. One of the qualifying conditions is to have swum for at least twelve hours or to have swum the English Channel, so I had my entry accepted. It was to take place in July of 1997. I was still training twice a week at Redhill and Reigate and as Easter came began training once again with the Channel swimmers. I knew now what to expect and there were a lot of new swimmers training for the Channel later that year. After our first swim we would go off to a local café and have lunch and swap stories from previous years, it made me feel like an old hand and it passed away the three hours break before we had to get in again.

On this swim I financed it totally as I was earning a better salary than before. The actual swim fee wasn't a great deal but there were other things to take into consideration, accommodation and flights had to be found but it all got sorted eventually. Hue was to accompany me and we would arrive two days prior to the race to get settled in and have a look around. July soon arrived and I was glad my training was over as I didn't want to hang on until August as I had done for previous swims.

We touched down in New York and grabbed a taxi which took us to a small hotel at the tip of Manhattan, right opposite Battery Park were the race started from. Our bedroom window looked out onto the Hudson River and we had a wonderful view of the

Statue of Liberty and just to the right the twin towers of the World Trade Centre. It was all too exciting and in the afternoon we took a circular trip of Manhattan by boat to get a feel for where I would swim. I'm glad the boat started from the same place and finished at the same place my swim would, as we set off the boat past the toe of Battery Park and headed off up the East river.

The first problem that I would face would be swimming alone until I caught up with my boat which would be mid river under the Manhattan Bridge, identifying it would be the problem but we decided the boat would watch for me not the other way around. We passed under the Manhattan Bridge and continued upstream, passing the Empire State Building and the Chrysler Building, the tide was pushing hard against the bow of the boat and I knew it would be a tuff swim but as it was early on in the swim I didn't worry too much. There is a place on the river called hells gate where the current picks up a notch and five rivers meet at that point, we were approaching it and I was visualizing what it would be like to swim this portion of the river, hard I thought.

We turned into the Harlem River and immediately the water calmed and was like sheet glass. There was the relief I would need after going through Hells Gate. We passed under several bridges and came to a railway bridge just before going out onto the Hudson. The commentator on the boat told us that at times he would wait in the river for the bridge to open as they closed it when a train was coming through. I knew for this bit of the river alone I would need a canoe to accompany me and I knew I would be able to hire one when I got to the meeting

That evening after dinner Hue and I sat in the bay window of the bedroom and watched a huge storm that was going on. There was a flash of green light opposite in Jersey and later we found out the power was out for several days, it had struck a power station. Early next morning we had a meeting of all swimmers and crew. We were appointed a boat for the day and we met the skipper. I didn't meet the man who was to accompany me in the canoe but would meet him on the day. The skipper was actually on his honeymoon and owned his own boat which was moored close by. We were all given T shirts, mine had swimmer on it and Hue's said he was crew.

My next stop was to get new goggles, the states have far more choice in their shops and I looked forward to buying a new pair as mine were old and leaked a little. During the day my ears started to really hurt, they had not been good since we got off the plane but now they were unbearable. I couldn't find a doctor and we eventually ended up at the hospital, I was glad to have insurance I knew this would cost a great deal. The doctor was terrific and I told him the next day I had to swim and he understood. He gave me very strong tablets and ear-drops and said he was glad I had come as the infection in my ear if left would have eaten away at the bone. The following day the pain had begun to subside and I felt well enough to compete.

It was four in the morning as we set out from the hotel to go to our respective starting points. Hue had to cut across town and find the boat just off of Manhattan Bridge, I was sent to Battery Park not far from the hotel where the race started. If you had told me I would be walking in Manhattan at four in the morning on my own I would have said you were mad but here I was. It was very peaceful and not a soul around, the sun was just coming up over the sky line. I had really enjoyed being in New York, it was never a place that I thought I would feel so peaceful. I arrived and soon others arrived as well. There were film crews and they interviewed some of the more influential swimmers, I was just an unknown so they didn't bother me and I was left with my own thoughts which were now heavily into the swim and the challenges which lay ahead.

One of the hazards is a sewage intake on the Hudson River which I knew I needed to steer clear of, another was the cruise liners docked in the Hudson but they left around one p.m. and I wouldn't be fast enough for that to be a problem. The cameras were now interviewing a man from Alaska who competed every year, he was bare foot and had arrived without shoes and looked very unkempt. I wondered where in Alaska he trained, it must be very hazardous with bear and the like. My mind wandered and watched what was happening and it was as if I were a fly on the wall almost like an outer body experience. Soon we were called to get undressed and get into the water. I had been looking forward to this as the water was a warm 68 degrees, the locals thought it chilly but to me it was like bath water. We all lined up the best we could and the horn sounded and we were off.

This was the first ever race I had been in as most of my swimming had been against the elements and was a solo event but here I was in an International arena with people from all around the world who were at a good standard, how would I fare in such a race I wondered. We rounded Battery Park, there were a good number of us, some were solo swimmers others relay swimmers and I thought it a shame that they hadn't separated us as the relay swimmers would be much faster away than the solo swimmers who were in for the long haul. As we neared Manhattan Bridge the boats were all strung out across the river in a line and already the main pack had separated. I fell somewhere in the middle of the pack and hoped my boat could pick me out, I need not have worried. As I came out the other side of the bridge my boat came up beside me and the canoeist had joined me. He came over and actually said good morning but all I could do was to wave in between strokes.

We made steady progress and already I could feel the sun soaking into my back as I passed the prison barge moored just off centre of the river and was used as an overflow to the state prison. We past to the left of an Island and I glimpsed the Empire state building, its lovely to see a lot of things as you swim. Normally while swimming in the English Channel all I could look at was the pilot boat and the crew busying themselves but now I was able to watch my progress as the land fell away to my left and I knew I was making progress. Occasionally my hand would touch a jelly fish, it wasn't shaped like the jelly fishes I had previously come across, it was more akin to a tennis ball but smooth and hard and I was pleased that it didn't sting, a real bonus!

We entered Hells Gate, the boat just ahead of me and to my right; the canoeist was next to me on my left and obviously feeling the same currents that I was. I dug into my strokes making sure each one counted, thinking about how my fingertips were entering the water and was my fingers together collecting every drop of water. Was my line flat with my head in the right position, eyes just above the water line? Was I using the whole of my legs and kicking from the hip, were my ankles free and not stiff? Lots of questions as edging my way up to the Harlem my mind was kept busy with these thoughts. The canoeist had gone far over to my left and was taking shelter from the high walls that rose from the water; just above I could see the cars going by above his head. As I stroked to the right another swimmer passed me, it was the man I had seen earlier being interviewed from Alaska and I wondered if I would get the opportunity to overtake him later. Hue waved at me from the boat which was encouraging.

Inching literally up the East River took every ounce of strength and I focused on reaching the Harlem River which I knew would be still. Putting my head down and controlling each stroke focusing on my next goal we turned into the Harlem, what a relief as I was surely making progress. The Harlem River isn't very wide and as I went under the first bridge it felt claustrophobic as the shadow of the bridge fell around me and I couldn't wait to get to the other side. People think that Channel swimmers wouldn't be scared of anything but I have lots of phobias, sea weed and bridges were just two I was finding out. A dead dog floated past just meters away and my boat crew tried to distract me so I wouldn't freak out which worked, I didn't find out about it until after the swim for which I was grateful.

I believe there are around fourteen bridges in the Harlem River, not that I counted them, I just concentrated on knowing the light just lay beyond their boundaries and pulled hard to get under them. We now stood off the last bridge which was closed as a train was passing over, just my luck I thought to get here when the bridge was closed. The canoe came over with my maxim which I drank in a couple of swallows, the skipper said I could make my way to the extreme left of the bridge where there was an archway, it was big enough for the canoe and myself to enter the Hudson but the boat would have to stay here until the bridge opened again.

I took my queue and followed the canoeist navigating over to the far left and under the bridge, the canoe went straight up in the air as he came out the other side and I realized the water was very rough. The water was so rough it was like a dish washer, pulling and pushing me everywhere, it was as much as I could do to keep a straight line and I even struggled with that. I spotted the canoeist and felt grateful I wasn't there out on my own, a hundred yards later and now in mid-stream treading water to keep my position of looking above the waves I could just about see my boat bobbing about. From their vantage position above the water I knew they must have spotted me and continued to swim.

The current in the Harlem pulls about seven knots Nick the Channel swimmer had told me when he swam it he was keeping pace with some of the vehicles he could see on the bank, it made me all the more cautious as I knew I must be approaching the sewage intake. When Hue and I had been on the circular tour I had the skipper point it out to me so that when it came time to swim I would be able to identify it easily. Spotting the intake some quarter of a mile away I began to swim towards the centre of the river earlier is better than later I thought to myself. For every stroke forward I was pushed a meter downstream and if I didn't put a lot of effort into this I knew there was a danger of being pulled into the intake, so putting everything in eventually the intake passed me on the left. This was fun, moving so swiftly that even if I didn't swim I moved at a fair rate of knots.

I was now approaching the piers where cruise liners had been earlier and was pleased to see that none remained and thought my passage would be safe but I was to face another hazard which almost proved fatal. As I neared one of the piers of which there were several, I noticed my crew looked very agitated and were waving at me, so I swam over to the boat. Just at that moment a huge hand grabbed the back of my costume and another my arm and they hauled me out onto the deck, engaging the motors and ran up stream. I was infuriated with them and wondered why when I was swimming ok would they ever do such a thing, the reason was soon made clear to me as I looked over my shoulder back at where I had been a huge tug with about fifteen barges attached came straight out behind us. The skipper of the tug could clearly see the boat and realizing it was motorized thought he had safe passage but could not see me in the water and didn't realize the hazard. The tug was only about ten foot off our stern and I knew it had been a close thing.

The skipper motored a little way up stream after the tug and barges had moved past us and once again I got back in and began to swim. Further down the river the boat pulled across my path and I had to tread water wondering what in Gods name was going on. It was a Sunday and what I hadn't realized was on a Sunday the river was just another play area for New Yorkers and on this occasion several ski boats going at break neck speed had been heading straight for me as they were unable to see me in the water even though we had a flag flying telling people there was a swimmer in the water. Recreational boats were not aware often of all the regulations of the water and hadn't got a clue when it came to observing waterway law.

The skipper pulled up beside me and gave me some more Maxim, he said that the finish wasn't more than half an hour away but I would need to swim as close to the wall as possible as the current if I were to be caught in it would sweep me past the finish. I was also to be ready to grab hold of the ladder and not to pass it as it was the only way of getting out. I didn't need telling twice, it had been an eventful swim and I had enjoyed it very much, even more so with the finish now in sight. There were lots of spectators gathered along the banks as I swam by, I didn't want to get too close to the wall as there may have been obstacles unseen just below the surface but needed to be in close enough not to miss the finish. The crowds were getting thicker and clapping and shouting, I could see the ladder as the wall to my left dipped in again and headed over as far as I could keep safety in mind. I grabbed for the ladder and with relief my hand held firm on one of the uprights. Hauling hard and with some help from above me I stepped onto the tarmac at the top of the ladder.

My legs were shaky but my heart had stopped racing, which up until that point I hadn't realized it had been pumping hard with adrenaline. Hue draped a towel over my shoulders and pulled me into a great big hug and told me how proud he was of me. Feeling numb now with exhaustion I crumpled onto a nearby bench and just sat taking everything in, I had just swum twenty seven miles around Manhattan Island and looking at my watch it had been just nine hours and seven minutes, I could barely believe it. Hue encouraged me to get dressed quickly as my body would stiffen and it makes getting dressed nearly impossible and he helped me as well. We were told to assemble at a hotel nearby which was hosting the awards ceremony; we could also get something to eat there and meet up with the rest of the crew.

At the hotel swimmers and crew were all mingling and chatting, I met a men from another American paper who also had been competing, he unfortunately didn't finish. He said he got as far as the sewage intake and was too close and had been sucked towards the intake and rescued by his gallant boat which had to navigate in between the huge wooden posts guarding the intake. He had grabbed hold of the ropes on the fender at the bow of the boat and they had hauled ass to get him out. That had happened twice and the second time the skipper didn't want to put his boat or crew at risk and ended the swim. I felt so sad for him he was obviously very depressed about the whole ordeal.

We grabbed a drink and some food and I thanked the skipper and was introduced to his new wife and I said how grateful I was that they had offered to help us. Everyone was called to gather around near the stage and they began the awards ceremony. The first swimmers home had safely been predicted and were correct. I was surprised when my name was called, I collected the prize for first lady home in the 40 to 49 age group, which there were a number of us in that category, and I was totally speechless and very surprised. It had been a wonderful day and a climax to the year.

The next day after a good lay in we got up and went down for breakfast, I couldn't stop smiling and Hue understood exactly what I was feeling. I felt elated that I hadn't failed and thoughts of my previous swim the year before crowded in, but now I was vindicated and it felt good. Having time now to look around New York, Hue and I went on a shopping spree, the clothes in Manhattan are an incredible bargain and soon we had so many plastic bags full of goodies we could hardly hold them. I had lots of presents for Emma and Phillip and others for the au pair, it had been wonderful just being there in New York and sharing it with

Hue, just wonderful!

That evening we celebrated and found a steak house just up from where our hotel stood and across the road from the twin towers of the World Trade Centre. At first we didn't think the restaurant was open as it had blacked out windows but on trying the door found it was open and went in. It was very posh and full of Wall Street business people. We were shown to a table with soft candle light, it was very romantic. The waitress came over with a trolley laden with lots of items and began running us through the menu. It was like nothing I had experienced before and she explained the different choices and ways of cooking each item. It took at least ten minutes before she came to a stop by which time I had forgotten most of what she said. Hue asked her to repeat it again but I know he was only pulling her leg. I chose a lobster as we were pushing the boat out and celebrating.

I have never eaten lobster and when it came up it was enormous, spilling over the sides of the plate. The waitress gave me some nut crackers and a small hammer and I sat with my mouth open not knowing what to do. Hue came to the rescue and helped me crack a few of the legs to get the meat out. I was grateful and felt so stupid; I should have known that was what they were for. We enjoyed the intimacy and it felt as if we were the only people in the restaurant, Hue had his hand over mine as we dined and it felt wonderful. It was late when we finally left the restaurant, they had departed us from the best part of one hundred pounds making it the most expensive dinner I had ever eaten in my life but we didn't care at that point in time and went back to the hotel for the celebrations to continue.

The time had come for us to go home; I had far too much luggage to put in my case, there were plastic bags everywhere. I am glad that all the airport restrictions were not in place at that time or we would never have got home. Hue had hired a stretch limousine to take us to the airport, I felt like a princess or at least royalty as we arrived there. While going through customs and placing my bag on the conveyer belt the security picked up something in my bag and I wondered what it could be that would cause so much scrutiny. At the end of the belt a security officer made me unpack the bag and the offending item was opened, it was the huge medal I had been given from the race officials and it drew a crowd of people. The security officer asked what it was from and when I told her it was from the Manhattan marathon swim every one clapped, I felt like a celebrity or a movie star.

Back at home the editor of the paper that I worked for wrote a piece on my swim talking about swimming across the pond which is a phrase used for the Atlantic Ocean which I found amusing. I was becoming a bit of a celebrity in my home town and people would often stop me and chat about swimming, normally they commented on the fact they couldn't swim and could not imagine doing such a long swim, I even had one person ask me what I did if I needed to go to the toilet, did I get out of the water? Some of the questions made me laugh. I began doing public speaking and had been invited to several venues to talk about Channel swimming. Many of the people I spoke to said I should write a book as it was so interesting and it is partly why I am now writing this book.

Nothing grand happened for the remainder of the year, it was back to business as usual, I would work until five thirty and the au pair would pick up the children from school and give them some supper before I got home. Hue would arrive sometime in the evening and we would watch TV together after dinner. Our relationship was what you would term as comfortable but there was never any commitment on Hue's side, he was as unrushed as ever and didn't see the need for us to get married.

Soon my mind was active again trying to think of another swim for the coming year, I had ceased training at Redhill and Reigate and would need to begin again in a local pool if I was to maintain my fitness.

A view of the 28.5 miles around Manhattan that I would swim.

View from my bedroom Window in New York, below was Battery Park the start of the Manhattan Marathon Swim.

CHAPTER EIGHT
Challenged to swim

In December we have the Channel swimmers awards ceremony where they give out the certificates for the year. I was still active and had done another relay that year and enjoyed the company of all my fellow swimmers and so went with Hue to the awards ceremony. We stayed overnight at the hotel where the awards were taking place, which was convenient. During the evening I noticed in the bar area a swimmer who was showing a swims video on a small TV and I happened by and took a peek. It wasn't a Channel swim at all, it was a swim of the Mediterranean; in fact it was the first ever swim from Africa to Italy, a swim of thirty six hours made by Martin Strell of Slovenia. He had in fact come to the dinner to challenge the Channel swimmers, to do the swim in the opposite direction from Italy to Africa. My interest was immediately peaked and I asked him for his contact details. Later that evening Hue and I talked about it, there was a lot of work in preparing for such a feat but decided that was the swim for next year. It was settled; I would give the challenge the thumbs up and contact Martin for further details.

Over the winter months I had time to put the initial plans together and to get a sponsor. Sponsors are notoriously difficult to get but in late January of 1998 I managed to get a sponsor from a therapy company. The owners were South African but they were trying to get into the UK market and with the abuse I gave my body we were more than compatible. I met the owners in London in February, taking a portfolio of the swims I had done to show them. I was introduced to their Marketing and public relations manager, a petite girl of around her early thirties. They agreed to sponsor me and as part of the agreement I would wear their costume for all photo shoots and they wanted me to be free to do interviews which I later cleared with my employers. The only thing left to do was to train hard.

I knew this time I was asking a lot of myself and needed professional help in training. Through my contacts at the paper I had done some advertising for a company in Oxted Surrey. It was owned by a young man of Italian descent who was very helpful. He offered to train me in his gym free of charge in exchange for some publicity and photos, it was all agreed.

Every work day I got up at five, it was no big deal as I was used to getting up early working for Royal Mail. I hurried off to the Gym which was about six miles from where I lived and started training. Not being used to gym work the instructor gave me a work regime which I had to adhere to and it went up in increments each month. For the most part I really enjoyed my time at the gym and it set me up for the day. The routine was a warm up followed by three circuits of weights and stretching. The reps started off as eight to a set but by the time it came for my swim I was doing sets of fifty.

At the beginning of the Easter holiday which was a long weekend, it was time to go to Dover again. It was much easier now that I didn't have to work on a Saturday, it gave me a lot more time to get ready and I didn't have to rush all the time. Ann one of the Channel swimmers would meet me half way and we would have a cappuccino and a croissant in the services at Maidstone before traveling on. We would leave one of the cars in the services which saved on petrol and on longer swims the passenger was able to sleep on the way home. I admit that on many occasions I have done a huge training swim and had to wind my window down to keep me awake on the way home. Because I wasn't working on a

Saturday I wasn't so tired and sharing the driving had been a great idea.

As we started training that Easter and being it was a long weekend, I stayed with Hue and the children at a bed and breakfast close to the ferry terminal. It made the whole weekend a family affair. After training Hue and I took the children to Samphire Hoe, a nature reserve built out of the waste from the Channel Tunnel, we visited Dover Castle with the children as well. Often during training Hue would walk up to the pier and wait for me to swim up that end. He would just do it to encourage me which was a lovely gesture. As it was early in the season and the swims were not too long everyone gathered together to have lunch and swapped stories and geed each other up. Some of the swimmers were first timers but others I had known for some time, it wasn't unlike a big family outing with Freda and Alison taking centre stage.

The water at that time of the year is very chilly but after three months of building up, it was plain sailing. I was due to swim in September when the water in the Mediterranean was at its optimum level and very warm. Everything was coming together nicely. I had booked the hotel which was one of the larger hotels on Pantelleria Island just off the foot of Italy and facing the straights of Pantelleria where I would cross to Tunisia. I had a boat in mind and the skipper had been contacted and agreed to be my pilot. It is very difficult when you are setting up a swim for the first time as everything must be organized, nothing has ever been attempted before and it's not like the Channel swims where all the boats go out every year and you have a host of boats fitted out correctly.

Ann was about to go and have her attempt at the English Channel but was very apprehensive about swimming at night. She wore glasses and without them it would be difficult. I arranged with her to do a night swim in Dover harbour with Julie and her husband who were both qualified divers and capable swimmers. If anything happened I knew Julie would be close at hand with her first aid ability. We met on the beach and Hue stood on the beach looking after our belongings while we set off. Ann had a night stick on her costume enabling us to see her easily and we swam either side of her guiding her. As we came close to the pier and nothing untoward had happened I tapped her on the shoulder and said she could make it to the pier on her own. She set off again; it was soon obvious that she wasn't ok, instead of heading to the pier she was heading out to sea, parallel with the pier. I chased after her and we swam back together to the beach. I hadn't realized her eye sight was so bad but had no solution for her.

A couple of days later she was called for her swim. I had been training with the other swimmers that day and had arranged to meet with Steven, another of the Channel swimmers and go to see Ann start her swim. It was close to one thirty in the morning when we arrived at Samphire Hoe nature reserve. The approach to the reserve is via a tunnel with a barrier just before you go in. We pulled up at the barrier and explained to the guard that we were seeing off a Channel swimmer who was starting just beyond the promenade and who the skipper was, at first he was a bit dubious about letting us pass but eventually let us through. We parked in the car park at the bottom of the hill and made our way on foot to the beach head. It was quite difficult in the dark trying to keep your footing.

Standing on the beach we saw two boats coming round from the harbour which I hadn't expected, the other boat was for a breaststroker making an attempt also. The two boats sat side by side about thirty feet from shore while Ann and the breaststroker swam to the beach. Steve said a few words of encouragement to Ann and we exchanged hugs. The horn blew on the boats and the two swimmers were off and swimming before you could blink an eye. We watched their progress for the first quarter of an hour, Ann was veering off to the left and the boat sounded the horn to get her attention until she corrected it again. Steve climbed back up onto the promenade and pulled me up behind him; crossing the walkway we went to the sea wall and looked out towards the boats. The breaststroker's boat was headed straight out but Ann's boat which was tracking her in the water was still veering off to the left. Steve and I watched for quite a while before heading back to the car.

On the way back through the nature reserve a jeep stopped us and asked if we wanted a lift, it was one of the reserve warders so we accepted as it was getting chilly, he dropped us right next to the car but not before telling us he had been concerned about us and thought we were committing suicide and had come to look for us. Apparently it had been done before and I was horrified at the thought. Back in Dover I dropped Steve at his car and he went home, I stayed and slept in the car in a quite car park at the end of the beach. At first I thought Hue would kill me if he knew I had slept in the car all night in a lonely car park but to be truthful I didn't care and felt quite safe.

September had arrived and my swim was about to go ahead. The team coming with me would be Hue, Julie as first aid and observer, her husband Rob as a diver and the PR lady Karen from the sponsors. We had realized that when we arrived in Italy the flights for Pantelleria Island would have stopped and I had faxed that to the chairman of Fina saying we were going to stop overnight on the mainland and would catch the early morning flight to Pantelleria. Unfortunately the chairman didn't get the fax and it was just by chance I phoned him as we landed out of courtesy, to say we had arrived safely. The chairman wasn't a happy bunny as he had arranged a few people to meet me at the airport, he was however very gracious and sent a couple of people to take us out to dinner. I had no idea he was going to send a welcoming committee but we were very pleased.

Next morning as we crossed the tarmac to board the plane we met up with the Tunisian judge also on his way to the swim. He was a short man, greying with glasses; he spoke perfect English and was very polite. When we landed a short while later we walked together with the Tunisian judge into the arrivals. It was a very small building, one side for departures and the other for arrivals. I wondered why there were so many people and cameras around and looked to see who the film star was or which celebrity had arrived but soon realized it was for me. I was shocked to say the least but soon realized that the Italians were mad about their sport so it shouldn't have surprised me at all.

There was a full TV crew along with sound booms and mikes as I was introduced to the chairman of Fina and the skipper and crew of my boat plus the hotel staff. Wow! It was all a little too much.

The hotel manager handed me a wonderful bouquet of flowers and a gift from the hotel and there were hugs and kisses as I went down the line of people there to greet me. They had sent a car to pick me up and we were whisked off to the hotel. Hue and I went up to our room and had a little chuckle to ourselves as we went; it was just too incredible to believe. Later we joined Julie and Rob in the bar by the pool before exploring the grounds further.

The bar we had left was the meeting place of a diving club and we had been introduced to the divers there, Julie and I left the boys and together with Karen walked around the grounds. There were two pools, one considerably larger than the first but was empty.

There were wonderful views of the sea and cliffs of volcanic rock just in front of the pool area and we watched the waves crashing against them. Just past the last pool were steps leading down into the sea where later I would have a swim and calm my nerves. We went back and joined the boys having a drink.

During the afternoon we had a meeting with the chairman of Fina and met some of the other observers. There were five observers by Fina rules but at this meeting one of the judges protested that Julie was an observer as well as a first aider and shouldn't it be someone independent from people who I had brought with me. I could have cursed that man. He was short with very dark features possibly Moroccan. He had on a prayer cap as worn by Muslims and was very objectionable. Next he was criticizing the fact that I had not had a medical so later that afternoon I found myself going to the local hospital to get a thorough check up. Julie, bless her saw how upset I was and sent me out of the meeting and said she would deal with it, I wasn't going to argue, unlike my Moroccan friend.

Hue and I headed off to the hospital with a translator in tow, the chairman had arranged for a taxi to take us there and we now found ourselves sat in the reception area waiting to see the doctor. I was astonished to see posters everywhere telling of my swim with a huge photo of me, it was plastered up all over the hospital and later in an ice cream parlour across the road. Hue and I just giggled at all the fuss but it was sweet. The medical had shown no problems and we took it back and gave it to the committee. Julie had by now come out of the meeting with some success.

The Moroccan had challenged her right to be there at all, saying I should have a doctor not a first aider but Julie stuck to her guns and won over the committee which just left the problem of finding another observer to fulfil the requirements of an inaugural world swim.

As chance would have it at that very hotel was an Olympic swimming judge who said he would willingly give up a day to come on such a prestigious swim and soon there was nothing holding us back, except the weather. All that evening and for the next three days it blew a gale. The sun was shining but the waves lashed the cliffs in front of the hotel. On the second day after we got to the hotel, the Mail newspaper and Carlton TV decided it was a no go and went home. We had a press conference for the Italian press and TV and told them we could not swim until the weather eased. I used the time to train and do another interview for the local TV.

It was hysterical doing the interview, we set up by the pool but the pool was far too salty and I decided to go into the sea off of the steps I had seen earlier. As I walked down the steps with the camera following me I slipped head over heels down the steps and none to lady like either. My legs were up in the air and I landed hard on the bottom step where it knocked the wind out of me. My face was crimson with embarrassment. It wasn't just my ego that got hurt; I had a huge bruise welling up on my thigh to boot. We decided to start the camera rolling with me already in the sea with a voice over, telling all about the weather and the hold ups we had to endure.

The following day was no better and the wind raged all day, I was due to meet the skipper and go over his boat to see if it was ready, the skipper wanted to attach an arc light which he needed permission to buy as it would be costly. Karen gave the go ahead although I had my doubts about swimming under an arc lamp at night, it would be like saying suppers ready, come and get it.

Just before I had set out for Italy there was a news piece on TV all about a fisherman and his son whose boat was attacked by a great white in the Mediterranean and his son cowering in the corner of the boat, he had caught it all on video. I didn't want to be the next person on the menu, no thank you! The tourist board would like you to think that there are no sharks in the Mediterranean but the TV had also done research for a show, were they interviewed fishermen about their catches and interviewed a surfer and they had undisputed evidence. The surfer showed his surf board which had a huge bite taken out of it. They also spoke to the survivor whose partner had been taken in twelve foot of water as they were swimming into a bay in clear visibility. He said one minute he was there and the next he had gone, just like that. It wasn't very inspiring to know all these things.

The skipper was a small muscular guy who walked round with no shoes on all the time. He had a lovely disposition and was always smiling. We went on board the boat and he showed us around. I think he had the hot's for Karen and was encouraging her to jump off the boat for a swim. She didn't swim to well but was up for a laugh and soon we were all in the harbour cooling off. Karen went in fully clothed, she really was a dare devil. We sat in the sun and dried off having a drink before setting out again back to the hotel.

The next day wasn't any better weather wise, the chairman had arranged for us all to go sightseeing to keep us from getting bored. We travelled down the coast and viewed a rock formation which looked like an elephant drinking the sea. Next we went to a former prison which had been changed into a museum. I was fascinated by the amphora which was dated at 500bc. That I thought was incredible, 500 years before Christ and they were still in perfect condition. The skipper who had tagged along said that was nothing, the best stuff was still under the sea, he should know as he had brought the amphora to the museum. We had a very pleasant afternoon which ended with us all going out for dinner in the town later that evening. We never paid for a thing and even though the restaurant was packed the chairman, who must have had some considerable sway, managed to get us in for dinner.

All the tension and waiting around wasn't doing me much good, I had not slept well or eaten properly for the past couple of days and the tummy trouble was back again. I really do suffer badly with nerves just before an event and it goes straight to my stomach.

The next day was a Tuesday, we had been there for four days

with no breakthrough in the weather at all, it was time to talk of alternatives as the weather didn't look as if it was going to play ball. Karen headed up the meeting with Hue, Julie and her husband and the skipper of the boat. We decided having come all that way and not swimming wasn't an option. I decided if I couldn't do the challenge that I wanted to be the first person to swim around the island, it had never been done before but if we hit foul weather we wouldn't be too far from port. So it was settled that is what we would do.

In the evening there was a cabaret show outside near the pool for the hotel guests which we were watching. All of a sudden the show came to a halt and the chairman appeared on stage, I didn't understand a word he was saying as it was all in Italian but I got the gist of it. He called us all to the stage and asked me what I felt about the Island and the Italian people and was I having a good time. Then he told me to say a few words about the swim and also had Karen speak her views as well. The whole place erupted with clapping. It is rather strange to be the centre of attention all at once but at the same time quite nice too.

I decided to get some sleep and left Hue and the others having a drink. Sleep eluded me and I just tossed and turned all night. At around five in the morning we got a call on the hotel phone to tell us there was an outside chance for the following morning. The weather forecast had said there would be no wind for the next twelve hours and after that was an unknown. I said we should give it a shot and started to get dressed as there was a lot to do before we set off in the morning.

When we went down for breakfast, which I couldn't eat, everyone was there all talking at once, excited that at last we were going to begin. Martin Strell didn't tell me that at this time of the year the sirocco winds blew most of the time. If he had swum the other way at the same time of the year, he must have been pushed most of the way. Never mind, we were here and ready for whatever the sea had to offer.

Karen and the crew left Julie and I around nine and headed for the harbour to fetch the boat down. The chairman had wanted us to hire a TV boat but Karen agreed with me it was too much money and not a necessity, but the chairman hired one any way, it was all too crazy! Julie and I sat in the sun for a while outside the café and I managed a coffee, not the best preparation I'm sure but all I could manage at the time. I had Julie grease me up with Channel grease and I carefully put on my hat and goggles making sure I didn't get any grease on them. Together we walked to the jetty to wait for the boats to arrive.

I don't know what the Chairman had said the night before but the jetty was full of holiday makers from the hotel, they had turned out to see me off. All the Italian Mamma's where especially happy, I think because I was female in what is a country dominated by males and I felt as if I were swimming especially for those ladies to hold up the female side of things. Children wanted me to autograph caps and t shirts, ladies wanted to hug me and kiss me and shake my hand, very bizarre.

The boats were now just in front of the jetty and it was time to get in and do my thing or something to that effect. Looking round the jetty there was a small ladder, a bit hard on the feet but made things easier. Before getting in I had a good look around as the rocks were volcanic and very sharp I had to navigate a path out into open sea. I climbed down the ladder and got in; the water was very warm and felt like silk over my skin. I never use sun screen when I am swimming as it tends to get all over the goggles and I really didn't want that to happen but it worried me that I would get very burnt but it was too late now for thoughts of suntan lotion.

As I swam away from shore I watched the bottom disappear, all I could see was a pale green hue of the water. I swam throughout the day stopping every hour for Maxim which was handed to me from the inflatable which barely left my side. Off to the right behind the inflatable was the film crew, they watched my progress with interest and sometimes I could see them filming and gave them a wave. The main boat was five hundred yards in front and I kept a close eye on their course as that was the boat I was following.

Later that afternoon Karen got in the water just ahead of me, I was surprised as I knew she didn't swim well. She was surrounded by divers so I knew she was in safe hands. I was even more surprised when thirty seconds later she got out and was wondering why she had got in in the first place. It was soon apparent that the water was teaming with jelly fish and they stung like blazes, no wonder she got out. The skipper had disappeared in the inflatable for the moment but was soon back but this time with a net. What was he doing I wondered but realized he was trying to cut a path through the jelly fish. I stopped swimming and shouted for him to stop as if the tentacles were to break off and get caught in my throat I don't know what the outcome would be but not good. He took the hint and stopped although he had got the net caught in the prop and had to dive in and untangle it himself.

I began to take pain relief which is allowed under swimming regulations as long as it is a recognized and cleared by the drug council. Taking maximum dose helped but I was covered in welts from the tentacles and wasn't having a ball. Night fell and the inky blackness fell all around. The boat was lit up like a Christmas tree I could easily pick out people walking on deck. Hue gave me a wave once or twice which was lovely, he had been really quite for the last couple of days and I wondered now what the problem was and would ask him when I got out of the water.

The boat captain came over with the dingy and said I should move under the arc light so they could keep an eye on me but I wasn't having any of it and told him I would rather swim in the open that under the light, he had to agree as he had no choice in the matter. I think I was a little bumptious but I had put a lot of work into the swim and that's how I felt, I had heard of fishermen using lights at night to draw the fish to them and it really didn't inspire me to be under the lights it would have flipped me out.

Julie had been in the boat for most of the day giving me Maxim and checking me over whenever I came over for my feed. I was getting close to the maximum dose of pain killers and the last four hours had been in a force five and very rough. I wasn't sure that I would make it to day break which I knew would lift my spirits which by now were rock bottom. I took another dose of pain killers knowing they were my last and swam on for another four hours. The sea was getting worse and I summed up my position and made the decision to abort the swim, it wasn't a decision I made lightly but summing up my options I made a good decision.

I told Julie my decision and she agreed, making my way to the side of the lead vessel I was helped out of the water very disappointed but glad to be out of the rough sea at last. I had swum for sixteen hours plus but a miss is as good as a mile my mum used to say and it hurt even to acknowledge it was over. The crew was very supportive and Karen gave me a huge hug before I went down into the cabin to put on something warm. Hue was his quiet self and I still wondered what bothered him and would ask later.

We arrived back at the harbour, everyone hugging everybody, the one person who I had not expected anything from was the Moroccan, and He simply said it was the most heroic swim he had ever seen. From anyone else I would have taken it with a pinch of salt but it really touched me. From the very onset of the swim he had been in opposition but this was a real turn around. I thanked all the crew personally and the judges and the larger part of the group went back to the hotel.

We ate dinner that night all together on one long table in the hotel dining room. The restaurant was totally empty and we had it all to ourselves. Over dinner we chatted together and then the chairman got up and made a speech and gave me a t shirt and photos of a famous statue which he explained was very important to the people of the Island. He also presented me with a porcelain jelly fish a reminder of my swim and asked if he could have my swimming costume. I was a bit taken back, why would anyone want my costume it was full of grease. He said he wanted to have it hung in the museum of sport in Rome and it didn't matter if it had grease all over it because it was authentic. I was honoured and went upstairs and put it in a bag and gave it to him. One day I would like to see my costume hung there for myself.

I eventually got out of Hue what had been plaguing him, Hue said he felt like a second fiddle and didn't like being in the shadows, he said he felt like a bag man. I had realized he felt so bad but didn't know what to say. The following day we got packed and left for the airport, I was still thinking over what Hue had said to me.

The reception in Italy at the Airport was manic, Tv,hotel staff, boat crew and the Mayor all turned out to greet myself and my swim team.

The training pools at the hotel where I trained for my Mediterranean crossing.

swimming the Mediterranean, eventually jelly fish and weather halted the swim.

Recovering after my eventful swim, Julie Byford doing first aid.

Receiving commemoration tee shirt.

CHAPTER NINE
The Loch Ness monster

Getting back to work I again dug in and focused on my work, things at work were not easy and I had taken a substantial drop in commission over the past year. I was now the advertising manager for the County Border News and had two girls under me. We would meet before work in a coffee house just across the street and I knew the management of the paper frowned on our meetings and thought I should keep a healthy distance from the team. I still had to go out to my own customers as well as collate small magazines or periodicals. It was a real rat race. At the same time I had tried doing a small business from home. It promised to be a real money spinner but involved a lot of house to house calls retailing clothing. To a degree it was successful but hard work. I then tried another small business, which had regional meetings that I always had problems in getting to. In the end they just flopped and died a death. Chasing money and get rich schemes was more hassle than it was worth.

The council house that I lived in was along with others going to be updated and the council housing department asked if I would like to move into one of the already renovated properties, in this case it was just across the road from where I already lived and two doors down from my friends Pat and Paul, so I readily agreed.

On the day of the move, with removal men everywhere my boss from work phoned. She wanted me to go into work as they were on deadline and struggling desperately. I couldn't believe they would phone me at home on such a busy day, didn't they realize I was moving and had two children to look after on top of that. I thought it totally unreasonable which didn't go down to well but they would just have to do without me, I had booked the day off and it was just too much.

Hue had stopped visiting so often and just said he was busy all the time. In fact he stopped coming all together but I did have dinner with him after a three month gap. He wasn't his normal self, he didn't hug me at all and by now although I loved him I had my hands full with work and the children.

I decided to do a swim of Loch ness later in the year and was struggling to get a sponsor but eventually found a sponsor through my work; it was a swim wear manufacturer called zoggs. They were a small company but had brilliant designs and gave me two costumes and glasses to get me started. I travelled to Scotland with my Channel swimming buddy Ann, we had found a place to stay at Inverness and caught a bus to Drumnadrochit, a small village on the northern shores of Loch ness where I knew we would be able to get information about the Loch. I had been talking to a man they called Willy the Boat; he did all the advertising for the loch and owned the hotel and house we would later rent. It was there at the hotel we were introduced to Adrian a Scientist who did research on the Loch and knew the waters about as well as any man and I picked his brains about which direction to swim and who to go to for a boat. He told me all about the water, the temperature and which side was best to stick to, by the time he was finished giving me the information my head was spinning. Adrian allowed Ann and I to visit the monster centre next door and as soon as business was over we went and had a look. It was very fascinating and although many claim to have seen the monster there was no hard evidence to substantiate the claim.

Ann and I took the next day to seek out the boat owner and strike a bargain with him to service the swim.

In June I set off in a car which I had been loaned by one of my garage customers, they had given it as part of their sponsorship complete with a full tank of petrol and together with Julie drove to Scotland. It was a wonderful drive and we pulled up outside the house opposite Urquhart Castle. It was a small cottage owned by Willey the boat, the hotelier up the road and had a camera on its roof filming the Loch 24/7 in case the monster appeared. The cottage was divided in two by stairs which led up to a living room and bedroom and a bathroom. Down stairs on one side was a huge kitchen and the other side housed another bedroom. It was small but very tasteful and had a definite Scottish feel to it.

The following day the Scottish swimmer who would be my observer sent by the open water swimming association arrived and we made her welcome. That evening we had dinner at the hotel next to the Loch ness monster visitors centre at Urquhart bay. After talking to the scientist Adrian we discovered that owing to weather conditions and the direction of the wind we would need to start at the opposite that we had previously arranged with the boat and I rang the boat owner to let him know. He wasn't pleased and told me he wasn't going to do it, he had no intension of getting up at the crack of dawn and motoring to the other end and he was sorry.

I was devastated and didn't know what to do, I began to well up and Julie couldn't but help notice. When I told her what had happened she was speechless. Just then Willey the manager came over to take our order and it was clear to him something was wrong, I told him what had occurred; he paused and then said to give him twenty minutes and he would see what he could do. True to his word he came back and said he had a vet who owned several boats and he would gladly do the swim with us, in fact he was on his way to the hotel and would meet us shortly. I don't think I have ever been so grateful in my life, everything hinged on the boat and now we would be ok if it was a suitable boat.

The vet was a tall blonde haired man quite handsome. He came in and introduced himself, his name was Ian. He sat opposite and ordered a drink. What a super guy, he was no ordinary vet but was hired in his capacity to cull the herds of deer which could become a problem if left to their own devices. Ian had several boats which he used in his job and knew the loch well. He was going to bring the boat down to the coast guards hut just in front of our cottage the following morning so that we could make sure it was what we needed and I thought what a kind chap to even bother but he really put himself out and nothing was too much trouble for him, my faith was restored in the Scottish people.

True to his word the following day at seven am Ian was waiting for Julie and me exactly where he had said. The coast guard had also turned up and was busy chatting to him as we arrived. I didn't have to look too closely but immediately was convinced the boat was just what we were looking for, together with the coast guard we discussed the best options on time for the following day and settled on 4am to meet back at the coast guards jetty in Urquhart bay to set off for Loch end.

Loch Ness is notorious for its monster but this time I joked that I was the monster. The water in Loch Ness is very cold, around 55 degrees and it is some 900 feet deep in places. I had decided to swim to raise funds for the Kent air ambulance and thought it would be a terrible crime just to swim for myself. Over the previous days we had done all the publicity shots for Zoggs and I had my first taste of just how cold the Loch is and my heart raced every time I thought about the swim and hoped for good weather the following morning.

We set the alarms for two thirty and got an early night as tomorrow would be a tuff day, both in the water and on the boat. At 4am we met Ian and loaded all our kit, it was pitch black and very calm, too early to tell what kind of a day it would turn out to be. Adrian had told me to stick close to the opposite shore until we passed Urquhart Bay and then to cross over and hug the near shore for the remainder of the swim and I was thinking over every detail of what he had told me as we began our journey to Loch End.

Now there are not many houses if any at Loch End and it was pitch black when Ian stopped the engine and said we were there. I couldn't see the end of the Loch and wondered how Ian knew we were there but he said we were about forty foot from the end of the loch. Being we were so close in I wondered about diving off of the boat or just gradually dropping in the water but Ian assured me there would be plenty of water under the boat and it would be fine to dive in. Julie fixed the night stick to the back of my costume and gave me a reassuring hug before I went over the side. Swimming into the shore in darkness isn't my idea of fun and I did say under my breath, "deep Joy" rather sarcastically as I was swimming to shore. My hand touched bottom and I ended up on a stone beach standing in the freezing cold wondering why they hadn't told me to start and then it hit me they couldn't see me and didn't know if I was in or out of the water. So I turned around so they could easily see my night stick glowing in the dark.

Ian shouted and Julie put the stop watch on to begin my swim. The water was so cold it took me some time to adjust my breathing. Just as the sun came up some four hours later we were just coming up to Urquhart bay but I had forgotten about keeping over to the other side and was now swimming right down the centre of the Loch. As we came to the opening of the bay I realized why Adrian had told me to stick to the opposite bank as the water in the centre was very rough but it was too late now my course was set. I focused on my stroke work to take my mind off of the waves which on occasion swamped me and came over my head, it was as if the water were going in two different directions at the same time and I started to regret not remembering Adrian's advice.

Eventually I was past the bay and could see the castle over to my right; it looked rather small from my prospective. I stopped for some Maxim, Julie had it in a flask to keep it hot and I steadied my body keeping my cup clear of the water. Loch water is fresh water and unlike sea swimming where there is a lot of salt, the Loch had no salt content, which means you are not as buoyant and tend to sit lower in the water making drinking difficult. The water was also a dirty brown colour from all the peat washed off of the hills and very cold due to the ice melting from the hills in winter. I was making good progress better than I had thought to be truthful.

As we proceeded down the lock I notice a car high up on the road side. I had seen it several times before parked in different places and realized that at least one person was following the swim. I gave them a wave but didn't think they would be able to see me but I was wrong so they must have had glasses as the person waved back at me. It was I found out after the swim Willey the hotel manager. At the time it lifted my spirits tremendously as I had begun to shiver. Shivering is the first sign of hyperthermia and when the shivering ends you become unable to comprehend things as your temperature drops. In some cases if it isn't caught in time death follows as the core temperature falls to low and the bodily functions cease. We had been on the Loch swimming for nearly fourteen hours and the end was now in sight. Normally that would have been enough to keep me going but I knew my body temperature was low.

I would end the swim at Fort Augustus which I had visited with Ann earlier in the year. It is a very pretty place with several loch gates making a staircase effect. I recognized the tree line off to our right as being very close to the end but my body was seizing up and the shivering from earlier had stopped which isn't a good sign. I had about a quarter of a mile left to swim but my body was starting to shut down and I called to Julie, she could see I was in distress and not making a lot of sense but she could also see the finish and pleaded with me to carry on, I turned over and slowly inched my way forward but it was no use and the Scots swimmer was getting undressed. She dove in and came up beside me, put her arm around me and hauled me into the boat, was I glad she was a big lass, I don't think I could have made it on my own. Soon Ian was phoning for an ambulance and shortly after we hit the shore an ambulance driver had a blanket around me and was putting me in the back.

Julie came with me to the hospital Inverness infirmary and soon as I was safe in bed she disappeared for the night. The ambulance driver asked me how long I had been in the water and when I told him over 14 hours he asked where my wet suit was and I told him I didn't have one, he was astounded. He said they had pulled people out of the Loch after half an hour wearing wet suits suffering from hyperthermia, how was it possible? He also said that when they took my temperature it had been off the scale and they were unable to read it.

I now lay in bed wrapped in a hot blanket which had been taken off of a radiator and it felt like I had died and gone to heaven, the nurses kept on talking to me not allowing me to go to sleep which is all I really wanted to do as I was shattered. Some hours later they did allow me to sleep and I fell into a dead sleep until morning. The nurse came in and said there was a reporter outside who wanted to talk to me and I said it was fine, so he came and pulled up a chair next to my bed. It soon transpired that he had come to do a story from another prospective about a girl who had died during the night doing an English Channel crossing and he wanted my opinion as a former Channel swimmer. Not knowing the circumstances or the swimmer it was difficult to comment at all but it was clear things had gone horribly wrong. Apparently the pilot had asked for the swimmer to get out and as I heard it later the trainer had refused.

Each swimmer has to undertake a six hour qualifying swim in local waters before they are allowed to swim the Channel, Freda our trainer makes you swim a ten hour session, so she knows you are fully prepared so I didn't know what had happened to this girl. It didn't help that I too was in the hospital with hyperthermia but that is life and my heart went out to her family who must have found it very hard to come to terms with their loss, even though she died doing something she really loved, it must have come as a real shock. Seeing that I couldn't really help, the reporter left and I was left to my thoughts again.

Later that day Julie came and picked me up, we went back to the cottage and I told her what had happened with the reporter, she was very shocked. Of course you are aware of the dangers when you do long distance swimming but it is so rare for things to go so horribly wrong that you put it out of your mind. I felt very down as we made our way back home again.

Pat had just been to a church in Biggin Hill and one Saturday having a cup of tea at her house I was telling her all my woes she told me how the church had changed everything for her and her family. I was half listening but it wasn't really my scene. I often went to Pats house when I felt low, many a time I had cried on her shoulder, she and her husband Paul were the salt of the earth and would give their last penny to help others. My life seemed one round of children and work, children and work and had very little happiness or time out. I felt lonely and depressed and was struggling financially, everything was a pressure.

I had for some time wanted to cut my ties with Hue, he was cold to me and distracted, when I spoke to him about it he said it was my own fault, I had moved thirty miles away and now had another job, I didn't go to football with him anymore and I had stopped going to the running club a long time before when my back was bad. He said I had put on weight and he didn't like that at all. It all sounded all too familiar and I was losing my grip. I just didn't know how to end it and didn't want to hurt his feelings but I did still love him.

Pat continued to bug me about going to church, it was a constant round of "it will be good for you" and "well it changed my life". Bully for you I thought but how could I ever have the time or commitment to go to church. One day while I was carping to her about how lonely I felt she said the church was having a BBQ and did I want to go, there would be no awkward questions and no pressure, it was just a meal with some of her friends, what had I got to loose, I didn't have anything else to do and I was lonely. The Tuesday night came, I wasn't going to get dressed up for the evening, and they could take me as I am or not at all was my attitude. It was to be a meal and pleasant company, which was all.

I didn't have far to go as it was at the bottom of my road in a house of a very affluent couple. There were around twenty five people there when I arrived with Pat and she busied herself introducing me. I didn't know what I was doing there and sat with my plate of food on my lap deep in thought when a man came and sat down next to me and started to chat. It wasn't difficult to like the man, he was very pleasant and was interested in my work and hobbies, the evening flew past and we said goodnight. I left with Pat and Paul and we walked home talking about the evening. It had been a nice distraction from my normal evenings of cooking and doing house work as by now I didn't have an au pair as the children were growing up and able to be responsible for themselves. Any way I didn't think any more about the evening but got on with life.

It had been several months since I last saw Hue, we chatted politely on the phone as if nothing had happened but the gap was already there and plain to see. I was really lonely and the visits to Pat and Paul's became more frequent, I popped in at least once a day, sometimes they would have tea at my house and other times we sat in their kitchen talking for hours, putting the world to rights. Both Emma and Phillip played with their children and they made me feel right at home and very comfortable. I didn't even need to knock before I went into their house; I just opened the door and shouted that it was me that's how close we were. Somehow I had become very niggled over the constant talk of going to church, if it had been anyone else but Pat I think I would have hit them because of all the constant nagging. But it was Pat and I did respect her but I just knew if I went to church with her I would feel trapped but I thought I owed it to her to go at least once.

The following Sunday I made up my mind to go to church but I didn't tell Pat I was going, she would have been skipping from the roof tops, instead I made plans to wait for them to leave and then turn up and sit as far as I could at the back. Phillip my son had been going to a church at Bessel's Green for quite a period of time and he had been on several camps with them and was now a Christian, sometimes he made me feel as if I was missing something, which began to eat away at my resistance.

It was now July of 1999. I waited patiently for their car to leave and watched as it drove off and then left in my own car. I knew where the fellowship was in the high Street and couldn't miss it as it was right next to Safeway's supermarket. I was greeted at the door by two people who were very smiley and gave me a hug which seemed strange but nice, it was ages since I had someone give me a hug but it felt really good. I found a seat right at the back, I could see the back of Pats head and just hoped she wouldn't turn around and see me. The service began and it struck me how different it was from church as I had known it all those years ago, when my parents had made me go. People were clapping and raising their hands which seemed strange but it didn't put me off, the songs had wonderful words and heartfelt sentiments it was all so different. The worship came to an end and we were asked to take our seats and say hello to someone next to us, wow this was really different from the memories I had.

The pastor began his sermon, previously when I went to church it was more of a dressing down and I was waiting for the rebuke to come but as I listened I was enthralled, not only did the rebuke not come but this guy was actually putting the reading into context for today's living. Practical use, now that was something I hadn't expected, it had all previously seemed to me a dead religion but this was something totally useful which I could apply to my every day situation. I was growing more interested by the minute. The man went on to speak about Peter stepping out of the boat, in fact everything he was speaking about appeared to be about water and it wasn't long before I thought God was actually watching me for my reaction, or he had a huge hand above my head pointing at me saying yes I'm talking to you. I felt myself actually drop down in my seat as he was talking.

As the meeting came to an end and the Pastor said not to run off but stay for tea and coffee I was just grabbing my hand bag off the floor when a hand came on my shoulder. All the way through the sermon I felt as if eyes were boring into my head and I was right. The man who had been sitting behind me now stood in front of me with his hand on my shoulder, I didn't know what he was about to say but what he said just blew me away. He said "are you aware that the Lord loves you". I was open mouthed and didn't know what to say in reply, he had really caught me off guard and tears started to well up in my eyes. At that moment I really didn't believe anyone loved me let alone sent someone to tell me they did. It was a real revelation and one that was to change my life completely.

Every Sunday I now looked forward to going to church and by September had surrendered my life to the Lord. Everything was so much better, I look forward to going to work and I could say I was even cheerful, which was a first under all the deadline pressures I had. My children stopped getting under my skin and I took time out to pay them special attention, finally I felt complete or nearly as I was still lonely at times. My life was starting to make sense at last and I began to feel an inner peace I had never known before. I started to go to the house groups on a Tuesday which was a more personal smaller group which I could share my struggles with.

It was at such a meeting one Tuesday evening that I broke down and told Liz who was one of the group about Hue and how I didn't know how to finally end things with him or what to say and I didn't have closure even though it had been months since I last saw him. Liz hugged me and began to pray over me. When she finished she said you must go and meet him and tell him about becoming a Christian and how that changed everything. He would have to commit or say goodbye it was that simple. It did seem simple and that's exactly what I did not knowing what kind of reaction it would provoke but it was truthful and I felt confident when I did again meet him.

We met in a lay bye and I hopped into his car and just came right out with it, what a relief and release I felt. Hue wasn't shocked but said he thought that is what I always wanted and told me he was pleased for me and just said goodbye as he wasn't going to commit to anything. I had done my bit and now felt complete relief and a new freedom; I gave him back his engagement ring and left him sitting in his car and returned home a new woman.

By December I had established a pattern of church on Sunday and group on Tuesday, my home group was made up of very different characters. Wendy was taking a bible course at bible school and lived at the house where I had the barbeque some months before; John and Liz was a retired couple living in a flat which was part of a grand house on the outskirts of Westerham. Pat and Paul were my neighbours and the couple who led the group were from Biggin Hill. There was another couple; the Ganley's, the husband was heavily into boats and he had done many transatlantic crossings bringing back boats to purchasers in the UK, we were indeed a mixed bunch of people from all walks of life. Liz had given me some Christian music which I played on the way to work each day, by the time I arrived at work I felt refreshed and ready for anything. It was during December that I was baptized as an outward sign of being a Christian, although by now all my friends and associates knew I was a Christian.

Christmas was approaching fast and I didn't want to have another Christmas alone in my house, I decided to go to Scotland for Christmas. I hired a people carrier as I didn't want to go in the works car and I would have too many things with me to fit into my car anyhow. The day before Christmas Eve I packed the car with everything including the Christmas tree and presents for Emma and Phillip. The two dogs which were puppies went in the back and Emma and Phillip had the back seat. I stopped frequently in the services and we walked the dogs so they could relieve themselves.

Emma had talked me into getting two dogs and I had bought a West highland white and a border collie. The pups were so cute but still very young and the stops were essential. We had just left Perth with hundreds of miles still to go when the car broke down and I just managed to get it off of the road but it was only a two way single tracks and every time a lorry went by the whole car rocked. I was glad I had a signal on my mobile and phoned the hire company who sent out a pickup truck to take us to the cottage on Loch Ness and then he put the car into a local garage for repairs.

It was late in the evening when we arrived and I was pleased to see that William the hotel manager had already decorated the cottage and had a roaring fire going in the hearth. It was magical. The children and I sat by the fire singing Christmas carols and then went to bed. Christmas Eve was bright and sunny although it had snowed during the night on the hills and I wished it would snow again for the children as there was no snow locally, it had all melted.

We had breakfast, William had lent me the hotel bus as transport and although it was huge compared to a car I managed to drive it safely. We headed into Inverness and found a small shop where they sold children's jumpers; I purchased two tartan jumpers, one each for the dogs as it was freezing. We filled up with diesel and got the remainder of our shopping and slipped back home. The Loch is so pretty at any time of the year but today it was especially so. I took the children to the hotel to see William and find out if there was a suitable place to walk the dogs. William told us there was a lovely walk not far from the hotel and we could leave the bus it was just down the road.

I put the jumper's on Ben and Sally and we set off. Everyone person we passed stopped us to pat the dogs, saying ahh there so lovely. They did look cute in their jumpers and I knew they would be just fine but had to keep stopping to roll the sleeves back up as they were dragging in the mud. The walk took us down beside the loch and crossed the road onto a footpath. As we walked with every step I felt renewed, the cobwebs were gently being blown away. We passed a field of sheep and Ben our collie was beside himself, this was his first encounter with sheep and he didn't know what to make of it. As we made our way back the way we had come the snow started to fall, lightly at first then the heavens opened. It was wonderful; Emma and Phillip couldn't believe their luck as we hadn't had snow at Christmas for years.

Christmas was great and we had a really grand time, back at the garage I enquired about the repairs to my car and they said the car would be ready the 30th the day before New Year's Eve. I had only planned on staying until just after Christmas and this would take me beyond the time I had allotted. I phoned the car hire company and because it was too far to come and get the car they agreed to pay my extended stay which was unbelievable. I would miss New Year's Day in Scotland which was a shame, as it was the turn off the millennium and Scotland was possibly the best place on earth to see in the New Year but I had to be back home. True to their word the car was ready on the 30th.

I picked up the car early in the morning of the 30th. We set of for home on New Year's Eve. I didn't stop until I got to Birmingham services where we all had a long rest and something to eat, it had been a long journey and I was glad of the rest. I got home late in the evening and was so tired I went to bed and missed all the celebrations entirely. I was going to go up to the church but it was all a bit too much, exhaustion got the better of me.

Picture taken just after being introduced to new pilot Ian. From left to right-Ian (Vet and my new pilot), Julie my medic, Adrian (Loch ness scientist) and myself.

Publicity photo call.

Loch Ness, a view from loch end where I began my coldest ever swim of my life.

The water was a very chilly 50 degrees.

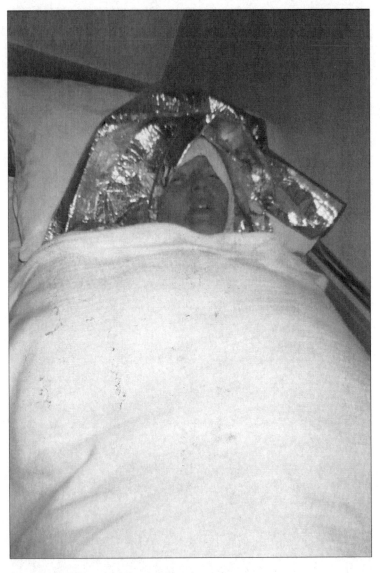

Recovering in Inverness hospital from hyperthermia

CHAPTER TEN
Be careful what you pray for
You might just get your wish

My neighbour Paul had one Sunday saved a chair for me, and Peter one of the congregations had gone to sit there when Paul told him it was for me, so he sat in the chair beside where I was to sit. That's how I first met Peter. He introduced himself as soon as I got there and when the service was over we chatted together. He had been single for thirteen years after the death of his wife, bringing up twin girls and as a coincidence. I had been on my own, well not married anyway for the same period. As we chatted I said it would be lovely if we had a singles group as I didn't get out other than work. Peter thought it would be a grand idea and he said he loved bowling and perhaps we could all go bowling. Together we asked several single people and it was soon all planned, we would meet the next Tuesday and go bowling.

Having become a Christian I knew God was interested in my life, even the smallest detail, for some months I had each morning gone walking in a field backing onto the houses where I lived. It was a place I could go to think and pray and worship which I did all the time. As I circled the field, which was very overgrown and hard to pick out the path, I would pray through the Lord's Prayer and at each section pray for specifics. One of the things I continually prayed for was a good Christian husband. It had to be a Christian, as it says in the bible, not to be unequally yoked, meaning marry a Christian not an unbeliever. I had always been notorious at picking the wrong person in the past, my track record wasn't good. I had two failed marriages and a man who could not commit himself, how had I got it so wrong. This time would be different, I wanted God to pick someone for me and prayed and focused on that detail, Please find me a good Christian Man to be my husband.

I had given up hope, it had been months and nothing seemed to be happening. I thought perhaps God intended me to be single. What would that mean to be single I thought. Perhaps God wanted me to put all my efforts into the children and so that's how my thinking went, until I was convinced, that is what God wanted me to do. I began renovating the house, small jobs as money allowed and had quality time with Phillip and Emma and things were going well, I had just finished all the renovations finally and life wasn't too bad except for work.

One Tuesday we had been working on a tight deadline and the stress had mounted throughout the day. Come finishing time, I said to a colleague that I was so stressed and she suggested we get a bottle of wine and go back to my place to unwind. Well I don't normally drink; in fact it had been years since I had a drink and as we sat talking and drinking and at this stage I had only had one glass, I could hardly speak. It must have seemed quite odd to my colleague. Anyway, she left me and went home.

I had for some time wondered why Peter had stopped greeting me in church. It was normal for everyone to greet one another and normal to hug you but Peter hadn't greeted me, nor hugged me and I wondered why. Having Dutch courage now I picked up the phone, I was jolly well going to find out what the problem was, had I upset him in some way. I didn't think so but he was definitely avoiding me, I was sure of it.

At the second ring came Peters familiar voice, I asked him if I had upset him and he sheepishly said no, so then I asked why was he avoiding me. There was a silence, he just said he had got out of the habit of dating and had wanted to ask me out but hadn't the courage to tell me so himself. Well I was relieved, and now feeling a bit woozy I collected my thoughts and said yes. We made a dinner date to meet at a Pub in Ide Hill the following evening.

I hadn't a thing to wear and cursed having made the date for the following evening but it was done and there was no going back. I wondered on the way to work if God was still in the driving seat but gave it all to him in prayer as I drove. I had been bowling with Peter and others on several occasions and enjoyed myself, on one occasion we all made plans to go to the cinema but only Peter and I turned up but I never thought anything of it. We did just watch the film, The Three Kings. I did like Peter but really didn't know anything about him, except that he was single and had previously struggled with drink but he didn't drink any more.

Work went slowly as I counted down the hours, I thought I wouldn't put on anything special that evening but would go as myself. In previous relationships I had always tried to impress and on this occasion I thought it best to take a new stance and just be myself and see what kind of a reaction that made. It was six o'clock and I sat gazing into the mirror as I brushed my hair looking at my reflection. I was now forty four years old, size 14 and reasonably fit. What would Peter make of me I wondered and the fact that I had two children and two previous marriages, I didn't really have time to wonder about these things, I needed to leave and find out first hand, picking up my bag I said goodbye to Emma and Phillip who were engrossed with the TV and left for my date.

The evening was a little chilly and I pulled my cardigan closer and buttoned it. Ide Hill was about twenty minutes' drive, quite a pleasant drive through country lanes and roads known mostly by locals so there wasn't much traffic to speak of. Peter had arrived before me, he gave me a warm hug and we took a place at the table he had reserved. The evening went smoothly and after dinner we sat outside talking until it got too cold and then went and sat in my car. We had so much in common. Peter was an excellent tennis player and I loved whatever sport was on offer. We had at one time worked close by each other without realizing it. We both had two children and as I said earlier had been on our own for thirteen years.

It was now in the early hours of the morning and we hadn't

even notice the time slipping by and we were preparing to go our separate ways when Peter asked if he could see me again. I think my reply would have been enough to put off most men. I just said not to bother unless he was serious as I had been so hurt by men in the past. Having been engaged for about eleven years and had a husband who went off with my best friend and another who was more in tune with his car than his wife I really wanted a better relationship, the one I had been praying to God about. Peter wasn't at all put off and just replied "why don't we get married then". Wow! What a statement, it took just seconds to realize that this encounter was from God, the very thing I had been asking for and here it was laid out on my lap. I didn't hesitate but immediately gave a nod in agreement and verbalized what my head was trying to say. Peter was serious and we agreed that we didn't want to wait.

The first thing we did was to go and see our pastor Gareth Wales. Bless him he was so sweet, he told us that we were old enough to make a decision and not a young couple so he would dispense with all the normal talk as it didn't really apply as we had both been married before but he did give us some other good advice regarding our children which we did adhere to and never regretted it for a minute. We set the date as July 22nd 2000 just after Peter's birthday. The first problem was the children, at this point they hadn't even met each other and we wondered if there would be any back lash. We talked about what their response might be but all of the talk was not founded as when they did meet they were brilliant together. Peter's twins Karen and Joanna were sixteen and my son was also sixteen. My daughter was a little older at eighteen and we knew we would have our hands full. One of the principals of the bible tells us that God is first in our lives then husbands are to love their wives and wives their husband and then the children come after those two things. That's exactly how things would be in our lives, God first, marriage second and then our children third.

When I told my colleagues at the paper they were amazed as they had never met Peter and didn't even know I was going out with anyone, it was a whirlwind romance and we were both caught up in every detail. My house wasn't large enough for everyone and Peter felt that his house had too many memories of his late wife and so we looked around for another house to purchase. Soon we realized it would be difficult to find what we wanted and Peters house was large enough and in an idyllic position. The house had five bedrooms and lots of rooms more than enough for our requirements but the house just needed to have a woman's touch as Marilyn, Peter's wife had been gone for thirteen years and the house was run down and definitely had been lived in by a man, if you know what I mean.

During my lunch hour one afternoon I went into one of my customers who ran a travel agency and asked if she had something for a honeymoon which was a little out of the ordinary. I had a thousand pounds to spend as my budget and I said I would return in an hour and see what she had come up with. Next I went to another customer who owned jewellers and looked at rings. They had a set of matching bands made with different colour gold's, they were stunning and together with a sapphire engagement ring I purchased the lot. Retracing my steps through Oxted High Street I called again at the travel agents to see what progress she had made. Sitting opposite the agent I listened carefully to what she had come up with and was pleasantly surprised.

The first thing she offered me was a safari in South Africa staying at a lodge, that seemed very different and South Africa was a place I had never been to. I knew Peter had only been over to Ireland with his work and to Bulgaria on a mission trip but other than that had not had a holiday abroad, this would be his first and I wanted something special as it was our honeymoon as well. The second thing she offered was a trip to Egypt. It was to include a week's diving tuition. That immediately spiked my interest as I had always wanted to dive and it was more than coincidence that Peter had mentioned it as well. Peter had been at a house group with church friends one evening, the ice breaker was if money were no object where in the world would you go and what would you do. He had told me this story a few weeks before and now I was being offered exactly that. The clincher though was when she said it included a trip to Moses Mountain, Mount Sinai and I thought the biblical connection was too much and stopped her in her tracks to say that was the one. I arranged it that we would stay at the Hilton at Gatwick airport for the night of the wedding and the following morning fly out to Egypt. I was really pleased with all that I had done and couldn't wait to see Peter and tell him the news.

Since we had decided to get married on most evenings we would sit and go over our wedding plans which were taking shape. We decided to introduce the children to one another and also planned a trip to Centre Parcs so it would make the transition easier in a fun place, as they had only now met once before. Centre Parcs proved to be a wonderful idea with all the family, Phillip even brought one of his friends with him as he felt a little outnumbered with all the girls.

Emma and I shared a room, Peter had his own room, the twins shared and the two boys had another room to themselves. The weather was perfect, it felt as if we had been a family for years and it was very natural. Joining both the families together was going well and I planned to move everyone to Peter's house in Tatsfield when I got back off honeymoon. In our church whenever there is a wedding the whole congregation chips in. Some offer to make dishes for the wedding and others offer their time to serve the food and act as ushers. We had chosen the meal and arranged for the cake to be made.

On the day of the wedding Peter had gone to stay with his best man, Vic Wichal and I had stayed with the children at his house. In between make up and dressing I sat on the patio in the early spring sun drinking coffee. I felt really nervous but never doubted Peter was the right man for me. He was gentle and very quiet and had a loving way about him which you don't often see in men. We had spent hours and hours talking and I knew he was a man of God and I think that's what I saw in him, a reassurance I had never known before that God was in charge. After years of insecurity it was like a breath of fresh air and made me love him all the more.

My daughter Emma and soon to be daughters Joanna and Karen were all busy in different stages of readiness, Phillip was already to go and looked so smart in his tails and gold cravat, he looked way beyond his sixteen years and very handsome Today he would give me away as my own father had passed away a job which I thought might be asking a great deal as there were speeches involved and he would have to talk in front of over a hundred guests but not a bit of it he was really looking forward to it. Emma, Jo and Karen all wore long gold satin dresses in different designs to enhance their figures and to show their age differences. My own dress I had bought with very little fuss at a shop in Caterham another of our papers customers. I tried on three dresses but fell instantly in love with this one, it had to be ordered from the states and only arrived two days before the wedding which was a bit hair raising.

Standing in front of a full length mirror I looked at the results, I never in my wildest dreams imagined that I would be dressed as a bride again as I was 44 years old but God knew different. I prayed in my mind thanking God for such a wonderful new adventure and a wonderful husband who must have been waiting for me by now. Fashionably late I think is the term. As I entered the church to the sound of Shania Twain's wedding song I was the happiest woman alive. Peter was waiting and as I finally faced him and held his reassuring hand I was overcome with love for him.

After the wedding and photos and all the things that go with weddings we sat together surrounded by our friends and relations. His brothers had come from Yorkshire and Scotland to be with us. We had put the top table right in the centre of the room with our friends all around instead of the traditional lay out. It worked very well and we didn't feel so detached from everything. When all the speeches were finished Peter asked if we could leave but we hadn't even cut the cake yet. He was so excited and just wanted to get the honeymoon under way. Friends of ours, Helen and Philip Norris had asked if they could drive us to the airport but first we stopped at their house and changed clothes and sat in their kitchen drinking coffee. We had already done all the family photos in their wonderful garden out back; it was so good just to have five minutes to take stock of all that had happened as we talked with them.

At the hotel the thing that stood out was Peters zest for life. He was so happy and because he had never stayed at a hotel before everything was new to him. He even asked the valet to give him back his case as he took it from us at the car. I think he thought that he was stealing it or something. Inside the hotel it was very grand with escalators going to the reception desk and a huge lounge area. At breakfast Peter was again looking at everything with his mouth open. He videoed all the array of breakfast foods it was so vast and tried most of them. It was not unlike being in the best toy shop in the world with a four year old, bless him!

Our honeymoon to Egypt was short lived. Firstly we found out that due to Peter's diabetes we wouldn't be allowed to dive and they returned our money for the course. Then along with half the hotel I became sick. It wasn't very pleasant, I really didn't know which end was the worst and cringed at the thought of Peter being in the next room but he was wonderful and called the house doctor to give me an injection, at least I could stop one of the symptoms to my great relief.

We did climb Mount Sinai early one morning with a guide. Starting out just after two we arrived at a hotel in the middle of nowhere but at the base of the mountain. It was pitch black and we were each given a helmet with a light on the front so that we could pick out where we were walking. The trail started off with a wide dirt path and after about twenty minutes became steeper. At the foot of the mountain were Arab's selling camel rides but Peter and I were determined to climb the mountain without help. The other young couple with us also on honeymoon soon stopped as his wife was suffering from the same problem I had been having. I think a huge number of our hotel had gone down with the same thing which was a great shame. We pressed on with the guide, it became very steep and with the heat very draining. After about an hour's climb we noticed small tents at the side of the path and as we went higher they became more frequent with less space in between and I'm not surprised as by now we were dead on our feet. We stopped the next camel driver that passed and asked if he would take us to the top feeling a bit defeated but it was really too much. He said that the camels didn't go any further as there were steps ahead which the camels couldn't go up. STEPS! I could hardly walk let alone climb a step but it was climb or wait for the guide to come back down as by now he was fed up with our slow progress and had gone on ahead. We began climbing the steps it was agonizingly slow but eventually we made the summit.

At the top was a chapel and I couldn't for the life of me think how they ever managed to bring building materials up so high but there it stood. The guide said the monks had built the church there to be close to God. We edged our way around the building and sat on a rock on the far side. It was incredible, we couldn't see anyone but there were hundreds of people gathered, singing and praising God and voices that mingled in all different languages but you were not able to make out a sole. The sun began to rise in the east and quickly crossed the valley floor and climbed the mountain, lighting up the path we had just walked up. When the sun rise was complete we were shocked to find we had been sitting right next to a drop off of hundreds of feet.

It was totally stunning the views and the atmosphere was one of ore and wonder, this was the mountain Moses had climbed to speak to God and he had brought back the Ten Commandments written on tablets of stone only to smash them and go through the whole process again. I think personally once was enough, he didn't even have steps to help him up and he was old when he had climbed the mountain, it put me to shame. By ten o clock we were climbing down the far side of the mountain which was all steps and hard going on the legs. We stopped several times as our legs felt like jelly under the strain.

At the base of the mountain is St Catherine's monastery, I had to put on a long flowing Arab gown to cover my shorts as is their custom but couldn't help wondering who else had worn it that morning and the odour from it didn't help much. The monastery was fascinating; it housed the holy burning bush and bones of former monks amongst other things. It was good to find some shade as by now the sun was pounding down. After the monastery we had just enough time to have a cold drink before we set out on the return journey to the hotel, it had been a memorable day and very different.

Because we had money back from the dive course we were able to go out for the day on a small boat to snorkel at an Island, it had been Peter's dream for ages. I wasn't too good on small boats and tended to get sea sick but on this occasion it wasn't a problem. The fish were amazing and the water as clear as a bell, we were able to see everything. As we were going back to the boat Peter disappeared and then I saw him he was sitting on the bottom with some divers who were buddy breathing, it was hysterical, Peter wasn't able to dive but he had managed to sit with the divers on the bottom only using his snorkel. I had to chuckle to myself watching from above. Back on board we got ready to get underway for the return trip, I had cut my leg on some fire coral which I hadn't realized until it was pointed out to me by one of the passengers but we managed to get it seen to.

The honey moon was wonderful and I wondered if one day we would come back to Egypt again, it is a very diverse country and the people are friendly. Of course the weather was very hot but it hadn't bothered us at all and there were plenty of pools around to cool off in. Married life was wonderful too, Peter was the perfect husband, he listened when I spoke and weighed things up before he replied which I would never get used to. The only problem I had was sometimes he would mumble and with his Yorkshire accent it made it hard to understand him at times and sometimes caused friction.

I hadn't thought about a swim for that year and so my mind set about thinking of a solution. It came one afternoon as I thought of how much I had enjoyed Scotland. I planned a swim across Scotland from one side to the other and put the idea to Alison who agreed it would be a swim worth doing. I used my connections with Duncan Goodhew the gold medallist to put it all together with a team of Channel swimmers. We measured the locks along the Caledonian Canal; the first swimmer in the water would swim their distance before entering the canal so that no one could say we hadn't done the full length of the canal. I arranged for six boats so that when we came to Loch gates the swimmer would get out of the water and walk around the loch gate and re-join a boat at the foot of the gates cutting out a lot of time. My coast guard friend arranged all of that. We had told the press of our intentions and Duncan was going to be at the start to launch the swim and for publicity purposes and he would meet us at Moray Firth our final destination.

Everything was planned and double checked so that nothing was missed out. On the Friday before the swim which was to be on the following Monday the water authority phoned to say they couldn't allow such a swim to proceed as it went against one of the bylaws which stated that you cannot swim in the Canal. I could have understood it if it had been one of the Lochs as they are very deep and cold but the canal hadn't even entered my mind. It was such a shame and difficult phoning all the swimmers as they were so looking forward to it and had trained really hard for the swim. I was bitterly disappointed.

A couple of days later at church we had a lady from Mexico visiting. She did remarkable work taking children off the land fill sites and housing them and schooling them against terrible odds. The children scavenged off the dumps eating peoples left over food and often got into trouble stealing and prostitution was common place at an early age. She brought them hope and gave them the tools to return to society again. I was really impressed by her and inspired and decided to raise money for her cause by swimming Lake Windermere.

As I left church that morning we went shopping next door to the church, after church there were always people I knew from church shopping and that day was no exception. Crossing the car park to put the shopping in the car I saw Rick Ganley with another church member. He had an affinity with the sea and I thought it would be wonderful if he would row for me. He not only offered he roped his friend in too.

So in August of 2000 we found ourselves heading for the Lake District were I had swum for Royal Mail once before, I had wondered if I might ever return again and here I was. Peter had booked us into a little B&B at Ambleside on the northern shores for the night. We met up with some of the Channel swimmers who had the previous day been involved in the Windermere Championships and talked to them about conditions on the lake and got directions for the boat hire place. That evening we had a splendid meal but as we stood outside directly after dinner on the veranda, my dinner came back again; I vomited everything and was feeling really poorly. It wasn't a good preparation for the following day. We got an early night as the following day would start early.

Half past five together with Peter and the other two men we started to prepare. I didn't need Channel grease as there was no salt content to the lake but put on Vaseline instead. Donning my swim cap and goggles stepped into the cold water. The boat had already left the jetty and was heading mid-stream by the time I caught up. I was in reasonable condition even though I hadn't spent a lot of time at Dover training wishing to stay with Peter for the most part and also I had church on Sunday although on some Sundays I had been down to Dover and got a good training session in.

As I left Ambleside behind the mist rose off the water, it was flat calm and progress was easy. Around lunch time we had just past the main town and were continuing down towards the two thirds point. I was now swimming near to the bank and was beginning to see weed growing under me which caused me to panic as I really don't like weed. So I decided to cross to the opposite bank some three hundred yards away where my crew got me to take some Maxim. They also hooked me up by phone and an intercom to the church sound system and I was able to speak to the whole church via the mobile. I remember saying something like "God is good all the time" and what the water and weather conditions were like and we were making good progress. While I was speaking on the mobile the crew was getting very anxious, they could see a ferry boat bearing down on us, it wasn't about to stop so they frantically rowed out of its path cursing. The church found it hilarious and I could hear laughter ringing down the phone. I hung up and swam on finishing in just over eight hours for the thirteen miles which was a good time and I was really pleased.

The following year 2001 I joined a team in Scotland at Loch Lomond. I left Peter at home for this swim as it would be too much money for him to come as well. Steven one of the Channel swimmers had put the team together and booked everything. We stayed at a delightful bed and breakfast right next to the Loch. The first day we swam across the loch just to get used to the cold, the water was dark brown just as Loch Ness had been and very cold just the same. The following day we went out for a walk above the bed and breakfast hoping to climb the hill behind it and get a better view of the Loch. We had not realized that during the night it had rained and now the hillside was like a bog but we were determined even though only one of us had walking boots on and the rest of us came back with trainers with mud caked all over them.

Next morning we set off for the boat which I hadn't seen, it was enormous, the owner used it for tourists to sight see around the Loch and we had it all to ourselves, I felt rather special. The swim was for the most part unspectacular and very cold, we did pass one of Scotland's famous golf courses and one of the swimmers said he believed it was the most expensive golf courses in Great Britain. As we passed some of the golfers playing waved at us I thought that was nice. I enjoyed the swim and the scenery and we had the pleasure of taking two hours off of the previous time set for the Loch and set a new world record at just under twelve hours for the 27 miles. It had been fun but I was glad to get back home to Peter as I had really missed him.

Time passed and the children went through all the problems that children do go through and having four teenagers in the house at times it was a challenge to say the least. I had talked about my work with Peter and we came to the conclusion that advertising wasn't possibly the best Christian job and so I began the hunt for a more suitable job. It took a year until I found the perfect job working in care at a Leonard Cheshire Home in Chipstead near Sevenoaks. They were a wonderful foundation to work for and I found the work really rewarding. I would go into work at seven thirty in the morning and work sometimes up until eight in the evening. My job was split between Physiotherapy and care which gave me a good insight into the needs of the residents and they soon found a way into my heart.

Emma had just started University at Epsom and Phillip wouldn't be far behind. By now Joanna was engaged to a wonderful guy called Matt hall who lived locally with other men from the church in an all-male church house. Things were changing and we didn't know how we would be able to afford to live where we were so Peter and I would talk about our options often. We decided as all the children except Karen would be off in a year or two that we would look at living abroad, during this time we went to France, and Spain in our hunt for a perfect place to live and although the places we looked at were fine there always seemed to be something missing and we realized it was a church family and God, we just couldn't seem to find the perfect place and so put it all on the back burner forgetting about it for the moment.

One Sunday we were at church and there was going to be a guest speaker from Mexico talking during the service. Peter and I took our seats towards the front of the church as the worship began. Nothing seemed out of the ordinary but soon things would change as the man from Mexico began to speak. I was totally riveted and hung on every word. This was surely what we were looking for I thought as I listened. We could combine living abroad with serving the church which would fill our time in serving the Lord and our need to be financially secure. I looked at Peter sitting next to me but he wasn't at all excited and the more the man spoke the more convinced I was that this was the answer. I was almost beside myself with excitement but there was still no reaction from Peter. When at last the talk ended and we had left the church for home I was bursting with excitement but he was just as normal as we drove home.

I broached the subject of Mexico and suggested we look into it perhaps living and serving there but it did nothing for Peter and he wasn't sold on the idea at all. I was mortified, I really thought this was a good answer to our problem and it would be so rewarding serving the church. When we had gone to Spain we had been introduced to one of the builders former clients at her house, she was sitting by their plunge pool knitting. We had a look around the house and it appeared wonderful but when we asked her where her husband was she said he played golf every day and they met up in the evening. That was all she had to say to put us off, life there was one continual round of Golf and wining and dining but God didn't come into the equation at all. Neither of us at the time played golf and we wanted to be part of the town not set apart from it with the British people. I was disappointed with Peter's apparent lack of interest to say the least but accepted Peter's decision to put it on hold.

An early start to our swim of Loch Lommond.

Loch Lommond team photo. From left to right, Steve Smith, Robert Lyle, Barry Creask, Janet Cook and myself kneeling.

Arriving jubilant after our freezing swim of loch Lommond. From left to right, Robert Lyle, myself, Janet Cook,Steve Smith and Barry Creask.

22nd July 2000. Peter & I got married with my children, Emma and Phillip.

CHAPTER ELEVEN
Out of the comfort zone

Sunday arrived and as we normally did we got ready to go to church. I was taking out the youth in our car to bowling while Peter was to attend the service. We parked out the front and I said goodbye as the girls jumped in. I had a Toyota Lightace which seated eight and the row of seats behind the driver turned so they faced the back row which made the vehicle ideal for carrying people, I think that's why I was required that Sunday morning to help transport the youth. We had a very pleasant morning, it was a lot of fun and the girls enjoyed themselves.

As I drew up to the car park Peter was standing waiting for me as I pulled up. He was so excited and started babbling something about a preacher; I had to slow him down to make sense of what he was saying. He slowly explained that he had just heard a preacher ask for workers that were self-sufficient to work permanently in Africa. I don't know why I wasn't surprised except to think why wasn't he interested in the Mexican preacher we had only just had? I said that's exactly what we should do as it answered a lot of our questions.

He opened the door and was half pulling me out to go speak to this man from Africa, when the preacher walked in front of the car. Peter stopped him in his tracks and told him we were interested in serving but could we get together over a dinner and chat about it, to which he agreed. We arranged to meet the following day at our house in Tat's field where I prepared lunch in the garden.

The preachers name was Steve Oliver and he came together with his wife Heather, they had been in a place called Clarens up in the Free State for the past twelve years and felt called to build a church there for both black and white. In the past Steve had many workers but had grown tired of training them and then they would leave. He was looking for more permanent people who were willing to serve. He had first come to Clarens on his holidays but someone had given him a prophecy, he was to go tend the daisies of Africa. Black people are often called the daises of Africa because they are prolific in number. Steve suggested we come out to Clarens and have a look for ourselves and see if we thought it was what we wanted.

When we got home we sat outside in the sunshine on a bench we had placed next to the front door overlooking the private unmade road outside. It was always a quiet place as there was no through traffic and the children tended to use the back garden not the front. Africa had really sparked our imagination and we talked excitedly about it. Phillip would soon join Emma at university and then they would be gone for at least four years by which time they would be independent anyway. Joanna was getting married to Matt, so she would be off hand which only left our daughter Karen. We felt she would be better off with us unless she wanted to stay behind and as she was now 18 was able to make up her own mind on the subject, if she decided she wanted to stay then we would honour her decision but hoped she would come with us. Our minds raced over all the possibilities and what needed to be done until we had exhausted the subject and all that was left was to implement the trip to Africa to look and see what it would be like.

April the 3rd 2003 we left with Joanna and Matt, Karen had exams, Emma was already at university and Phillip was fast approaching exams and needed the time to study. While we were away Emma was to visit her Dad in Portugal and I thought that might be a good distraction for her.

I didn't know what Africa would be like as the only information was what I learned in school which is not a lot and what I have seen on TV. They had coverage of the fights during the apartheid years and pictures of Ethiopia and the famine of that country where children had popped bellies and it was like a dust bowl. Landing at Johannesburg International airport it was apparent that the latter view was wrong. It wasn't a dust bowl but very modern. We got our hire car and set out following directions from one of the elders at Biggin Hill who had been to Clarens previously.

The roads around the airport were good quality and city soon gave way to country. The Free State is very much the home of the Afrikaner farmers, looking around all I could see were field after field of maize and wondered if we would be living in a field as there wasn't anything else to look at. Four hours later we started to see mountains in the distance as we turned onto the Clarens road; it was a pleasant change from just fields. We dropped down between two mountains and I was surprised at how green everything was, huge poplar trees lined the bottom of the hill and were now turning a golden colour, it was like an oasis in a sea of farm land, we had arrived at Clarens. Steve's farm was just outside of Clarens some twenty five minutes further on towards Fouriesburg. We turned off the main road and took a sharp right entering an unmade road and passing the sign for his cottages we made our way to his farm.

Steve came out to greet us as soon as we arrived and was followed by Heather and her children. They had friends from Harare staying with them, Brian, Cathy his wife and Gregg who is mentally impaired; Brian was to preach that Sunday at church. We are shown to a small cottage where we were to stay until we left on the 16th. The cottage was pink with a thatched roof and had three bedrooms, a bathroom and a large sitting room. We made ourselves at home and unpacked our luggage. We were all exhausted after the long trip and headed off to bed. In the morning as I opened the back door of the kitchen Steve's collie dog Shadow was outside begging for food. I made some cereal and put some out for him to eat which he ate with relish. He was a lovely dog and was joined by some ducks which Heather kept, they were very noisy and I wondered if they would wake the others up as they were still fast asleep. I made breakfast for the others as they got up as we were going to church, the church was for the English speaking community and we were due there at 8.30am. Heather showed us where to go as Steve had already gone with Brain and Cathy and Gregg. We took the turning into Clarens by the petrol station, turned immediately right and then left and parked up in front of an odd shaped building which was the makeshift church as they hadn't yet built their own church. Brian and Cathy came out and greeted us and we met some of the teachers from the school and we stood chatting in the sunshine before going inside.

We started with worship and I knew most of the songs all except for a couple, Steve introduced us to the church and stated our intentions to live and work in Clarens for the church. Brian then began by allowing Cathy to speak about their time in Zimbabwe. It must have been difficult for her to speak and I could see she was trying to quell the tears of so many years of oppression, it was very powerful. Brian then spoke of the plan God had shown him for the poor. He spoke from Psalm 41 regarding Gods Protection for all those who serve him and care for the poor. His vision was wonderful and he went on to show a video which he used to teach the black farmers how to cultivate the land by hand, leaving a mulch called Gods blanket to protect the seeds from soil erosion and drying out. He gives this message to as many people who will listen including elders. He teaches about going back to Gods basics not unlike the Garden of Eden and we are to be the stewards.

After church outside we talked to Steve about our visas and then went off for lunch. We went to a restaurant called the Highlander at the top of the square, we all ate too much especially Matt and I prayed his stomach will hold up to the onslaught. We had booked a Sundowner quad bike ride for 3pm the following day which was to last three hours. Wednesday we had booked a two hour pony trek but for now Jo and Matt were going off to play golf with Steve.

Peter and I went for a walk down to the river; we were joined by Steve's dogs Ruby and Bentley. We walked to the bottom of the drive which was mainly shaded by sycamore trees. There was nobody to be seen in the servants quarters as we passed, normally the children line the fence and wave to us as we come and go.

Crossing the road into the sunlight we join the dirt track leading down to a deserted Boar house, one of the very few left standing, passing the house on our left we headed down hill as the track winds left and right. We entered a small copse of trees, the grass stung our legs as we walked, sometimes the path came into the open and then quickly dives back under the trees. The path came to a dried river bed which I assumed filled with water during the wet season. Passing over the river bed we made our way to the Caledon River. Besotho children played nearby in the water and waved enthusiastically, one shouted that he was friends with that side meaning he was friends with Steve and the others just laughed. We said our goodbyes as we retraced our steps with Ruby heading us up. It was a lovely walk but very hot.

We went to meet Steve and Matt who were just coming in from their game with Steve's son Cameron. Watching them from the club house on the final green Matt had a good chip so close to the hole that Steve gives it to him; Steve putted a four footer followed by Cameron. After drinks Steve and Heather went home and we went off to the Highlander for dinner and then back to the farm for the night.

I had a wonderful conversation with Brian's son Gregg after breakfast, we talked about Hyacinth Bouquet from the TV series, Gregg has a great recall for detail and soon we were both laughing. Brian and Cathy were leaving for Durban before returning to Harare, what a delightful couple they were.

I sat outside looking out over the farm; it was a wonderful place and lovely first thing in the morning. I could see the heat haze across the mountains and together with the poplar trees golden in the foreground it would have made a pretty canvas for any painter. It was by now mid-morning and the time was getting on as we headed out for some light lunch, but not so light. Jo was determined to make up for her lack of pancakes from the previous day.

We only had time for a quick bite as we were due at the quad bike place. We were able to practice a bit before going out on the farmer's front garden which I was very pleased about as I had never ridden before. Peter our guide went ahead of us as we passed the first two farms, we followed sat together on our bike with my Peter driving followed by Matt and Jo, Matt was driving their bike. We got to our first downhill section which led onto river bed full of boulders. I was surprised the bikes coped with all the boulders and hoped they were coping better than my backside. The guide flew up the bank on the opposite side of the river and we followed but the bike just came to a halt with our combined weight, Matt and Jo just missed going into our rear as they weren't too far behind. It took three attempts but we finally made it. The ride made its way half way up a mountain before we stopped and took in the wonderful views and the sun setting in front of us. We all had a fine layer of dust by the time we got home and Jo unfortunately had cow dung on her legs as well as matt had gone through some cow pats not realizing that Jo would get the back lash but it was very memorable.

I phoned Phillip and Emma in the UK when I got home, their father had passed away just as Emma was to go and visit him, he had been having treatment for cancer and now she would be going to his funeral instead. They told me that they were not going anywhere as his wife had already had the funeral and it wasn't worth them making the trip as he was already dead and buried. lmy heart went out to them, it was so sad that they wouldn't have a chance to even say goodbye to their father. I had to forgive his wife and hoped it was the grief and not a malicious act on her part and prayed that Emma and Phillip would come to terms with the loss of their Dad. I was so engrossed in my thoughts about the children that I took the wrong road and was now heading for Golden Gate; thankfully Peter was awake and soon realized my mistake. It had been another glorious day but we were all exhausted and went to bed.

The next day we were running a bit late and set out for Clarens more asleep than awake as we turned onto the Golden Gate road, past Sandstone Gorge. We turned onto a dirt track and followed it for about 3km until we saw Bokport the riding stables. We were all given mounts, peter had a black horse which was a bit slow, Matt was on a mare called Arizona and Jo had a horse called Andrew and I had a little bay filly called Falcon. The man who owned the stables was an Afrikaner with boar heritage and I guess he still held a grudge with the English as he didn't say anymore to us but spoke to everyone else in their own language and totally ignored us all. I was told later that during the change when apartheid ended he led some of the riots and would have preferred to have kept things as they were.

We set off downhill getting used to the motion it's been years since I have ridden and it was as much as I could do to stay on but soon a group were cantering and I gave it a go. I think the word stiff comes to mind! Thankfully after about twenty minutes we got to a plateau and we all got off to stretch our legs. The views are stunning but I was already feeling the impact on my back from all the jogging and we had only just begun. The ride passed through and over a river and ended up surrounded by game, buck and antelope were everywhere, very magical. I wasn't too sad when we got back to the stables and wondered how on earth I would ever walk again; it took two attempts to even get my leg back over the horse. It was a lovely thing to do but we all agreed it was a SORE point. As I went to bed that night my legs were bruised from all the riding and I'm sure the others felt the same but didn't say so.

Wednesday came, we were off to Lesotho today for a church meeting which is held under trees and later we were to go to the home affairs office to see about our visas. We crossed into Lesotho via Caledon Sport a border point about twenty minutes from Steve's house, John the pastor who we were going to see in fact just lives right opposite where Steve lives, but it took a good hour to go all the way around through the border crossing. John spoke perfect English and is waiting to marry a local girl in Lesotho but has to pay a Lebola first. Lebola is not unlike a dowry which is paid to the father of the bride. In times gone by it would have been a number of cows but today it is normally given mainly in money, although blankets and other items may also be involved. The more intelligent the bride the more the father will require as Lebola. It seems unfair that he has waited for nearly five years to marry.

The Bethlehem home affairs couldn't help us, they told us to go to Welkom about two and a half hours away, this is due to corruption and so they have centralized the visa section. Steve tried to contact them but with no joy and we chatted about our future role in South Africa. Heather had about thirty women doing embroidery in the house; she is trying to empower the ladies, so that they can earn an income. Steve had spoken to us before about the importance of empowering and not just taking over but as we didn't know quite what we would be doing when we arrived we put it to the back of our minds.

Steve tried ringing Welkom again and this time got through. They were asking for police checks, our marriage certificate, all of our birth certificates and we needed medical cover as well. Now we felt much better although it was a lot of things that we needed to do but it was a start.

Matt played cricket with Steve's boys in front of their barn for a while until dinner. We decided to go into Clarens once more to our favourite restaurant were we met the girl who played piano on Sunday, she was due to go back home and had been there since September the year before. The following day we were to go and help out at the school. We understood that not all the windows had been put in and a team from Swindon was to come out shortly to paint the outside of the school, as long as all the windows were done. The head wanted to get all the furniture in place to utilize what she had. While we were talking it crossed my mind that we had to get things for the braii the next evening. A braii is an African word for Barbeque.

I woke early from a dream the following morning, it was freaky! I dreamt Jo and I had spent a night in a house in the township after working there all day. A man with dreadlocks had entered the house after setting fire to houses and cars. There were dead people in the water. As he came in he pulled back the covers and poured petrol on our bed. I jumped out of bed and started giving him the gospel, asking him to repent and God would be merciful to him, where I got the courage from only heaven knows. As I continued talking the man he put his can down and started to listen. I was prompted to stick to only the facts and not to mention what he had been doing. He fell to his knees and repented and then left. It was so real it frightened me rigid but I didn't mention it to anyone.

We went to Clarens later that day to pick up some kebabs for the braii later that evening, it was to be our last day in South Africa and I knew I would really miss the place and all the people , we had left Matt and Jo asleep while we went into Clarens and the school was the first stop. Four panes of glass had already been put in but there was nobody around. We took photos for our church back home in Biggin Hill as they liked to keep abreast of everything that was going on. As we left there was a lady looking after about 14 children, she didn't speak English and all I could get out of her was in Africann's and I didn't understand a word, I did get some wonderful shots of the children though. Their faces were a picture of innocence. Bought lots of presents for Emma, Phillip and Karen back at home while we were in Clarens along with some kebabs for the braii.

As we arrived back at Steve's farm two of his dogs, Bentley and Shadow came out to greet us, it was only about one thirty in the afternoon and Heather was in her garden. She came over to greet us asking if we had a good morning and we chatted a while and then went inside. Peter told me he was struggling with going back home and just knew this was where we should be and I agreed. The thing that had been missing in our previous excursions abroad was the church, but here in Clarens we felt so at home and so welcomed. Later that evening as the braii was well underway we were joined by the head of a local school his name is Gavin Northcote and he was accompanied by his wife Lynne. We joined them outside on Heather's stoop. Gavin and Lynne had been in Clarens since the 1990's and had originally come from a place just outside of Durban. While we talk about possible houses for us to rent when we come and we discovered there was a huge amount for us to do when we did and we felt really good about it all by the time we went to bed.

We were up at six thirty and I fed shadow, Steve's dog as he was scrounging outside the kitchen door. Peter joined me outside in the sunshine and we worked out again our finances for coming to South Africa and after went inside to pack up our luggage for the flight home. Heather had tried to contact the airport to confirm our flights home on several occasions but with no luck. By eight forty five I was all packed, Peter was in having a bath and had packed all but his wash gear as I set about making breakfast for us all. I tried to use up all the oddments left in the cupboards but what was left would go to the maid. Steve had gone off early to the airport to meet the Swindon team and it was a shame that we were not able to see them.

It was very hot again and I waited for Peter as it was nearly lunch time and we had decided to go into Clarens for lunch one last time before we head off for home. Check in at the airport was four fifteen and Heather had checked all the flights were on time as we said our final farewell's to them. I looked forward to meeting them all again as I knew we would be back and I said goodbye to their dogs which I had become very fond of as we climbed into the car, waving frantically as we drove down the driveway. Even with the aircon on it was still very hot. Before going for lunch we stopped off at the school to say goodbye to the head Margaret and to see all the children.

As we drove up to the gates of the school all the children came out to meet us, their smiles are huge I have never been greeted in the joyous way that these children had greeted us, it was lovely. Margaret stopped her class to come out and say goodbye, I hadn't expected her to and felt really privileged. The children sang and danced for us as they had to practice for Sunday's day of celebration, when all the local churches were coming together. The harmony was fantastic as they sang and I thought who needs guitars and pianos when you have voices like these children. It had struck me several times before how well the Africans can sing, their voices are like angels. They all gave us huge hugs as we were leaving and I felt a tear well up as the gates were closed behind us.

We passed Steve on his way home just outside of Tweeling with the Swindon team and we all waved, the boys from Swindon looked a bit cramped in the back of his bakkie and I'm sure they were tired; it's a long flight from the UK even if it's a direct flight.

As we drove we all talked about our own experiences of Clarens and the Free State. I was struck by the food which was lovely and fresh and healthy but my lasting impression of the Free State was the huge skies and open spaces with jaw dropping scenery. Jo was impressed with the people, they all talk to you even when you don't know them and are a lot friendlier. Peter said how stress free he had felt while being there and how united the church was a big plus for us both.

We arrived at the airport in plenty of time and even had time to look around the shops and have a drink too. I saw some African themed linen that would go well in Jo's bedroom. At the book in the man attending to us was a real pain. He kept on about we should have checked our flights, which we had done through Heather and then he said there were no seats. I wasn't best pleased and just said the flights were booked and paid for months ago and was he going to honour our booking. He eventually found us seats together at the back of the plane and I did give a huge sigh of relief. I thought he must have got out of bed the wrong side; we had finished boarding by half past seven and took off for Athens where we caught our on-going flight to London's Heathrow airport.

It was now May of 2003 and there was so much to do in preparation for our emigration, but first we had to see what the elders of our church in Biggin Hill thought about us going out to Africa. It would be a permanent move and once we had taken the steps to move there was no going back. First we sought out the lead elder Gareth Wales and we found him in his office at the church. We had made an appointment to see him in advance as we wanted him to know we were serious about the move.

He welcomed us into the office and sat us down with a cup of tea and together we prayed that God would make known to us his will for our lives. Gareth outlined all the financial aspects of moving and living abroad which we were grateful for but he didn't outwardly encourage us which came a bit hard. Next we sought out Dave Gillard; he was the elder in charge of evangelism. He listened but didn't make much in the way of a response. Next was Ray Lowe who had started the church in Biggin Hill many years before and was now an apostolic elder. He gave it the thumbs up and told us we would be spoilt with all the good food and the countryside was to die for, which made us feel a little better about things.

I knew from the outset that this was an immense undertaking, one which I felt ill equipped for. I prayed in earnest that God would take all of the plans from me, as it was far beyond my capabilities, there was just too much to do. We needed to sell our house in Tatsfield and buy a small place for Phillip Jo and Karen until Phillip went to University in September. Karen was to fly with us to South Africa and it looked like we would have a wedding in September for Matt and Jo when they would move into whatever we had bought together. Peter and I would need somewhere for us until all of our goods that were to be shipped to South Africa arrived there and not only that but it had to be a place that accepted dogs as we had two dogs as well. It was all too much and I needed God to intervene or none of it would ever get done.

CHAPTER TWELVE
God in all things

It was hard to know where to begin exactly; Peter and I would each evening sit in the garden and talk over what we each felt should happen. And on one evening Peter had a bright idea. Instead of paying an estate agent we should make our own advert and post it. I had been an estate agent and managed an agency for a while and quite honestly I didn't think it stood a hope in hells chance of succeeding but we had lots of time and I guess I thought we should at least try, it was a start anyway. We jumped on the computer and began putting together an ad for the house. Even Phillip and Emma got involved. Emma was doing a graphic design degree, so she should have a clue and Phillip was computer mad and helped us get to the appropriate programme. It looked very professional when we had finished.

The following weekend I took all the adverts and went into Westerham, stopping at several newsagents and placing them in the window. I managed to get a further two into newsagents in Biggin Hill and then came home. When I arrived home I was shocked when Peter said he had already had two calls while I was out. The following day the first couple that had rung came and had a look at the house and they liked it but would give us an answer the following day. The next day we had another couple come and have a look, it was really amazing and later that evening we had confirmation the first couple wanted to buy. They were cash buyers as he had his own business, I just couldn't believe it had happened so quickly.

We began throwing away old junk that had accumulated and pared everything down to the bone. Most evenings found us cleaning paintwork and trips to the tip etc. I was concerned that we did need somewhere for the children but should not have worried. About a week after the house sold our friends from church phoned. I had forgotten we had a conversation about nine months prior saying we might be interested in their flat, they were about to immigrate to France and they gave a price which we couldn't believe. It didn't take much thinking about and we purchased their two bed roomed flat in Biggin Hill.

The flat was just off of the main road and part of a complex of four flats that made up a house, they were newly built not more than about six years old and right on the high street close to the shops. It was just perfect and would be home for Karen, Jo and Phillip when we sold the house.

Next thing was to find a place for Peter and I plus the two dogs which wouldn't be so easy. I phoned several places for rent but they were either too expensive or would not allow pets. Then I tried bed and breakfasts and guest houses. I didn't mind where it was as it didn't really matter but the same thing happened they were either too expensive or didn't take dogs. I was quickly running out of options and time was running away with us. One Sunday Peter and I went out for a drive into the surrey countryside. While we were driving peter remembered a place he had visited years ago called Abinger Hammer. He said he thought there was a caravan place there which we might look at.

I didn't really like the sound of that too much but went with the flow and sure enough we came across the caravan sales outlet he had spoken of. I didn't think we would find anything worth looking at and just thought it was a phase Peter was going through, what he must have be thinking that we could really live in a caravan for three months, I don't think so! It wouldn't hurt to look through and it would pass an afternoon. It was very warm that afternoon and lent itself to the ambiance of the occasion.

Inside we were shown around by a salesman, he first took us to a small four birth caravan, it was second hand and appeared rather cramped, I remembered we would have two dogs with us as well. We told the sales assistant why we wanted a caravan for just three months and how we were just waiting for our furniture to be sent to Africa and then we could follow as soon as we got the all clear it had arrived. It wouldn't take more than three months we had been told. He scratched his head and took us to another caravan and then a mobile unit but all were either small or bad design, nothing was just as we wanted it. Just as we were about to leave he said he had one more caravan but it was a collector's item. If we did want it just for the three months and brought it back he would buy it back from us at the same price he had sold it for.

He took us around the back of the showroom and across the yard to where this caravan stood. It didn't to my eye appear any different in design on the outside to what we had already been shown but he opened the door and helped me inside. It was like a little tardis inside and was full of gadgets. It even had a shower which I was pleased about. The end of the caravan went down into a double bed and at the other end it had two bunk beds that were easily installed. He said we would need to buy an awning large enough for the dogs which would make life easier I thought.

In no time at all we had all the paperwork done and we had bought the awning which he showed us how to erect. It was exciting as I had never been camping other than to a caravan already prepared for a couple of days but this would be totally different and for a much longer period. We said we would notify him when we wanted the caravan and he only needed a couple of days to get it cleaned inside and out prior to us picking it up. I was really relieved when we left as it was another link in our chain that was completed.

The next thing on the agenda was to arrange shipping of our furniture to Africa. Because of my work at the paper I had connections to an international shipper. One of the girls, Lorraine Chapman who I had worked with at the paper, her husband had his own shipping company and I knew they had a connection with

South Africa. I gave Lorraine a call and made the arrangements to come and visit her at the shipping office the following week on the Saturday.

As Saturday came we made our way to their shipping centre which wasn't far from Westerham and Lorraine came out to meet us. It had been nearly two years since I had last seen her and we very soon were happily chatting away. I told her that we were going out to Africa to live and serve our church there and she was a bit surprised as she didn't know I had become a Christian but was happy for me. I introduced Peter and we got business underway. It would take just over three months for the furniture to arrive and we made arrangements that the furniture would come to the yard on the day we moved out of Tatsfield. She also said that if we purchased any new items to go to a large outlet as they would add what we bought to the shipping itinerary and there would be no VAT. We both thought that was a capital idea as there were many items we were giving to Jo for her new house when she got married. On the Sunday we went off to Ikea and M.F.I. to get the things we would need to replace and had them sent to the shippers.

The last thing we had on our list of things to do before hand was to arrange for the dogs to go into kennels before we went and to arrange their flights but that would have to wait until we knew what date we were going. I looked up kennels on the net and found one close by that did international shipping and gave them a call. I had to give them the date which I already knew and they would arrange for a vet to give both dogs an identity chip which is injected close to the skin between their shoulder blades; they would also have to have inoculations against tick bite fever which is rife in South Africa. The good news was that there is no quarantine in South Africa and they would be allowed straight in the country which I was very surprised at.

We kept the children up to date with all that was going on and they all seemed happy, all except Phillip. He said one day" it's normally the children that leave not the parents". I understood the sentiment behind his remark and I knew I would miss the children terribly but they were growing up now and he would be at university for at least four years but it left a gaping hole in my heart all the same and I have never forgotten his words on that day. Jo and Matt had set a date for their wedding, just to add to the mayhem. It was to be September the 6th, I didn't know how that would fit in with the timing but it was a plan and all part of the arrangements that had to be done before we went off to South Africa.

I had been working for a couple of years at the Leonard Cheshire home in Chipstead and had grown very fond of the residents and the lake which it sat beside. On my last day of work not a lot of work actually got done. Barry one of the residents took me for lunch at the pub just at the bottom of the drive. I didn't realize it was all a rouse, while we were out they erected a marquee on the back lawn and laid out a buffet. All the residents sat in the back garden waiting for me to return. It was so lovely and I couldn't help but cry. I would miss them all terribly. There were a number who had become like family, we swapped emails and phone numbers and finally I said goodbye. It was very sad and I knew I was closing a chapter of my life forever.

Peter on the other hand was having a wretched time. His colleagues had laid on a farewell buffet but all his bosses had taken leave for the day. It was a personal shun to Peter, they had tried on hearing about him going to South Africa to move him into a job they thought he wouldn't like to get rid of him. Unfortunately they hadn't read his CV and didn't realize he was a tool maker and put him in a little back room to sort out production problems. It was right down Peter's street and he had just loved it, but he did think they would have been a bit more gracious when it was time for him to leave.

The house was finally sold in early July; it was an incredibly hot day that day. We had put stickers on everything that was to go to the flat in one colour and used a different colour for South Africa and a further colour for the caravan. Jo and Matt were going to have our sierra and we managed to sell the shogun to friends that just left the large Toyota which we would use to pull the caravan but we would deal with that when we got back from our travels. All the goods for the caravan and South Africa were stacked into the garage so they wouldn't get mixed up with the things for the flat. Our solicitor had not called us and it was getting late, we had so much to do and the new owners would be at the house soon. We tried the solicitor but he had gone for lunch and just as we were getting agitated Roy Fanning who had sold us the flat arrived to say we could go ahead and start to move things into his old flat.

We loaded up the Toyota and had a large hire van which we loaded as well and set off for the flat not more than ten minutes up the road. There was Peter and I along with all the children heaving boxes and crates up two flights of stairs as the new flat was on the top floor in all that heat. It was an all-out race to get things done as speedily as possible so not to keep the new occupants waiting. On our return to the house their removal lorry was already there and waiting to get in. We had to allow our removal lorry to first empty the garage of all the items going to South Africa which really got up the noses of the new people. When we came back for the third and final load the Mother in law of the new owner was ranting and raving saying we were inconsiderate and how her daughter who was expecting a new baby couldn't stand the strain of waiting. The way the mother acted you would have thought her daughter was about to drop the baby any minute and why had she brought her along, it would have been better if the mother had kept her daughter out of harm's way until the move was complete.

The unfortunate thing was the Mother in law couldn't keep a lid on things and soon was ranting and swearing at Peter. Well if there is one thing that gets right up Peter's nose its being sworn at by a lady, it was hot, very hot and everyone was tired, but oh no she had to carry on and on swearing and ranting. I could see Peter was going to explode as he was glowing red in the face. I have never seen Peter loose it but on this occasion he lost it big time. I had to go out and separate the two of them and then spoke to the Mother in law. I managed to calm her down but Peter couldn't stand there anymore and went to the top of the road where I met him with the last load of furniture.

Back again at the flat the sun was losing its power thankfully as we climbed the stairs for the last time. The kids sank into the settee and collapsed, it had been an unforgettable day for all the wrong reasons but we were finally in. There were boxes everywhere but it was too late to start unpacking, Peter and I had to go and put up an awning on our caravan and put away all the things we had brought out of the house for the caravan so it would be a long night for us as I didn't want to leave it as a caravan is such a small place and unless it is tidy it's impossible.

We said goodbye to Jo and Phil and Karen and headed off to the caravan. We had found the most perfect site at the top of Westerham Hill not more than five minutes down the road for which we were eternally grateful as it meant we could keep in contact with the children. We first had to go and collect the caravan from the sales yard and bring it back to Westerham Heights which would take us almost until it got dark if we were lucky. The only place we had difficulties with our new baby on tow was actually on Westerham Hill itself. It's a very steep hill and with the caravan it made us very slow going uphill and cars were beginning to hoot behind us but as it was Peters first time towing we just ignored the hoots. We pulled in just at the crown of the hill much to the drivers delight behind us as by now we had quite a line of cars behind.

The site was one large field with a tap for collecting wash water and a pit for waste which was at the far end of the field as far away as we could make it in fact. Next to the field was a small unmade road which I would walk the dogs on later but for the moment we had to get set up before darkness fell. Neither of us had put up an awning before, the salesman said it was a piece of cake. I wondered if he had ever put up an awning either as it took forever. We ended up with a Tilley lamp in the darkness trying to finish the final poles. When it finally went up it was huge and more than enough for the dogs. The site was deserted we were the only people there which was a blessing with two dogs and first time campers. We were all set for the night, water tanks full wheels clamped, eclectics on and awning up, what more could you want. We gave one another a hug of satisfaction when everything was done; we were certainly done for the night and ready to hit the sack but I first had to walk the dogs.

By now it was pitch black as there were no street lights on the site, I found the torch and set off with the dogs. Ben didn't need a lead as he walks most of the time to heel but Sally given anything to sniff she would be off on her wanderings. So I put Sally on a lead and we set off across the field and onto the unmade path to see where it went to. I don't mind the darkness and it doesn't worry me at all and we set off at a pace down the lane. The lane opened onto a clearing off to the left and then goes right ending in front of a cottage. Lights were burning inside and I felt like I shouldn't be there so we quickly retraced our steps throwing twigs for Ben whenever I found one in my torch light. When I got back to the caravan Peter had already made the bed up and was under the bed clothes but awake.

I let both dogs into the caravan as the awning was never meant for them to sleep in overnight but was a place to put them during the day while we were around, an extension of our new home so to speak. I settled them both down and put on my night clothes and jumped into bed, thankful at last to rest after a really long day. The morning came all too soon; I took the dogs out first thing so that they wouldn't have any accidents. The field was large enough to throw balls for Ben which he just loved. We had breakfast and washed up all the dishes before laying out the chairs in the awning plus a little camp table. I prepared the vegetables for later that evening as we sat talking.

It hadn't crossed my mind until Peter mentioned it but now we had a caravan we were able to travel and didn't need to be on the same site for the full three months. We discussed our options; perhaps we should go and visit all of our relations, they were certainly all spread around the country, time was not an issue to a degree and we needed to see them all before we left anyway. Peter was so excited and went off to fetch his map of the UK. We were soon plotting a course around the British Isles which would take us all the way to the Scottish borders.

Some days after work Jo, Karen, Phil and Matt would come down to the camp site to see us and have a cup of coffee. We even had a visit from Emma one weekend which was lovely. The dogs seemed to like their new environment and as we had not had any rain I was very pleased too. The only down side was the bed, It had begun to make my back ache but there wasn't much I could do about it so I tried to forget about it.

At the end of July having put all the wedding plans into place we felt it would be fine to set out on our travels. The first place we were to go to was Durham as that is where Peters Brother Kenneth lives with his wife Dylis; we would take a few days to get there as we decided we would like to see something of the country on our tour. The first stop was at a service station. We pulled in and walked the dogs before getting ready for bed. Just before we settled down Peter looked at the map to see how far we had come, he thought it was nowhere near far enough and we up sticks and travelled on for a few more hours before settling in for the night.

The following morning when I looked at the map we were right on top of the place we wanted to stay at which was a school. Well I say school loosely, it was more of a children's summer school for horse riding. We pulled up in front of a very grand house which is where the children had their dormitories and mess hall. Our pitch was in front of the dressage ring. As it turned out it was one of the best spots on the whole of the site as we were able to watch the children going through their paces. I wandered around with the dogs to stretch their legs after being cramped for so long in the caravan. I came across a chapel, it looked really old and thought I would explore later.

We stayed at the site for a further day, enjoying the country air and views. I even went walking with Peter around a reservoir nearby, the dogs loved it and after putting the dogs into the awning we went off to see the chapel as there appeared to be people working on it and we wanted to be nosey. It was explained to us by the owner that they were getting ready for a wedding the following day. The chapel and the mansion were all part of an estate which they had inherited. To keep the mansion they had to let it out during the summer months to get enough to keep it in good repair. It seemed such a shame to have to go to such lengths but it was no different to what the National Trust was doing for other owners all around the country and it meant that lots of people get to enjoy it. Gazing up to the arched window at the far end of the chapel I asked the owner how old the chapel was, it was 16th century and had been added to at later stages making it a reasonable size for a family home.

The following day we paid for our site and headed off for Durham and parked the caravan just on the outskirts of Durham down a very narrow lane. I did think if anything is coming the other way we wouldn't be able to back up at all. Crossing over an old rail track which looked as if it had been abandoned years before we turned right in the farm gate while I hopped out to unlatch it. A smart looking lady came down to the gate and met us along with her dogs. She showed us where the hook ups and waste was and left us to settle in. There were about a dozen caravans on the field already and one or two came over and said hello. We had a spot of lunch and then went to see the owner and pay for our pitch, while we were there she said we would be able to go straight across the road opposite and walk the dogs in a field which they had just cut. I took the opportunity to walk the dogs as soon as we had finished with her as they had been in the caravan for ages.

Ben was the first out and instantly makes acquaintance with the owner's dog, he was shortly followed by Sally who I think was very comfortable and not wanting to move but had to stretch her legs. Crossing the road just beyond the gate we entered the field the owner had spoken of and I threw the Frisbee I had brought for Ben, like a whirling Dervish he chased it at top speed and almost rolling over in his efforts to get to the Frisbee. Hand in hand Peter and I walked the field stopping near the river to try to get a better glimpse but it was too overgrown and impenetrable.

Ben and Sally come with us to Kenneth and Dylis's house but we did have trouble finding it. We had passed it at least four or five times before we stopped to ask someone, Peter hadn't recognized it because it had been years since he had been to Durham, normally his brother and his wife came to Kent to see him. It was good to find them in good health. Dylis suggested we go and have a look around the cathedral and get some lunch. Walking round the town and over the bridge we approached the cathedral from behind and climb a very steep hill next to the river, finally coming out in the car park of the cathedral. I bought some items in the visitors shop before we stepped inside. On the notice board I found details of an outreach to Lesotho and marvel at just how small the world is. Lesotho is just across from Steve's farm, you could I suppose almost cross into Lesotho on foot from where he lives.

Outside once more and into the sunshine we stand deciding where to go for lunch. Peter remarks that I haven't yet tasted northern fish and chips. I must admit I really had no idea what all the fuss was about, how could they be any different from Southern fish and chips? I was about to find out. Firstly they don't keep the skin on the fish and the portion I had was enormous, secondly, they fry the fish in lard not oil which makes all the difference in the world, it was a completely different dish. I was astounded at the difference between the fish. Late in the afternoon we headed off back to the caravan for the night.

Next morning we had breakfast and went to explore the rail tracks just around the corner. There were no rails anymore just the impression that they left behind making almost a feel of a private glen but in miniature. The grassy turf under my feet was springy and in places still had dew where the sun hadn't yet peeped through. Ben and Sally were beside themselves, chasing too and fro, I had to be careful what I throw for Ben as when he was just a pup I threw a stick which landed and went into the ground, because he is so quick he ran straight onto it lodging it in his throat. These days I just throw balls or Frisbee's. It had been amazing how all through our travels we hadn't had a drop of rain at all, truly blessed. In the afternoon we made our way to Peter's Uncle Billy who lives in Friday Thorpe in the Yorkshire Dales. We found him with his workers in one of the old cow sheds. He is getting on in years now but in stature is as youthful as a thirty year old. He took us round the other side of the farm in front of a grand house owned by a Lord and Lady. Opening the door of the stable, he revealed the most wonderful blue merle Collie; she was surrounded by about eleven pups. This was his working dog as Billy often did beatings for the Lords pheasant shoots. He took us out onto the fell and showed us where they went shooting, I was amazed to find out he used a tractor on some of the steep inclines as they looked far too steep and at his age as well, wow! What a character, and his agility belies his age. We had the most wonderful day, I wished I could have put all the pups in my pocket and taken them home with me, cute!

Next stop was to see Peter's Brother Barry; some years before he had lost his wife to cancer, she had battled for a while but had succumbed to the illness in the end. He had the most wonderful house in a small village lying close to the borders of Scotland, in fact Hadrian's Wall ran very close by. We found the camp site with ease but had real trouble getting the caravan through the gates as they were so narrow. The camp site was in a wooded area with some permanent chalets dotted around. The grounds were extensive and we walked there with the dogs. Behind us were a group of people getting ready for a wedding, the weather would be perfect for it. We settled in and then went off to find Barry's house.

Barry was a keen gardener and often opened his garden to the public to raise funds for the cancer hospice; he was just getting the garden into shape for another such opening when we arrived. We went and sat outside in the sunshine and had a cool drink before heading off to the village pub with Barry for lunch. After lunch we walked back through the village to his house and sat in his drawing room talking about his late wife. He wondered how he would be able to meet another lady to be part of his life. He had joined the badminton group and other groups but to no avail, Peter and I wondered if it might be that his house was like a shrine to his late wife. Everything was just as it was when she was alive even down to her clothes still hanging in the wardrobe, shame! We spent a further couple of days in Carlisle before setting off home to Kent again.

On the way home we were to meet Karen our daughter at Alton Towers for the day and we were heading in that direction. It was early evening, and while traveling on the M6 we passed under a motorway bridge. I don't know what happened but one minute we were heading along the road and the next we were spinning out of control. The rig which was seventeen foot plus our car, span 360 degrees and ended up behind the yellow line parked the wrong way at the top of an on ramp. What is so incredible is that we had passed through bollards placed nine foot apart for road works without any of them moving a hair. And to top it all off we were perfectly parallel parked but now facing oncoming traffic.

I was shaken to say the least; it was as if we watched the world go by in slow motion. I got out to check the dogs in the caravan and to see if everything was ok. As I opened the door to the caravan I was shocked to find nothing had been disturbed as was as it had been prior to the accident. I closed the door and caught up with Peter who was inspecting the connection between the caravan and car which amazingly was intact. I could not believe on a four lane motorway that we had just spun out of control and had come out of it without a scratch. Peter and I both agreed we would need a police man to help us stop traffic coming up the on ramp so that we could turn the caravan around. I walked to the front of the car to see a police man coming towards me across the motorway, it was a miracle he was so quick. He said he saw it all on camera but didn't believe his eyes, especially when he saw there was nothing wrong with our rig or car. It had indeed been a miracle. The police man unhitched the car and allowed us to take it to the opposite end of the caravan while he spun the caravan on its axis and hitched it up again. Soon we were off once more but shaking in our boots and couldn't wait to make it to the next exit to get off the motorway. Luckily it was our exit and we made it safely without incident to the caravan park.

The caravan park was a long strip of land up on top of a hill, very neat and tidy. Late into the evening we were joined by a tent right next to us, it was a bit unusual as only caravans were allowed. I was making dinner and went to the tent to ask if the owner wanted to join us for dinner. It was a young French boy. He had cycled from France to see his friend and surprise him but had an accident on his bike and the owner of the caravan site allowed him to pitch his tent to make repairs for a couple of days. His name was Rene; he was charming but very hungry. We had chance to share the gospel with him during the course of the night but it was getting late so we went off to bed.

The following day we had agreed to meet Karen and her friends who lived at Swindon to go to Alton Towers together. We had a fabulous day and were quite tired when we got back home. Her friends were real live wires and full of energy, I think I must have gone on just about every ride at Alton Towers. We took Karen and Rene to the local pub at the bottom of the lane for a game of darts and some food before settling in for the night, Karen went back to her friend's house and we would see her when we arrived back at Westerham Heights again.

Rene had not repaired his bike by the following morning so we decided to give him a hand. Putting the bike into the van we went into Derby town to look for a bike repair shop. We did find one but it was incredibly busy, so we left the bike there and took Rene for some lunch while it was being repaired and picked it up later. On the way home we asked him where he was going to, he said his friend lived in Sheffield so with the bike and his tent and all his equipment we set out for Sheffield. Rene didn't understand why anyone would want to help him at all, let alone drive hundreds of miles out of their way. If it had been my own Son I should have liked someone to help him as we were doing but pointed out that is what Christians do. The bible says love your neighbour as yourself and this was a reflection of what God had done for us, and it was our pleasure to pass that onto others.

We made it back to Westerham and parked up in the site at the top of Westerham hill, there were a couple of other caravans on site when we arrived which felt odd after having the whole field to ourselves. The furniture was by now well on its way to South Africa but wouldn't arrive until October, we were just biding our time until it arrived, well that and getting things organized for Jo and Matt's wedding in September. Jo was getting really excited at each piece of the puzzle was put into place.

It was July 22nd 2003, our Anniversary, we had been married for three years, wonderful years in which I had grown to love Peter even more. I had purchased an old hamper from one of the charity shops that proliferate the high street and filled it with lots of goodies. It was to be a surprise for Peter; he hadn't thought I had enough time to even buy a present. The caravan I had noticed on one of my many walks with the dogs was parked near to the North Down way. I had walked part of the way before we had gone on our tour. There was a spot in particular that was very pretty, it overlooked Westerham village, and was high up on the downs. From its vantage point it would be a brilliant place to watch the sun set. I didn't tell Peter where we were going and disguised the hamper and carried it myself. I regretted carrying the hamper later as it tore the muscles of my arm. We found the most idyllic spot and sat and had the picnic as we watched the sun go down, most romantic.

On the 6th of August we had Jo and Matt's wedding, the morning was hectic as we crammed into the tiny flat doing makeup and all trying to get ready in the small bathroom. From an outsiders perspective it must have looked hilarious as we took turns frantically to get ready on time. The church was literally only just across the road but as traditions go we were going to be fashionably late. The weather was perfect with not a cloud in the sky and I couldn't but help notice that since we had gone on our travels it had not rained once and it had been five months. Who would have guessed it when we first took the caravan that we would be blessed with such a fantastic summer?

The ceremony was lovely but I would say that as I am biased just a bit. Around six o clock Matt and Jo wanted to make a move as they were going to follow in our footsteps and stay at the Hilton for the night before flying out to Egypt for their honeymoon. When I went to get the car from the car park it was filled with balloons and I could hardly see out of the front window. I got Jo into the car just about with balloons popping and Jo squealing and drove straight to the flat so that we could empty out some of the balloons as it was a positive driving hazard. I remember when they had come back from honeymoon the balloons were still up in the trees where they had landed weeks earlier.

Now that Matt and Jo were back from honeymoon Phillip was off to University and Karen stayed with friends until we were to leave for South Africa. We sold the caravan back to the dealers at Abinger Hammer and true to their word, they gave us back what we had paid for the caravan in the first place, it was yet another miracle. Looking back God was in everything we had done right from the start and he is a faithful God. The weather had been outstanding; we had found the caravan against all odds and been able to see all of our family around the UK without paying for accommodation. The accident on the busy M6, with traffic all around, was nothing short of a miracle; to this day I don't know how we managed to get between the bollard without misplacing them and with not even a scratch on our car or caravan. Early in the year I had prayed for God to help me with all that was to be done and miraculously everything fell into place, there were so many things that could have gone wrong. It would have only taken one part of this very complicated chain to break and the rest would have all been history. I never once worried about the detail as I knew God had it all in hand.

During our wait to go we had a prophecy from Roy and Francis Fanning, the couple we bought the flat from. They said we were not to worry about where we would live God had a house just for us. It was while working at the Leonard Cheshire home one day that I made a phone call to a contact I had been given who would be able to rent a house to us. He told me they had stopped renting and were now trying to sell the houses and I asked how much. It was within our budget and over the phone I said yes as I remembered Roy and Francis telling me God had a house for us so I was confident to go ahead. The man was astounded and asked, didn't I first want to see the house. I didn't want to see the house as I just knew it would be fine God had promised us it would be fine.

The last week before we left was a real roller coaster of emotions. Whenever I saw the children I wanted to cry and got very emotional at each last hug from friends. It was an endless time of crying, I hadn't realized it would be half as hard as it was. Karen was staying with friends and we had been at friends too. They brought us down to have lunch with Matt and Jo before it was time to leave. The dogs were at kennels and had been vetted the night before; they would be waiting to board the plane soon. All that remained was to say goodbye to Jo and Matt. I was very fond of Jo, although she was Peter's daughter I had become her new mum and it was really difficult leaving her. She had only just got married and was about to embark on life's adventure for herself. As we were driven away towards the airport my heart broke. I looked at Peter and he was visibly crying along with Karen. We had no idea when we would see the children again and couldn't disguise the pain we were all feeling.

6th August 2003 Jo & Matt got married prior to us leaving for South Africa

CHAPTER THIRTEEN
Gods Plan

I cried most of the way to the airport, I hadn't for a moment thought that things would be as tuff, leaving everyone behind was so difficult but I just knew God had so much in store for us. We had booked a one way ticket to Johannesburg International as we were not making the return journey and we now stood in front of the desk handing over our passports and air tickets. The stewardess looked at the tickets quizzically and told us the airline could not fly us today. I thought she was joking but the smile was soon wiped off my face, she was absolutely serious. It appears that if you are not a native of the country you are flying to, you are required to have return tickets. Dumbfounded wasn't the word that sprang to mind, it was more outrage. The airlines had sold us a one way ticket without telling us any of these rules and as we stood there, mouths wide open my dogs were already being put onto a plane we might not be able to catch. A manager was called to assist us, she told us that we needed an onward flight ticket or they wouldn't fly us and if we went across to the ticket office and got a forward flight to Swaziland then they would take us.

It was too late to argue and time was ticking, my dogs were on that flight and I had to be on it too. At the ticket office we bought three onward flights to Swaziland knowing full well we would never set foot in that country and then went directly back to the luggage counter to try again. This time there was no problem and soon all of our baggage was checked in and we had to dash to make the flight. As we stood waiting to board the plane that blank look that Peter sometimes got was firmly fixed and I asked him what the problem was. In our haste to leave he had left his bum bag with all the currency in it on Matt and Jo's settee. I couldn't believe it, what a mess, we had barely enough for coffee's, well it was too late we would have to make other arrangements when we finally touched down in South Africa.

The flight was direct to Johannesburg but very boring, the films showing were either too violent or I had seen them already and like most air travel unless you are in first class forget the leg space, cramped comes to mind. The flight was overnight which was a shame as I have always been fascinated with the dessert and we were going to fly directly over the Sahara desert but wouldn't see anything. Peter woke early and squeezed my hand as if to say everything would be fine, the reassurance was welcomed as lots of different images had crossed my mind during the flight. We still didn't know what Steve had in mind for us to do but we agreed we would be flexible and ready to serve. As we came into land the thoughts that hampered my mind fell away and were replaced by shear relief at having arrived, I wanted to do a Pope and kiss the ground.

Steve and another elder from the church called Justice were waiting in arrivals for us after we had collected our bags and cleared customs. Customs, ah yes that was another story. Steve had asked us to get him some Blue cheese as it was something he relished. They sold blue cheese in Heathrow and innocently I had bought some for him, not realizing it is one of the banned goods which you are not allowed to bring into the country. When I read the customs declaration I knew we had to declare it and so we went through the red channel and declared the cheese. After explaining it was for our pastor the customs officer allowed us to keep it as long as we disposed of the wrapper thoughtfully. I really thought we would be prosecuted for bringing in an illegal substance and was happy he had let us off.

Steve and Justice waved to us as we came through customs and entered the arrival area with smiles and hugs, we had arrived on South African soil for good. I didn't know what to feel, relief and anxiety flooded my body as we walked to Steve's car, it had been a long tuff road but we were here at last and ready to serve. We gave Steve the address to pick up the dogs, the depot wasn't far from the airport and the dogs had arrived ahead of us. They were vetted once more to see there were no ill effects from the flight and we waited at the front of a huge warehouse for them to be brought out to us. I didn't realize they were still in their shipping crates. A fork lift truck with both crates set them down in front of us. Their leads and collars were hung on the outside of each crate. Ben and Sally must have heard our voices and began barking furiously as they were let out from their crates, it was a joyous reunion. Steve was using his bakkie, the dogs just fitted in next to the suit cases nicely and we set off for our final destination of Clarens.

The dogs settled down in the back of the car as Steve drove as by now they were used to being carted around in our caravan. Four hours later we turned onto the Clarens road and ahead I could see the mountains which marked where Clarens stood. We were filled with joy as we came through the pass and were dropping down into Clarens. As we passed Titanic Rock at the neck of Clarens Steve turned to Peter and said "I don't really know what to do with you both but as you were a mechanical Engineer and tool maker, perhaps you should look after the school and be its caretaker". He then said over his shoulder, "you're a swimmer and the school could use your skills to teach the children swimming".

I thought to myself that what he had suggested was fine and I would do that but there had to be more. By the time we had turned into Clarens I felt God laid on my heart HIV. I had a care background; it wouldn't be too difficult to learn all that I needed to work in the field of HIV. I didn't say anything to Steve but later mentioned what I felt God had told me to Peter.

At the house we met Glen McCloud the agent I had bought the house through, he was waiting outside for us to arrive with the keys. Glen was in his early sixties, tall with greying hair, a really nice man who I had spoken to on the phone months before. Now he stood rather anxiously waiting for us to take the first look at our new house. He said he was hesitant about everything as we hadn't seen the house before and it was way out of his comfort zone. He handed me the key and said he would come back in a half hour but he couldn't wait around because he felt so uneasy with it all. I understood but reaffirmed what God had said to us through Roy and Francis and told him he had nothing to worry about but he still went away leaving us to open up the house.

As well as buying the house we had bought a small farm that Steve had sold us during our wait to come to South Africa. He had first shown us the land on our visit but told us he had a consortium that was supposed to be buying it but they were messing him about and would we be interested. We had fallen in love with the farm. It overlooked Lesotho and was breathtakingly beautiful. We put it out of our mind as we thought the buyer would be mad if he didn't buy the piece of land and didn't think any more about it. It wasn't until months later as we were out shopping in Croydon that we had a surprise call from Steve. The land had not been bought by the consortium and Steve had just heard that we had purchased a house and thought we didn't want the farm. He was phoning to see if his assumption was correct. I didn't even glance at Peter as I said we loved the land and would go ahead and purchase it. I don't know what was going through my head at the time but would find out later it was a God thought.

As we entered the house we were pleasantly taken back. It was far bigger than we had thought, having four bedrooms and three bathrooms. The bedrooms were on either side of a large open planned living room and kitchen complete with breakfast bar. God had certainly come through for us, he is so faithful and the house was far beyond what we had envisaged, much better in fact. Glen was relieved when he finally came back, he shook Peters hand and said farewell and left us to our new home.

There wasn't hardly anything in the house as our furniture was another nine days before it finally arrived but Steve had spoken to the church ahead of our arrival, making arrangements for camp cots and a bed from his guest house to make us comfortable. A knock came at the front door. As I opened it I was confronted by a front tire of a push bike, the occupant was still in riding position and didn't get off. It was one of the congregation, one Martie Du Plessie. She handed me a large thermos and said to return it as soon as our furniture arrived, at least we would be able to make hot drinks. Then without another word she about faced on her bike and rode away. Next was someone from the church with a large plate of food for the evening, we were quite taken back by all the hospitality. Each day the same thing happened and either we found a dish of food waiting for us when we got home or the person would hand it to us in person.

Sunday arrived and I was looking forward to the service at the Martie Lotz hall. It was now early October and the sun was already hot as we pulled up outside and parked on the grass opposite the entrance. The hall was rented from the local council for our church meetings. It was an odd shaped building not unlike the Sydney opera house. Inside we took our seats, somehow Peter because he was talking when the service started was at the back of the church and I was front row. During the service Steve asked us to join together with the person sitting next to us and pray for each other. The emphasis was on what plans God had for each of us. I was at the front praying "God open the doors on HIV for me" while at the back, the man Peter was praying with was praying "God send someone to pray together with me for those infected with HIV in our townships". As soon as church was over Peter knowing what God had placed on my heart, told me of his prayers with this man who at that time remained nameless. It took a full three weeks before I got to speak to Johannes; every time I saw him in church by the time the service was over he was nowhere to be seen. Johannes was very pleased that God had heard his prayers and said he would be in contact shortly.

It wasn't very long before he came one day to our house. He wanted me to go with him to pray for a young teacher who had succumbed to HIV and was no longer able to work in the school as she was too ill. We found her outside of a shack in Kanana a small township on the far side of Clarens. She was sat outside in the sunshine and had just given a private English lesson. Johannes introduced me in perfect English as there was no need for an interpreter. This lady lived together with her Mother, Brothers, Father and daughter. Her mother worked part time to make ends meet and they all lived in a small brick built house and the over flow, in a shack which adjoined the house. It was a miserable existence and the odds where stacking up against this young lady all the time.

As we walked back home I felt the overwhelming odds of what we were about to do crowd in on me. The devil sometimes clouds our thoughts with inadequacies and doubts and on occasions, it was all too clear that was what was happening. I felt inadequate that I could not have been of more practical help but we had made a start, comforting her with God's word and with our physical presence and getting alongside her, and I knew prayer was a powerful tool.

Nine days after we got to South Africa our furniture arrived; it took a further two weeks to get the house straight with pictures on the walls. Something's do however take a little longer, such as the two dressing tables we had purchased back in the UK. I have never before seen such an array of instructions and would defy a civil engineer to construct those dressing tables from the instructions given. Have you ever seen a dressing table with an outer skin, at first I thought they had given us two separate dressing tables and we now had two too many. Only one of the dressing tables had a glass top although they were supposed to be identical. Strange! Eventually we discovered how it all went together, the dressers were solid and it had been a good purchase.

Steve tipped us off that there was a bakkie in good condition at the garage in Bethlehem and it was an excellent buy, in our travels we called in to take a look. We wanted to purchase the car but we needed a bank account before we could do that. The salesman gave us a brown run-around in the meantime. It was a complete heap and had very little to no brakes and conked out all the time. I couldn't believe the salesman had actually found a buyer for it, who in their right mind would want such a heap. When that car went back I thought we had scored as he then gave us a white Mercedes, I was completely wrong on all counts. On the Mercedes we were instructed to pull out a wire from under the dash and pull out a fuel release. If you left it on by accident the car wouldn't start. It failed one evening at the top of a hill in Clarens and we found ourselves pushing to get it started, very dodgy!

At the bank the red tape was horrendous, the bank in the UK wouldn't deal with the SA bank until they had received a letter of permission from us which took two weeks, it actually ended up taking a month to get an account open.

We soon made friends at church as their welcome was overwhelming; we took the people straight to our hearts. Life here was great but you don't need to look very far to see extreme poverty. The township folk could really teach English people a thing or too as in their poverty they reach out to each other. They sing at the drop of a hat and really love their children; their lives are very family orientated.

Steve had asked me to get involved with teaching the children to swim and close to our house was a pool that was empty of water and had been empty for the past 18 months. We made an appointment with the janitor who showed us around. The changing room ceilings needed some repair, the pool surround needed attention and the pool itself had developed a large crack at its base. In the pump house it was the same story and was a mess. We had a specialist look at the pool, he thought it was only superficial mostly but the filters needed backwashing and the sand in the filters needed replacing to get it all up and running again. It would cost a staggering R6000 a month to keep the filters going and that was without wages. The sums sadly didn't add up and we had to shelve the idea of starting the pool up again.

Karen had made herself busy at the school and Jo, one of the teachers had taken Karen under her wing and was encouraging her to teach, wonderful! Karen grew immensely in those early days both in her attitude and in her Christian life, taking on new projects as if she were a natural. We also notice that a certain young black guy had taken a shine to her and we believed the feeling was mutual. It was soon evident that our assumptions were right, his name was Morena Legoabala and he lived in Kanana. It wasn't long before they began to go out together. We didn't realize this would have any repercussions until later.

Peter was busy with the growing list of maintenance jobs, the play equipment needed repair and he had made flower baskets out of old tires and had to hang them outside each class. He also made coat racks for the children's bags and coats as space in each class was at a premium and the lighting in some of the class rooms was a bit suspect and needed replacing. He planted trees for shade and roses to give ascetic appeal in the play area and entrance to the school, we were very busy. The other job we had picked up was taking one of the elders, Petros, to restock his church shop which found us going all over the place to get the best prices.

I still didn't have a position but felt God laid on my heart again the Aids situation. Johannes came the very next day along with a friend. He wanted me to talk to his friend who had put himself at risk of HIV some years before and was now left wondering if he had the decease. It took over a month for me to convince him to go and be tested. His wife didn't want anything to do with him and thought as he had served in the armed forces he might have put himself at risk and she didn't want him to touch her. The problem had now got to such a pitch that the wife wanted to be tested too but Johannes's friend took a lot of convincing. It was as if he was afraid of being afraid. It was too difficult for him to even go to be tested at the local clinic, he thought word would get out into the community and he would be disgraced. It was my pleasure a little later to take both him and his wife to be tested at Bethlehem about thirty kilometres away.

It was a little more discreet using the Bethlehem clinic as nobody there knew the couple. We waited nearly six hours before they both came out of the clinic; we had waited by the car. They were jubilant as they came out; we hugged and danced in the street not caring what people thought of us. All the years of living in fear and the division that had separated them both melted away. I just want to give God all the glory, he had laid on my heart a compassion that I didn't know existed and I just knew I had found my calling and purpose.

I heard the lady Johannes and I prayed for was now back at work and was very much encouraged by the news. The couple we had tested that were HIV negative was so overjoyed they had begun witnessing to others and encouraging them to go for HIV testing. Next Johannes introduced me to a young mum who was positive and we prayed for her and her family.

Peter was getting to grips with the work at the school as the January term began; already the boggy road which led to the school had been addressed and was a vast improvement and the class rooms all now had black boards to work on.

Johannes and I were asked by a Nursing Sister to talk at a local school in Bethlehem but what we had not realized was that the school had designated the day an HIV day and invited all kinds of people to talk. When we arrived there were around three hundred children all waiting and seated just in front of one of the walkways which was doubling as a stage. The people who were due to speak were a local police man, a welfare worker and the Sister who we had met previously. She asked if I wanted to talk first or last and as I wouldn't have a clue what had been said as it was all in Sesotho I chose to speak first with Johannes interpreting for me. I talked about the varying ways that innocently a person could pick up the HIV infection, such as sharing a family member's toothbrush and sharing a razor. Then feeling confident that I had the audiences full concentration I asked who was going to the mountain camps during the holiday for initiation rites. All the children put their hands in the air, somewhere waving two hands. Ok I thought, here goes and plunged into a factual account. I told how the circumcision was carried out, without sterile implements and how that could lead to HIV spreading. The whole place went absolutely quite, you could have heard a pin drop, although what I had said was true, I don't think we will be asked back there again for a revisit. God had given me the confidence backed up with a strong biblical message, I knew the children needed to be well informed and I felt confident in what I had said, even though it was tuff. I knew God had been right beside me as I had talked and my earlier prayers for his help had indeed been answered.

Peter and I stayed flexible in our plans, sometimes we were a taxi, sometimes we were the gofers, sometimes the counsellors, whatever it took we had trust and faith that God was in control and he kept opening doors for us. Each day brought new challenges and we never knew each day what the Lord would put before us but took each day as it came.

Phillip, my Son came on a visit and it was during a white water rafting experience that one of the people who was on the raft approached me to ask if I could help counsel her and her boyfriend. They wanted to be tested for HIV and both were negative but the door of friendship had opened again. We had chance to whiteness Gods endless love to them and they soon wanted to come to church. I know I shouldn't have been amused by Gods work in our lives but I was just bowled over every day.

The following day Cynthia one of the English volunteers came to see me, she had been troubled and was left feeling inadequate after visiting someone in Kgwbetswana a small township opposite where I lived and asked if I would go with her to talk to a Father as she felt sure he was HIV positive and was showing signs of Aids. As we walked through the township towards the house we were to visit we passed an elderly lady coming in the opposite direction. It was soon clear she needed shoes as the ones she wore were not much better than a mass of holes. She stopped beside me and said something in Sesotho; I didn't understand a word but understood the sentiment. Bending down I took off my Nikes and handed them to her and she gave me her worn out shoes. I had to put them on as the road surface was scorching my feet but inside I secretly shuddered.

Cynthia and I spent a few hours counselling the Father before I returned home. Peter took one look at my feet and asked what on earth I had on my feet, we were both soon laughing hysterically at what seemed an absurd and odd thing to have happened.

Johannes came the next day and asked if Peter and I would take the teacher that I had prayed with months before to the Doctors as she was now very ill. When I saw her I was shocked at the loss of weight, she was so light I picked her up myself and put her into the back of our bakkie on a mattress. It would take a full hour and a half to reach Qwa Qwa where the doctor would be able to see us. Her Mother had decided to come with us and now sat on the back seat.

The doctor was in between a herbalist and a witch doctor or as they call them here a Sengoma. He gave me a list of medication as long as your arm. We went off to Bethlehem to fill out the prescription before heading back to Clarens with the teacher still in the back. On the way home I felt prompted to ask if we could take the teacher to our house to look after her. The mother I knew had a job to go to as well as looking after a houseful of people, how would she ever manage to give her only daughter the attention she would require? With Johannes interpreting the decision was made, they would all come and stay at our house; I would show the Mum how to administer all the medication and look after the teacher myself.

It was a truly blessed time when God showed me in microcosms what HIV was all about. The family needed counselling and I got a good insight into the workings of the clinic and local hospitals. I was given first-hand knowledge of what it was like to be infected and live day to day with HIV all in this one case scenario. Eventually we had to take the teacher to the District hospital for pain relief as it was evident that she was in the last stages of Aids when there is no longer any immune system to fight off the infections that now took over her body. At that time antiretroviral drugs were not an option as they hadn't yet been rolled out in the Free State.

We took the Mother to the hospital twice a day to see her daughter and twice I had cause to speak to the nursing sisters. They had left all the windows of the ward open and the patients only had a sheet on their beds. When I asked about a blanket they just said they didn't issue blankets until all the visitors had gone or they would take them. On the second occasion I asked for pain relief, they told me they needed a doctor to prescribe pain relief and there wasn't a doctor available. I couldn't believe what I was hearing, no doctor. I pressured the sister again and she told me the only doctor around was in casualty. Peter and I went off to find the doctor who turned out to be most helpful, she prescribed pain relief and when the patient asked to go home the doctor would not release her because she was responsible for her for thirty six hours after the release and she felt the patient was not well enough and might die. Three days later she did die, it was very sad, Peter and I did all we could for the family, we even had the house groups go and pray for the family. The Mother and daughter are now a firm part of our church today because of Gods compassion and love they received.

We began to gather those in the church who had a heart for serving the sick, they gathered at our house and together with Steve and Benson who heads up HIV for our church in South Africa we laid plans to organize ourselves. The group stood at fifteen people and we decided to call the group People of Hope.

I lead the group as I was the only person with care experience. At first I went out mainly with Johannes after a while things were not moving fast enough for him and he got disillusioned and left. I then went out with my son in laws Mother, Liesbeth. She is a wonderful lady and we soon become firm friends. We would go out just after nine in the morning and finish around five; sometimes it was later depending on what we were doing and worked as the need arose. People would knock on the door at all hour needing help, Liesbeth also had her fair share of callers asking for help. It was not unusual to find us at the hospital at one or two in the morning with a patient. Gradually more people worked alongside us and we had formal training.

Peter and I went off to Pietermaritzburg where Benson taught along with his wife at Gateway, Gateway was once a prison but New Frontier Church's restored it and it was used for HIV teaching and empowering work. It also has a school, women's refuge and pregnancy crisis centre. The old prison cells were refurbished to enable those training and helping to stay in the prison block. It wasn't a time I remember fondly, after the first night we stayed in the prison cells we had no sleep at all. The top part of the window was missing and the road behind the prison was a main road. That combined with the freight trains all night long sleep was impossible. The course however was a real blessing, Beatrice, Bensons wife is a natural at teaching. We came away from Pietermaritzburg crammed with knowledge and raring to go. All the other information I needed I just read up on.

Karen and Doug saw each other most nights but soon we were called to a meeting with the elders regarding the pair of them. There had been rumours and as they were the first black white couple the church wanted to make sure things went well as it would pave the road for other mixed race couples to get married. Steve wanted us to send Karen to Cape Town to stay with another black white couple who lived in a township. We didn't have enough expertise to counsel Karen as we didn't know enough about the culture and she should have some idea what it would be like in a mixed marriage, the highs and the lows, so we agreed. Karen was not to go into the township with Doug or walk holding hands together as in Besotho culture this would indicate you were sexual partners. We agreed they would do all their courting at our house so that there could be no rumours until they were married. It's good to be accountable to each other and it is a biblical principal.

Peter had started to work on building the church on a piece of land behind the school, it was made with cement blocks made on Steve's farm and later thatched. He would go to the site and supervise the work there and then together with another volunteer fetch the blocks for the walls. It was full on all the time, up and down to the farm fetching the thousands of blocks required. We had a couple of church meetings in the church before it was fully completed which was very cold. Eventually it was painted and the floor concreted. Peter had built his own home in Tatsfield and the experience he had gained there was invaluable while working on the church.

Doug finally popped the question to Karen on the 5th of April 2004 but it would be almost another year before they were married. The plans for the wedding went reasonably well but the numbers for catering were a problem. In Besotho culture everyone is able to come to the wedding whereas in English culture only those who are invited come to the wedding. We wanted a mix of the two and decide to have open house for the wedding with cold drinks and cake available outside the school while the photos are being taken. After the bride and groom return we had a formal sit down dinner for invited guests which worked out well. We were told there was a lot of interest in the wedding as it's the first black white marriage in the Free State. Each day the number went up, we started with two hundred people then increased it to three hundred, but on the day over five hundred people arrive. It was a lovely wedding and they made a wonderful couple. They had their honeymoon in Victoria Falls and then returned home and moved into the small houses at the bottom of the street.

Peter began to clear the land on our farm to prepare for building our house there but during the time they began to dig the foundations Peter was taken ill and rushed to the Medi-Centre in Bethlehem. The doctor ran tests on him and sent him to a specialist in Bloemfontein where they discovered he has dysrhythmia of the heart. While he was in ICU I said to Peter, did he think building a house was a good idea now that he was ill and we agreed to stop the work. The same day Steve phoned to tell me the workers that we had hired to dig the foundations were a bunch of cowboys, he wanted to send them away. I could do nothing from Bloemfontein and asked Steve if he would be so kind as to dismiss the workers which left Peter and I wondering what we would do with the farm land we had bought. We didn't have to wait long to find out, about an hour later we had a phone call from a golfing consortium, they wanted to purchase the land from us at quite a huge profit for us. God is so good and we want to pinch ourselves, who else could with precision timing come up with such a plan.......

On October first 2004 we had been in Africa for a whole year. In that time People of Hope had increased to twenty people. We had managed to get uniforms for them all. They were recognized throughout the townships and had made great strides, they saw six new cases of HIV every week and I prayed God would send more workers. We started to get funding from our old church in Biggin Hill; it helped with food and gave a little to the girls for working with us.

Late in October 2004 we were joined by our Daughter Jo and Her Husband who have come to live with us in Clarens they have the bedroom on the far side of the house with a separate shower room. It takes several months for Matt to settle in, at first he is bored and the atmosphere in the house is awful but after Peter and I speak to him he finds himself getting busy with church activities. He helps put in the kitchen work tops at the church and got involved in the youth; he even played golf with Steve. Jo is fully committed to the school and gave all of her time there. At first she was a little shy but soon got the hang of it. So now all the Dickerson children were here in South Africa along with their husbands, my children were still in the UK, Phillip was at university and Emma had now finished and started work in Brixton London, not the best of areas and I worried about her all the time.

The group, People of Hope continued to make huge strides and hosted many church teams from the UK and around the world. Teams worked together with People of hope in the township, both the visiting team and People of Hope benefited from the experiences they had together.

There was a family that we were looking after, the Mother was HIV positive but the three children proved to be negative. They all lived together in a small shack high up on a hill looking just East of Larola where I lived. The shack was made of corrugated tin and the door was not quite square on its hinges. Inside it was perpetually dark unless the door was pinned back to allow light to penetrate. As you stepped inside you entered the kitchen area, to the left was a light blue 1950's cabinet which houses dishes beside the cabinet was a wonky chair, heaven knows how it stays upright and opposite the door was a small stove. It's just large enough to take a nine inch log of wood and was the main source of heating in the shack. The bedroom was divided from the kitchen by a net curtain and was very dark as there were no windows. Inside I could just about see a double bed with a heavy quilt on it and next to that with no space in between was a dressing table. Clothes hung from the draws and it was near nye impossible to put anything inside it as it was so close to the bed.

The eldest was a girl; she was thirteen, then a boy who was eleven and then a seven year old boy. The children slept on the floor in the kitchen beside the stove for warmth, they didn't have even a mattress to sleep on and just had one single blanket each. The mother slept on a foam mattress in between the kitchen and the bedroom and the step father slept in the bed on his own. Most nights when he got in he was blind drunk and collapses on the bed. All the care we show to the lady is in vain and after suffering for many years she finally died peacefully in the local hospital. The children were left at the hands of the step father who threw them onto the street and they found shelter in a hut owned by friends that isn't yet complete. Peter and I discovered them one morning and were horrified the man had just thrown them out to fend for themselves. We built a shack for the family and soon the two boys were adopted by a church family and went to live in Bloemfontein. The girl, Jamina came to work for People of Hope and was a welcomed addition. He brother went to live with her we think to protect her but soon it is clear he too was taking advantage of her and wanted his girlfriend to move into the one bed roomed shack and made it clear he wanted her out. One of the girls in People of Hope took her to live with them, which was a real blessing. Eventually she was harassed by immigration and we had to get her back into Lesotho where she is living today with a Christian family. They encouraged her to go to school as she wanted to become a nurse.

Another lady I became very fond with was about 80 but called me Mama, quite sweet really. I began by massaging her hands which were damaged due to a stroke. She could not understand why a white person would want to bother with her and why they would ever touch her was beyond her comprehension. Every time I massaged her hands she would cry. It wasn't a cry of pain but a cry that was from an over flow of joy. She and her husband both gave their lives to Christ one evening in the centre of their kitchen. It was a privilege to witness the moment.

There are hundreds of examples of work that we did with People of Hope, some stood out more than others and will be remembered for years to come Praise God!

Jo and Matt had to leave the country due to immigration problems and settled in Ireland where they joined a wonderful church. Doug and Karen moved into a larger house on the edge of Kgwbetswana and are both now employed in the Clarens. Doug worked for estate agents, one of the first black people to work in that field of work. Karen worked at a gift shop locally, after trying her hand at working in restaurants; she found the work better and the hours better in the gift shop.

on left Lizabeth Lengoabala leading her new team "People of Grace ".

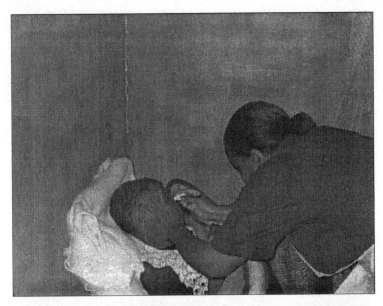

Despite all odds, our teams are building "bridges of friendship"and the community is changing it's attitude towards HIV/AIDS.

My daughter Karen with her new husband Doug. Doug was the reason Karen changed her mind and made her stay in South Africa

CHAPTER FOURTEEN
Abraham and Sarah
Blessed with children at
The age of 99 and 90 respectively.

Matt 25v40
The King will reply, I tell you the truth,
Whatever you did for one of the least of these
Brothers of mine, you did for me.

In the summer of 2004 we had a visit from some of the young girls in the church; they called at our house to speak to us. I invited them in and they sat down on the settee, at first they didn't know where to begin, there were three girls and eventually the girl on the end plucked up courage and began to speak. She wanted me to go and see a small baby they had come across. She said it almost made her cry when she first saw the child and they believed she had been neglected and wanted me to take a look. It would be very difficult to do anything without the parents' consent but about two weeks on I did have chance to see the child for myself.

I was working with Liesbeth that day and we had been visiting the sick, she took me to a house in Kanana that I had never been to before and introduced me to a couple. They had a small little girl about four who was playing in the kitchen so we had gone into the bedroom at the mothers request to talk about her problems. There on the floor in the corner was a small bundle, at first I thought it was dirty clothes but it began to moan and I realized it was in fact a child. Because it was crying now I was able to go and pick it up and the mother as I thought, gave me a rundown of all that had happened to the child.

Her name was Rafilowe and she was just around two years old.

Her mother had died from HIV and the grandmother had taken her to Lesotho. At that time she was a normal healthy girl. While the grandmother was in Lesotho the child became very ill and stopped moving, not knowing what had happened she bought the child back to the Aunt in South Africa, who I had assumed was the mother, and just dumped her on the Aunt and left. Reading between the lines I began to get the full picture. Because Rafilowe had a problem eating and she didn't move it was evident she had become the last in the house hold to receive attention and because she didn't speak she never complained.

I felt compassion for Rafilowe and my heart went out to her, what could be done for this little fragile bundle. I asked the Aunt if we could help by taking her at the weekends, that would give the Aunt some well needed rest and I would be able to give the child a good look over and see what could be done for her. The Aunt readily agreed as Rafilowe was just another mouth to feed and I felt she was relieved to pass the responsibility onto someone else.

At the weekend I went and picked Rafilowe up and brought her back home. We decided she would sleep in the back room next to ours as I would be able to hear her if she cried. She didn't move a muscle and it was quite safe to put her into a normal bed as she didn't move and wouldn't fall out of bed. I placed a plastic bin liner under her sheet to protect the mattress in case of accidents.

The first thing to do was to give her a bath as she was very dirty. Peter went out and bought her some disposable nappies as the rag she had on was fit for nothing. The problem with bathing, she was as small as a baby. When we weighed her she only weighed 3.5 kilos, I had seen bigger babies and she was over two years old. As I stripped off the damp and soiled clothing, what I found was an emaciated little pop bellied baby. It was a sight I will never forget as I placed her in the hand basin which was now doubling as a bath, she was so fragile. Her arms were like match sticks and her legs although long were painfully thin. It must have been a shock for her having a bath and she continually cried but I soon had her in warm towels and snuggled her close.

Peter took to her immediately; he took her from me as soon as I had redressed her, placing her in the crook of his leg so that he had a good look at her, and he chatted away merrily. It might have been a one way conversation but there was a whole heap of things that were said. On the Sunday we took her to church for the first time. She was a little show stopper and everyone wanted to hold her and have a look at her. Sadly on the Monday I had to return her to her Aunt.

This went on for a couple of months. We had bought her new clothes but every time we visited to pick her up she would be in rags. All of her clothes smelt of wood smoke and I wondered how her little lungs would hold up to the onslaught. One such weekend I spoke to Peter about my concerns for her and he agreed that the best course of action would be to take her permanently. So when I returned with her to the Aunts house I put the question to her. She was delighted and we returned home with Rafilowe. It was the first major break through with the child.

We were not sure if she could hear us or not as she couldn't speak but often as one or another of the dogs barked she would flinch. We decided to have her hearing tested along with some other things. The specialist that tested her ears was at Monapo Hospital in Qwa Qwa, we had to make an appointment and be there early in the morning. It wasn't until the afternoon that we were seen by the specialist but it was worth the wait. She put head phones on Rafilowe and sent through a signal to her, I don't know how they measured the response as she didn't talk but they were able to evaluate her and said she had full normal hearing. I was so happy when the specialist told me I burst into tears. I can't imagine what passers bye must have thought but I didn't give a hoot, she could hear, it was a miracle. Peter hugged me and together we said a prayer of thanks to God that Rafilowe could hear our voices and know she was loved what a break through.

Next we had her eyesight tested. We were not able to get it done through the conventional routes but paid for her to be seen by a specialist privately. I sat with her on my lap as the specialist tested her eyes, sometimes in the dark and other times with a scope, looking into her eyes. He was very thorough but the answer was not good. She had damaged retners and would not be able to see ever. It was a real blow, somehow I thought it would be fine just as the hearing test had been, I left his office feeling a bit depressed, our little girl would never see the wonders of our world, or see our faces, the faces of those that loved her.

One afternoon, while at a friend's house where we had purchased our Labrador, we had chance to meet a doctor. He was a friend of the family we were having tea with. He took one look at Rafilowe and said she had been exposed to Meningitis and was possibly brain damaged and we should have her looked at. It all fitted into place, Lesotho was a hot bed for Meningitis and that would explain the paralysis and the lack of sight. The doctor said we should get her bones checked out as well.

We made an appointment at the provincial hospital in Bethlehem, it was another early start and we stood in the queue for hours waiting to see the specialist. Eventually it was our turn. He checked out her bones and said they were fine but wanted to do more tests on her and gave us an appointment to see another paediatric specialist in a clinic at the hospital. We had to be at the clinic and registered by eight thirty that Friday and as we sat in the clinic people just stared at us. It was filled completely with black ladies, we were the only white people there but we were not going to be put off. While we were there, we were able to witness the gospel to a number of the ladies.

When we got to see the specialist I was really taken back by his attitude. He asked why on earth we would even bother with this child, in his opinion she was a lost cause. I didn't even give his words breathing space before correcting him and saying she was a child of God and deserved every love and bit of attention he would allow. He went very quiet and just got on with the examination. He prescribed some multivitamins and put us in touch with a dietician and that was the end of his consultation. We had to go to the same clinic on many occasions but fortunately we didn't see him again.

Rafilowe thrived and soon gained weight, her best weight was ten kilos, although it was under the weight for her age, she had come on in leaps and bounds. She would often react when I came into the room, sometimes she would be making her baby noises and stop as soon as she heard my voice, she was such a delight to have around and for most of the day we took it in turns to cuddle her. Peter would often sit her on his lap and sing to her, he had quite a repertoire of songs. Little did peter realize that he would begin with babies again at over sixty, I was 48 years old and I never imagined having any more children but here we were, happy as school children? It reminded me of Abraham and Sarah who in their nineties God promised children to. Sarah had been barren and unable to have children and God promised them a child of their own but Sarah didn't conceive until she was ninety years old. At 48 it isn't any easier, Rafilowe had an awful sleep pattern and most nights she would wake, crying. It reminded me of my time at Royal Mail getting up in the early hours of the morning. I looked like I had been on a red eye most of the time. I also developed muscles in my arms I never thought I would have again, it was from all the lifting and carrying as most of the time I had her in my arms. Contact with her tiny frame was as important as speaking to her, as she was unable to see.

Rafilowe soon became ill and was admitted to the children ward at Phekolong hospital in Bethlehem. They found she had pneumonia due to food getting trapped in her lungs which set up an infection. She had, we were told a lazy flap in her stomach which allowed food to enter the lungs sometimes and she would be vulnerable to pneumonia for the rest of her life. So we knew her life expectancy would be shortened but didn't know by how much, it was a devastating blow. Often pneumonia would ravish her tiny body, all I could do was to be with her in the ward and hold her. I repeated over and over how much we loved her as if by doing so it would make everything alright.

She continued to get pneumonia on a regular basis and we wondered how much more her little body would take. We often visited the local clinic with her to see the dietician and the speech therapist who by now had become firm friends. One day as we were visiting the speech therapist told us she might be able to get us a contact at the top hospital in the country in Bloemfontein and we left it with her to do some research on our behalf. She knew that Rafilowe would have more chance of survival if she could have a shunt directly into her stomach. This would ensure food got directly into the stomach and didn't go into the lungs causing infection and would increase her life expectation.

Late one afternoon we got the call we had been waiting for, we could meet up with her friend in Bloemfontein and she could make all the necessary arrangements to see the consulting doctor there. It would necessitate us leaving at three in the morning to make the seven o clock appointment but that was not an issue. We got everything ready the night before so that we had a smooth start the following day. I double checked I had everything as once we were on the road it would be too late to come back home should we forget anything. I was becoming an old hand at getting everything ready by now.

We set out for Bloem with Rafilowe sat in the back in a baby chair, she didn't seem to mind the ride and slept for the better part of the four hour journey. When we got to the hospital we had to find the speech therapist, she would make the arrangements with the specialist. We caught up with her and she phoned the specialist and before we knew it we were going up to the specialist's office she had agreed to see us even though we had no referral. The specialist was in her late forties going grey at the temples; she was wonderful with Rafilowe and soon put us at ease. After evaluating Rafilowe she made an appointment the same afternoon to see another specialist who dealt with stents, he was at another hospital on the far side of town. After we had seen him the doctor wanted us to go back and tell her what the specialist had said.

It was a lot of messing about but by now we were well versed in the waiting game that makes up South Africa's health system. Rafilowe was as good as gold and everywhere we went people just adored her, I think we witnessed to more people through Rafilowe than at any other time, doors just opened for us. We even found ourselves praying for the nurses on the ward. The doctor we saw at the University hospital told us he could do the operation in two days' time and we were to return to the hospital at nine and get her checked in. What a relief, finally we had a doctor who was sympathetic to Rafilowe and we were delighted but very tired. Instead of going home we decided to find a bed and breakfast In Bloem until she had her operation. Two days later she received the stent that was so vital to her wellbeing.

Rafilowe never did get back to a normal diet that she had before her bouts of pneumonia but had a specialist powdered food which we bought through the dietician. The dietician kept a close eye on her progress she monitored once a week.

Steve came to see us at home he had something mysterious he wanted to talk to us about. He sat down in the living room and after some chit chat and over tea he told us what was on his mind. He felt we were giving up our ministry for the sake of one child and robbing thousands of others by doing so. Phew! It wasn't something I had considered before. Peter and I listened closely, he definitely had our attention. He felt it would be better if we found a good home for Rafilowe, maybe with a local family and he left us to think about what he had said.

Now Steve had often thrown us curve balls and this certainly was no exception, I didn't even see it coming. But on every occasion Steve had always been right, even if at times we didn't want to see he was right. I had come to trust Steve's intuition implicitly. Peter wouldn't have any of it; he was enraged at first and then just didn't get it at all. As we talked together we got back to basics, why had we come to South Africa in the first place? It had been to serve God and to serve Steve in his ministry. We didn't have a choice when we analysed the situation; God always came first in our marriage without question, but what a hard decision, a decision that consumed our every waking hour.

Jo and matt had to leave the country as their passports didn't allow them to be in the country for more than three months and the home affairs were not sympathetic to them staying. They had been to Welkom to the home affairs Office and when they returned Jo was in a real state. They had been told they had a month to leave the country. They were due to go to Thailand for a holiday and knew that when they returned they would have their passports stamped for a further three months which would give them enough time to think about what they would do.

When they returned they decided to leave the country but didn't want to go back to the UK, they felt that would be a retrograde step. Instead they contacted a friend from Biggin Hill who was now living and working in Ireland. He had been asking Matt and

Jo to join him there for some time, so when they contacted him he was pleased to oblige and have them stay with him. It was sad seeing them go, they had grown so much during the time they had been with us. Matt had taken hold of his responsibilities with both hands and made the most of the opportunities he had been given. When he had first arrived in South Africa he would have been the first person to say he was a square peg in a round hole but now they were both equally sad to be leaving.

A couple of days before they left Jo came to me one morning and told me she was pregnant. She was in tears and I gave her a big hug. I think it was because of all the upheaval but it was a joyous time and not a time to have tears. I believe she wondered how we would take the news. It was for them a difficult time, they were going to a new country, new house, and new friends and to top it all, they were having a baby, wow! God did look after them and they made the transition well.

We looked around for people we thought would make suitable parents for Rafilowe and thought about different scenarios but nothing we thought of was really what we wanted. We shelved the idea until we could come up with a better solution. About a month went by and we remembered some nurses we had met at Bloemfontein national hospital, they had given me their number and we felt we should call them and see if they had a solution.

Their names were Henrietta and Antoinette, in stature they were both very small but they had huge hearts and we had been very impressed with both of them while at Bloem. They came up with the perfect solution, there was a hospice for terminally ill children attached to the National hospital which they sometimes worked in and they felt this would be the perfect place. Henrietta said she would phone me back after talking to the head of the home to see if she had space for Rafilowe.

The call I had been dreading arrived, they had space for her at Sunflower House and we could go and see for ourselves what it was like. We set off with heavy hearts to Bloem and the National hospital. It was almost unreal the whole journey, we were parked just in front of the home, not willing to get out of the car, we just sat there looking at the building. We did eventually get out and we didn't speak as I picked up this little bundle of joy we had come to love and carried her into the home. I kept telling myself this is just to look; there was no danger in just looking.

The matron showed us around and we met the other children. It seemed a happy place, although we knew many children had died there, it was the nature of the beast. Many of the children had been there for some years but all of them seemed happy. We said our goodbyes to the nurses outside and drove away. We stopped on the outskirts of Bloem at a service station to feed Rafilowe and took a seat outside at one of the tables. We were both very quiet; I broke the silence and asked Peter what his thoughts were. He said it had been better than he had thought. I was thinking just the same, it was the best solution we had come up with that seemed plausible.

Back at home I knew our time with Rafilowe was coming to an end and I hugged her close never wished to let go. I never knew I could love a child like Rafilowe, if you had asked me, I am sure my answer would have been that I thought it wouldn't have been possible, but here we were. I loved this child so much, this child who could not give me any affection back, I loved her with every fibre of my being and I knew Peter felt the same way, he was crazy about her. We had tried everything to give her a normal life but the truth was she would never be normal. She needed looking after 24/7 and her prognosis wasn't good. At least at the hospice they had doctors on call, but would I ever be able to see it through to the end when she would inevitably die? How would I cope with that if she were to die here in our house? What would the authorities say about it all? The answer was, we would have to place her in the home, that would release us to get on with our ministry and I knew Steve was right.

A week later we were on our way back to the home to place Rafilowe there for the last time. I have never before felt as numb as I did on that day. With every item of hers that I folded and put into her bag my heart just crumpled.. It was as though life itself had been sucked out of me and I could do nothing about it. As I finally handed Rafilowe to the Matron I could bear it no longer, I had to leave Peter to finish up. He was crying as he came out to the car, we just held each other not willing to move on, despair filled every inch of the car as we sat there holding on.

I cried most of the way home and the first couple of days without her were awful. Peter just sat in the chair holding one of her teddies; he didn't have to say anything it was plane to see it was pulling him apart. It was the largest thing God had ever asked us to do and definitely the hardest. It was a couple of days before Christmas, everything felt flat, Christmas should feel wonderful, children make Christmas and we wondered if we had done the right thing in taking Rafilowe to the home.

We visited her often and met up with the two nurses while we were there. They had decided to move to Clarens and start another leg of the home there. They had become disillusioned with the system and wanted a change. This would be an opportunity to completely change their life style and to really care about children. We were pleased for them both.

Our old church at Biggin Hill was sending a team out during March and as March approached I was really excited. It had been some time since we had visitors from Biggin Hill. Peter and I decided to bring Rafilowe home for a holiday while they were in Clarens. It would be good for them to see the little girl they had heard so much about. It was a wonderful time; Rafilowe looked good and had put on a bit of weight when we picked her up. We both made a huge fuss of her as we knew our time with her would be short and she would return to the home again so we were going to make the most of the time we had left with her. As the week came to a close we took her back to Bloemfontein but this time it wasn't as hard as the first time. When we said goodbye we knew we could visit whenever we wanted and could take her home occasionally.

April 2nd we had a visit from Henrietta and Antoinette, they called about ten in the morning which was a little out of the usual for them. I made a cup of tea for us all and we sat talking. Henrietta broke the news that I had feared. Rafilowe had passed away early that morning from Pneumonia, she had suffered complications and it was too much for her tiny body to take.

I thought the world was falling in on me as I sat listening to the news. Our little girl was dead and I wasn't there to comfort her. It was beyond comprehension and for a while I just could not allow it to register. Peter came over and gave me a cuddle without speaking, words were not required, I knew he was feeling as bad as I was and we just cuddled there for what seemed like eternity. My heart thought what an awful mother I must be allowing my child to be put into a hospice while my head told me it was better she died in the hospice. I just could not shake the feelings of guilt.

Plans had to be made for the funeral; we wanted to cremate her body but had to ask the Father his wishes even though he had not contributed to her upbringing for the past two years, the uncle and Aunt had to be consulted too. It is customary in Besotho culture that they wanted her to be buried, we made all the arrangements. The ball was in our court, we made no provision for ancestor worship, which is common in Besotho culture. Normally when someone dies they hold a midnight vigil and then march to the graveside. We decided instead to have a small service for family and friends at our church and then go directly to the graveside.

It was a miserable day the day of the funeral, it had rained most of the night and it was what I describe as a grey day, that was how I felt inside, grey just like the weather. A few of our close friends came to the funeral and we praised God for Rafilowe and her life however brief it had been, it had been a shining example of God's love and compassion. We loved Rafilowe as much as any parent could love their child and miss her dearly

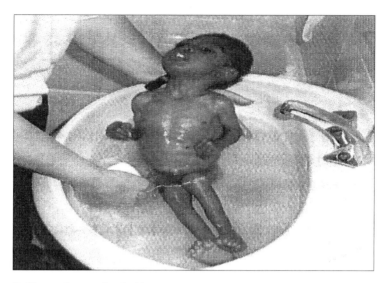

Refilowe when we first had her

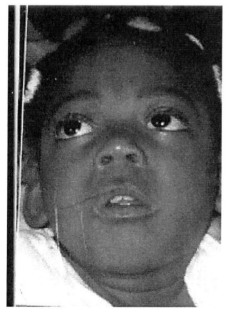

Refilowe slowly put on weight to just under 10kg

CHAPTER FIFTEEN

Psalm 68 v 9-10

You give abundant showers, O God you refreshed
your weary inheritance. Your people settled in it, and
from your bounty, O God, you provided for the poor.

Monday 8th January 2007. Peter and I set off for St Lucia for a
week's break but when we arrive I discover we have booked for
the wrong day and we are left to book into a bed and breakfast as
it is too far to travel back in one day. We found a wonderful bed
and breakfast in one of the back streets called the Hornbill. To
make the most of our time there we booked a trip up the estuary
and we bumped into a young couple from our church that are on
honeymoon, which was a bit awkward. The boat we travel on was
built by Len Basson; Len has been in Clarens now for about two
years and built his house just across the road from ours. It's quite
weird how we were on the boat that he had built. We saw lots of
crocodiles and hippo and had a wonderful day. The following day
we travelled via Richards Bay back to Clarens and decide to bring
my Daughter and her Husband Douglas when we came on the
correct date, silly me!

I booked a swim for Margaret the head teacher of our school
and a group of boys to swim the Midmar dam and we had been
training really hard. It's difficult to train in the Free State as pools
are at a premium.

I had been training a group of township children to swim; we
started from scratch at a small pool on the road to Bethlehem.

It's part of a tourist complex but is only sixteen meters long but ideal for our purposes. The golf consortium that was buying our farm said they would sponsor the boys to go and swim the English Channel in the UK as a relay but they changed their mind as the recession took hold. The boys were so disappointed at not going abroad, it was a real shame, I had even costed the trip and put in a business plan but to no avail. So we had to change our plans and now the idea was that they swim Midmar which was the largest open water swim in the world and they swim Sterkfontien Dam which is about an hour away.

Most Sunday afternoons are spent in Clarens old water reservoir, they call it the kloof and it backs onto the North East side of town on a nature reserve. It meant we were able to cut the cost of training as it didn't cost anything to swim at the kloof. The down side was that the boys had been told while growing up that they were not to go near the water as a large black snake lived there. I don't blame the parents they hadn't time to teach their children to swim and made up stories to keep them away. It didn't help that one Sunday while we were swimming we actually did bump into a snake. I had gone in with the boys and we were swimming on the far side of the kloof when the boy recoiled next to me and said something touched his leg. I looked into the water to see a wrinkle swim away. They are most venomous but as I understand it they are not able to strike while in the water, well that's the theory anyway.

In mid-January and the boys were able to swim for a full hour, they were almost ready for their competition but there were a few things I still needed to go over with them. At Midmar there are lots of life savers around but because there are so many people in the water it's impossible to see who needs help, so I would need to teach them to tread water and raise their hands at the same time.

The church was moving into a new phase as Steve was called to do apostolic work for the poor worldwide. He had just gone to a meeting in Dubai to talk over a world strategy for going into untouched nations where Christianity was outlawed, in February they meet to talk over poverty worldwide. I prayed that we would be used in some capacity for Gods glory, we wanted to serve the poor globally and the waiting was killing me.

When Steve arrived back he met with us about People of Hope and wanted us to go back to basics and to revamp the team. It's good sometimes to take time out and just assess the past, that way through looking at your strengths and weaknesses you are able to see the right way to go in the future. While we looked at People of Hope we realize we had only been touching the surface, looking after those that were dying but not getting to the root cause. Since the beginning of the year we saw twenty three of the people we were looking after die from aids and the message just was not getting through. So it was decided to HIV test in the homes and to educate in the homes.

I approached the two nurses that now live and work in Clarens and they agree to help us without charge. Hilder, the sister who runs the local clinic had arranged for us to have some testing kits from the clinic as she realized HIV is out of hand and requires some drastic measures. She trusted People of Hope implicitly as we had now been counselling for four years and the girls were well versed in what was required. HIV was now affecting one in three of our township folk and Hilder told me that all the ladies being tested during pregnancy were infected, it was a sorry state.

In the first month that we began to test in the home we covered forty tests which was wonderful as due to the stigma very few got to the clinic to be voluntary tested. At the same time we were able to teach the whole family about HIV. It's sad that you have to wait to treat a family member with HIV before you are able to speak to the families but the truth is that until you have access via a family member it was not a real scenario for the family. They have all heard about HIV, its everywhere they turn and they have heard it a million times before but it always happens to someone else. But it became real to them and they began to listen when it was in their own family.

During this time together with a few of the more senior ladies of People of Hope we are able to write a teaching manual and everyone in the group had their own copy. It was a real blessing; each person was working from the same base line which was wonderful.

Peter and I were continually praying for the group's maturity, both in Christ and in their medical knowledge as we always wanted to hand over the group to the local people of the church. They lived in the community and spoke the language, we knew this was the only way to sustain the group; it was all about local people, neighbours looking after neighbours, not government throwing money at the problem.

At the beginning of May Peter and I set off for the UK and Ireland, we have until mid-July in the UK. During our stay I am looking for several things, firstly Peter and I need a break after the traumatic death of Rafilowe and we have three weddings to attend and the birth of our first Grandchild. We are doing the trip on a shoe string and will be staying with church people the whole time; God is so good in his provision. We started at Durham and went to see Peters now aging Brother and his wife Dylis and then travel to see his other Brother Barry. The visit finds his Brother well although getting older he is still able to get around. His wife's Dylis helps when they go out she does all the driving. It was wonderful to spend some quality time with them, we visited some of the local attractions and I went to church with Dylis although it was a lot different from what I am used to in Africa and I felt it was a bit stiff, I'm more used to clapping and dancing and the service being led by the people not being led from the front.

We left Barry and made our way to Solihull where Rachel and Kieran two of the young volunteers that stayed with us were getting married. We stayed with a really nice church couple there, it's amazing we travel all the way across the world but find the body of Christ is willing to look after us as if we were their own family; it reminds me of Paul on his travels during bible times. The wedding is wonderful and is held at their New Frontiers church, they have church in what was an old print house and there is a stack of room. Afterwards the reception is held at a golf club about fifteen miles away. Emma knows Rachel from when she was out in Africa and she was invited to the wedding as well which gives me time to catch up with her. It's wonderful to see my daughter once again, she is now going out with an Irish man and appears very happy and I can't help but wonder if he will be the person she settles down with.

After Solihull we go off to Buxton and the church in the Peak, Tim is the pastor there and our church has a great relationship with his church. We stay with a couple called Andy and Harry, their church is held in a school hall and I was pleasantly surprised at how many young people attend. Tim's son plays in the worship band and his wife Becky sings too. After church we go to friends who are putting up Tim and Becky and their children while they look around for a new house to live in. While at Buxton we go on a small excursion with Sue Reed, she is one of the congregation. She takes us out into the dales for a walk. Her house is an old mining cottage close to a mill. Down below where she lives in the valley is a small river and on the opposite hill sheep graze in the mid-afternoon on the lush grass. After we had dinner with her and her husband we go to the cinema to see a film about Nelson Mandela.

The following evening we are to talk to Tim's church in the coffee shop they run within Buxton town. During the talk that evening I was showing some slides of our work in South Africa and while I am showing the slides I come across pictures of Rafilowe and found it difficult to talk as sorrow overwhelms me. Tim's churches have agreed to fund People of Hope out of the profits from the coffee shop which is a wonderful outpouring of their love for the church.

After we visited Buxton we made our way to Manchester airport and caught the early morning flight to Ireland. Matt would be at work but Jo and Alison a lady formally from Biggin Hill and who now lives in Ireland would be at the airport to meet us. They watched the plane as it came into land from the open fence at the other side of the airport. The drive down to Edenderry didn't give away much about Ireland as it is mostly motorway. Edenderry was a small town based around a compact High Street with shops crammed on either side. At the centre of the town on the left was the start of the Grand Canal, which ran just in front of Jo and Matt's house which was situated on a new estate. Their house was rented and was large and inviting. It had a small back garden with an alley at the side and I notice that next door were two large Rottweiler dogs which was a bit disturbing knowing Jo was about to have a small baby and the reputation they have. Most of the six weeks we were with Jo and Matt, it rained. We arrived just five days before she gives birth to a bouncing boy they call David Peter Hall, Peter was his middle name as both his Grand Dads are called Peter. On the night before she has David Jo said she was unable to sleep. In Ireland it doesn't get dark until well after 11.30pm and I took her for a walk along the canal bank in the dusk. It didn't do the trick and the following day they induce her into labour as she had some complications and they did'nt want to put the baby at risk.

It was all hands on deck, we were back and forwards to the hospital, Jo looked remarkable after her ordeal and made a swift recovery. Shortly after she came home the two dogs from next door got out and were rampaging the streets causing havoc. I told the police but they were not interested, sure enough a little boy was mauled and put into hospital. Peter had been out on the estate as soon as he realized the dogs were loose, telling children to keep off the streets until the dogs could be put back inside, it was an accident waiting to happen.

During our stay I was able to get Jo into a routine, we also visited their church in Mullingar, and I had enough time to swim in one of the local lakes, which was freezing. It felt much colder than the English Channel, and I thought I must be getting soft.

We flew back to Gatwick and picked up a car from the airport, one of the very few luxuries we have allowed ourselves during our stay. When we went to pick it up there were no cars in the row we should have chosen from and so the man allowed us to choose from the next category up but there was only one car in that line so the choice was made for us. It wasn't too sad as the car we picked up had a GPS which would prove invaluable to us over the coming weeks. We headed off to Bristol and another friend who we had come to know through our work in Africa. They visited us with a team of volunteers and said if we were ever in the UK to come and look them up so here we were heading to see them. I wanted to get their church involved in supporting People of Hope and we intended to speak to their church the following Sunday.

When we arrive and Pauline and Mike have arranged a huge

barbeque so that people were able to talk to us about our work, how wonderful. They were an amazing couple and God was using them powerfully. On the Sunday we went to the Anglican church where they are members, it's a real eye opener, The Anglican priest there was doing a service all about the poor and our talk fitted right into what was being said, Gods timing is so good. The church agreed to fund our work for the next few years and I felt this trip was going to be such a blessing in laying foundations for People of Hope. In the evening we had a wonderful meal with Pauline and Mike and also Bill and Sheila who we had met in South Africa in that same visiting team. When they came out to see us they brought hundreds of pairs of under pants and I will always remember Bill with under pants on his head. He is a hulking great figure of a man and has a full beard and with the pants on his head looked hysterical. What a blessing they were and very committed Christians, they so wanted to help with what we are doing in South Africa. We had a wonderful time of fellowship with the small group at Bristol but sadly we had to move on, we met up with another volunteer who had stayed with us in South Africa, Angela.

We drove to Camberley near Gatwick airport, we would have to pick up Doug and Karen from Gatwick in a few days and go to my Son's wedding but for the moment we went to catch up with Angela. Angela really made us welcome, she lived in a small terrace house with her sister and daughter. Her sister made me laugh all the time, they fought like cat and dog but I think its all pretence or most of the time anyway. We did a presentation of our work to the church there one evening before we set out to pick up Doug and Karen. They stayed with church friends in Biggin Hill while we stayed with the Lee family also from Biggin Hill.

It's sad to think that while we were living in Tatsfield we didn't get to know the Lee's, the only contact I had with them was when Jo and Matt got married and it was Janet who decorated the registry table where they sign the register, I was quite taken back by her generosity. While at their house we attended a Christian conference at Brighton, it is an annual event for leaders and we chose to drive the church mini bus and take all the guys from

Biggin Hill to the conference every day. I also had a speaking engagement with the Monday group at church; mainly the elderly and I spoke about our work in South Africa. About thirty or so people turn up and we have a really blessed time soaking in the presence of God. The people we spoke to were genuinely moved by what we shared with them.

It's a real shame we chose to drive the mini bus, it took ages to park and by the time we got back to the conference centre the first seminar was almost over. One evening on our way home from the conference, we had a phone call telling us not to join the M25, there had been an accident, we had to take two detours to get around it. The motorway was blocked with cars and we didn't get home until 1.30am, we had to up and go the following day at 6am. Eventually our time at Brighton conference was over; we had seen most of our church visiting from South Africa and friends from Buxton at the conference.

Back at Janet and Kevin house things were very bubbly and buoyant, we celebrated Peters 64th Birthday on July 16th in their front lounge and for the remainder of the time played lots of Wii, for the uninitiated it's a computer generated game which was lovely and had us all in raucous bouts of laughter. We left the Lee's house and set out to a small village near Ashford in Kent. My Son Phillip and his Fiancé Mary had chosen to get married in the village of Great Chart at a Norman church there. It was picture perfect as we parked the car across the road. All my children would be together, which is an achievement all on its own. Emma had travelled down from London and Matt and Jo had brought David over from Ireland and Karen and Doug had travelled down with us in the car.

The rain which had threatened us the whole of our stay had cleared up and the day was again bright and sunny, perfect! I was really excited for Phil, he had grown into a delightful young man and Mary was a real joy, I just knew Mary would be a real blessing to Phillip. The reception was at Mary's parent's house about a mile away. They had put a huge marquee on the front lawn. They lived in a quaint farm which is very old. The farm is extensive and has its very own Oast house which would be wonderful for the photos. There was also a small pond on the farm, Mary kept her horses there and had some of the photos taken with them in the background. I was so thankful Phillip found Mary again after so many years. He had first met her while we lived at Westerham when he was around thirteen. He used to go to a youth meeting which was held each week by her parents who were deacons of their church at Bessel's Green near Sevenoaks. In the years in between they had gone to respective universities but because Phillip kept up his Christian Summer camps as a leader he kept his link with the family. It was Mary's Father who had brought them together when Mary returned from Uni.

When it came time to go home we said goodbye to the children, not knowing when we would see them all again, it was really sad. I picked up my new Grandson and just cuddled him not wishing to break the connection, it is a price we pay for working in Gods kingdom and it isn't always easy.

September 2007.

Since being back in South Africa things had been hard, our money was almost gone but there was hope on the horizon as the golf consortium appears to have made headway and the sale of our farm looked imminent. It had been over two years since the golfing consortium first approached us to buy our farm, we had been at this stage before earlier in the year and wonder if this was really going to be the final sale.

The group People of Hope had begun a forum, Steve decided with a lot of revelation that we needed to expand into schools and farms and the community at large. The forum was made up of counsellors, trainers, net workers, transport and logistical personnel. It had been hard to let go, problems and misgivings dogged me and had kept me awake at night. I knew this was a work of God and I pray for his peace in it all.

November 2007

The forum was well underway now and Val was heading up the education. We had enough people in the group People of Hope to split them into two teams. Each team had a mature Christian to lead them. We decided that quality of work was more important than quantity, they each took six families and as each family was educated and counselled they moved on to another family. The impact was wonderful and many people come to the Lord through the ministry.

During this time we had a house full of guests as we had a conference at church. We had five house guests and all are from Lesotho. They were fascinated by the mod cons of the house, including the dishwasher, toaster and shower. It was three days until I was able to get a hot shower as by that time I got there all the hot water was gone, due to them having long hot showers.

We had another miracle during our work time with People of Hope. I visited one of the new brick built houses in the newly established township of Pahameng that day. One room was full of young girls braiding hair, the girl doing the braiding was the daughter of the client we had come to visit. We found her locked in a back bedroom; they said they had locked the door as it wouldn't close without the lock being on. The client as I will call her had badly ulcerated legs which had become infected. She sat on the bed swishing the flies to keep them away. The client refused to go to hospital as she had already lost her husband and one of her children in that very hospital. I managed to get the two nurses to visit and dress her leg but they didn't like the look of it.

The following days were a round of cleaning and dressing the leg, Henrietta, one of the nurses said that the leg had gangrene which was very sad news. The client would either die from not going to hospital for amputation or she would die through the operation as she had a heart condition on top of her already gangrene legs, not much of a choice for my client. I managed to talk her into going to hospital if I could get her to a different hospital, it was a tall order but it gave us a glimmer of hope, she agreed. I stepped out from her bedroom and past the large number of young girls who seemed to collect at the house, out into the garden and phoned a doctor who was a friend, it was a long shot but I had no options left open to me. With great relief she agreed to get her a bed at the provincial hospital in Bethlehem.

Peter decided on his way into Bethlehem to look up our client and see how she had progressed after her operation to remove her gangrene legs, we had been praying hard for her recovery. When he called to see her he couldn't believe his eyes, she was sat up in bed laughing, her legs had been saved against all odds and they were treating her heart. Our God is a mighty God and faithful to those who love him. Wow! What a turnaround from not wanting help and needing amputation to complete recovery.

End November 2007.

I had taken a lady to Bethlehem to the hospital her CD4 count was 31, the doctor told her that her lungs and kidneys were failing, she was told to come back to the hospital for treatment the following Tuesday and we realized if she was to make it through to the following Tuesday we would need to help her and give her a lot of tlc. We took her to our house, washed her then tucked her into bed. The lady gave us permission to disclose her status to her daughter who was around fourteen or fifteen years old, it was very sad but made what was coming up a little easier. As I went into the bedroom with some soup and her medication I was already too late. The lady gave a huge sigh and passed away peacefully. We got all the family together and broke the news to them. After a death there are always lots to do and we set about arranging the funeral for the family and the undertakers etc. It's all part of the work we do as People of Hope and although we were too late for the lady the remainder of the family all became Christians due to what they had seen. It was now the 1st of December 2007, during the evening Karen our daughter called at our house for a blanket. Outside her house in Kgwbetswana a man has fallen over in the road and Peter and I went and help her. It was getting late and he must have been on his way back from the local tavern as we could smell the drink just by standing over him. He was cut on his head badly so I put on a pair of gloves to have a closer look. I took his blood pressure and it wasn't great so we called an ambulance but it was well over an hour and it still hadn't arrived. We used a large blanket to lift him into the back of our bakkie as the ambulance was nowhere to be seen by this time his brother had appeared and we drove together to Bethlehem hospital.

On arrival at the hospital I went off to get some more gloves to transfer him into a chair as there was so much blood but by the time I returned to the car the nurses had already got there with a gurney to transfer him into casualty. The doctor took one look at him after putting up a drip and said he needed to be x-rayed and stitched but the x-ray department wasn't open so they would admit him. We took his brother home to Clarens, he wasn't much better himself and I was left wondering about the extent of drinking that goes on in the township.

The golfing consortium agreed to pay ten per cent of the sale price to each of the farmers to enable them to have an extension to the contract as the government had held up the sale of the land. It was a blessing as we were now down to our last R200 at the bank, Gods timing is wonderful and he never fails to amaze me.

The husband of a young couple who we had been looking after passed away today. Both he and his young wife were HIV positive. After the funeral we took the wife to our house, she stayed with us for a while as the family of her dead husband wanted to strip her house of all its belongings. While she was with us Peter and I together with one of the People of Hope took out all the furniture and distributed it amongst all the church members living locally so that when his family arrive at the house it will be empty. It seems to be a common practice amongst Besotho people but leaves the widow helpless and we were glad to help. I had chosen to call the wife Pearl, her Sesotho name was unpronounceable and Pearl really suited her as she was precious. She settled in and was not frightened of the dogs; she appeared to understand a lot of English which was a relief. Tomorrow we must go to the clerk of the court to get a court order so she is able to keep possession of her furniture.

Pearl had been renting her plot of land and we got news that the landlord was going to throw her off for non-payment of rent. We had another miracle that day; it turned out that the landlord of Pearl was no other than the child of the lady I had looked after before she died at my house. Because of the grace shown to her Mother when she found out I was involved with Pearl she never pressed for payment and allowed Pearl to live on the site rent free. Gods light had truly penetrated her heart and she gave grace because she had been shown grace, what a glorious God we serve.

I went to see the two nurses as they had moved their base to a house in Larola where we lived and I wanted to catch up with them. Peter had last year had an ulcer removed and was bleeding and I wanted to ask their advice without having to put Peter through going to the doctors again if it all proved unnecessary. She told me to take him to the doctor as it might be a new ulcer and she was very concerned for him. Bless Peter, he had been very tired of late and by four in the afternoon he often went to bed.

Henrietta actually phoned Peter and convinced him to seek medical advice so we phoned his surgeon who performed the last operation. Dr McAlpine asked to see Peter right away. When he saw the surgeon he had blood tests taken and the results were back in a few days so I was able to take him home again.

As the year drew to a close I had time to reflect on what an eventful year it had been. Who would have thought we would see so much progress with People of Hope. In a year we have been praying for nurses to join us and then we got two, it's a bit like waiting for a bus then two come together, God has a great sense of humour. We had done our first testing in the homes with the help of our two nurses and started to implement a training package in our group. We had managed to arrange funding for the group for many years to come and gained some wonderful friendships to boot. We saw three weddings and the birth of our first Grandson and had miracles as well. It's never dull working for God and every day brings challenges. My daughter Karen often asks what have we got planned for today, who needs to plan, I tell her, God has it already planned, and we just go with the flow.

Emma my daughter arrived in Cape Town with a friend and was coming up to see us over Christmas; it would be so fantastic to see her again. She came in by plane into Johannesburg with her friend Peter on the 23rd of December just in time for the festive fun. I had thirteen to dinner on Christmas day and it was pure mayhem but wonderful all the same.

On Boxing Day we were visited by a dozen or so children from the township, we gave them all sweets as there was so many still around. They opened Christmas crackers, I think they had never seen Christmas crackers before and it was a delight to see their faces when they pulled them.

Emma was only with us for a few days and on the 27th of December left for Cape Town again, she was flying back to the UK on the 2nd of January, as the coach pulled away taking her to the Cape I said a quick prayer for God to keep her safe as I didn't know when I shall see her again.

During church the following Sunday, Steve was preaching he was talking about how heaven would be when we get there. I couldn't help but shed a tear when he said those that had died who were disabled would be fully restored. I thought about Rafilowe, blind and paralyzed and dying at four years old and prayed she had been fully restored. Val gave me a picture just after her death of Rafilowe running through tall grass. She was bounding across the field, full of life and as she ran she waved. Val said when she glanced up she saw that she was waving to Jesus and he was waving back. It was such a wonderful picture and I cling to that picture even today.

My besotho team of lads competing at Sterkfontein dam, their 2nd ever swimming event. They went from non swimmers to competing in just one year. I am so proud of their achievements.

My son Phillip with new wife Mary on their wedding day 7/7/2007

CHAPTER SIXTEEN

Acts 20 v 24
However I consider my life worth nothing to me
If only I may finish the race and complete the task
The Lord Jesus has given me, the task of
Testifying to the gospel of God's grace.

Every year as I enter the New Year I find myself praying, "God increase my borders, have your hand with us and bless us". It's a prayer I often say. I am not the sort of person who makes New Year resolutions as many of you are. I always think by the end of the first week I will have broken most of them. However going into 2008 after the year I had before I did hope and wonder if it would be a good year.

The year began with Emma going back to the UK, I always miss my children when they go home and wonder when I will see them next and this was no different. It's hard being a mum of children who are in another country. I wonder how they are getting on, are they struggling. I always wish they would phone more often as I know many parents do but Africa sometimes feels a million miles away. All of my children are Christians and I know they understand why I was there in South Africa which is a real blessing, otherwise I don't think I would be able to do the things I do.

Peter was due to go to see his specialist during the first weeks of the year and as he had been very tired and had some bleeding I was a bit anxious. The specialist had become a good friend and we felt comfortable with him. Peter was booked in to the hospital that day as he was going to have a scope to see if the problem was ulcers which he had suffered with since he was a young man. When he was about 20 years old he had an operation to take away the lower part of his stomach which held an ulcer. Surgery then was rather radical and it left him with a huge scar over his abdomen.

Dr McAlpine was a tall young athletic looking Dr, he looked as if he had in his time played a lot of rugby, I don't know if he had or not but that's how he comes across. On his desk were photos of his family and he was very gentle in his mannerisms. We had called into his office that morning just out of courtesy before Peter checked in. Dr McAlpine was pleased to see us and we were soon chatting about family and the like. He assured Peter it would be a mundane procedure and the most he expected was an ulcer. It turned out to be an ulcer which was treated with tablets and we were both relieved.

One evening during March I had just made dinner and Peter was as usual in the bathroom washing up. I heard a very faint cry and realized it was Peter he needed my help, it was more a croak than a scream and I didn't exactly run to his aid as it didn't sound urgent. He was standing bent over the sink in the bathroom as I opened the door, even then it didn't sink in he was in trouble. The blood was dripping from his mouth and my eyes fell on the blood on the floor then up the bath panel and splash back. I have seen a lot of gory things since working with the poor in the townships and although I suppose I was running on auto the numbness hit home. I was keeping stable more for Peter's sake than my own; I didn't want to panic him.

I sat him on the floor as I think he would have collapsed anyway and rushed to get my cell phone, I had the number for the ambulance service logged in as we were always calling ambulances in our field of work. I hit the button trying not to allow my voice to give away my true feelings; inside I was a mess but outwardly a picture of confidence. Giving all the details to the operator a feeling of some relief came as I knew help was on its way, sure enough an ambulance with two medics arrived and started to extract information from us. Shortly after the ambulance arrived they were joined by a paramedic who had been about 20 minutes away at Golden Gate National Park on stand bye. Their vehicles were parked on our steep drive still with their lights flashing, it was all surreal and I had trouble even thinking so I just tried to stay out of the way and watched as they stabilized Peter.

They had to get him into the ambulance but the entrance to the bathroom was too tight, the angles were too acute to turn the stretcher through the doorway. Now Peter is a large man and the hope they would physically lift him was out of the question although if they had no other option I think they would have tried but instead they asked him if he could manage to get out onto the stretcher. It was painful watching as he crawled on all fours out of the bathroom and into the dining room to get onto the stretcher. We were on our way after what seemed to me like years had passed. I sat in the front with the driver to give the medic more room to manoeuvre in the back as we drove. I don't think anything was going through my mind at the time; it was like being in limbo.

They got Peter into the trauma room and accessed his situation and he was stabilized and kept in ICU overnight. Next day Dr McAlpine did another scope and found Peter had an ulcer that had bled and his previous operation had refluxed back into his stomach causing the ulcer. They upped the medication but to no avail and due to Peter's lack of response to medication, his situation became much worse. The second night when I went to leave the hospital they were putting up units of blood in preparation for the operation he would undergo the following day to remove his bowl from his stomach and lower it to stop the reflux.

Karen Doug and I all stood outside of ICU after the operation anxiously waiting to see how he had faired during his operation. Dr McAlpine had told me it had been a success but I don't know about you I always want to see for myself. Peter was in an isolation room with a nurse all to himself, I suppose that is what ICU is all about, individual attention. He looked pale but was sat up in bed as if nothing had happened. It was only the mass of lines hooked up that gave away the real story. I was glad to see him in such good spirits and when we left I felt at ease.

It was very different being home alone; Peter couldn't hog the remotes for the TV for a start. It would only be for a short while so I really didn't worry about being on my own, it was after all temporary. I had time to do house work and go to prayer meetings and house groups; they didn't interfere with Peter's visiting hours. He was in Hospital for about two weeks and when he came home at first he had bed rest as he was still a bit weak after the operation. He also had some bad side effects from the Morphine and kept having anxiety attacks. He said he felt an impending feeling of doom and totally out of control. I managed to get him some medication which helped and he soon got past it and back to his normal self.

It was such a relief for him not to feel tired by four in the afternoon, he was able to walk the dogs which he hadn't been able to do since we arrived in Africa. It was like having a new man around the house; repairs that had been outstanding for ages got repaired. Peter was more alert and chatty and more romantic. I had forgotten what his arms around me felt like but as we stood in the kitchen and he hugged me I knew how God had yet again come through for us and I felt grateful to be standing there with my husband in his arms, I admit there were times especially after he collapsed I wondered if Peter was going home to be with God. The thoughts soon drifted out of my mind as I turned and gave him a kiss and held him close.

At the end of June we booked a holiday, it was to celebrate Peters 65th Birthday and our wedding anniversary. Before going to Egypt Steve had us in the office to discuss handing over People of Hope. I was relieved as it had grown in momentum and was going at break neck speed. We now had 23 volunteers and it was time to hand the project over as we had always intended to do and with Peters recurring illnesses it was time. Steve was relieved we felt the same way about the project and it wasn't until after I had left his office I wondered who he had in mind to take over. The following Sunday at church I told him I thought Topsy the church secretary was the right person and he said I thought I had told you who I had in mind. He was very apologetic at not having told me it was Topsy he had thought of and we both laughed. God is so good sometimes and he had placed her name on my heart, it was a real relief we both had the same person in mind.

Topsy is a very mature Christian and although she had no

medical experience it wasn't about that. It was more to do with attitudes, Topsy was the perfect choice, and she had the ability to look at things from a Godly perspective and knew the language and lived in the township. She willing took up the challenge as I knew she would, God had so plainly given her name to me I just knew she was the person to take on the role and lead the project, I was totally at ease with the idea.

In South Africa during July it is mid-winter and freezing, Peter had always been a sunshine person so Africa was not in the picture. I thought it would be romantic to go back to Egypt as that is where we went on honeymoon. Picturing our honeymoon brought back smiles; we had a wonderful time there, snorkelling in the pristine seas. The fish were amazing, so many different varieties and the clarity is something else. I recalled climbing Mount Sinai, it almost killed us both, and the heat and breathlessness is unbelievable but all worthwhile just to see the view as the sun comes up over the Holy Mountain. It was an incredibly romantic time one I wanted to capture again and so we booked for Egypt once more. I couldn't get booked into the same hotel or the town we had stayed at previously but made the booking for a hotel just up the coast.

Egypt was just as I remembered it as we landed, the smells and the heat were over powering, there is a certain smell the dessert has that is like no other and its one of the things that most struck Peter about Egypt, he remembers getting off the plane and smelling this dusty smell and it brought back all the memories once again. We were not able to go straight to Sharm El Sheik but had to go first to Cairo, so we decided to stay for a couple of days as we wanted to see the pyramids. We joined a coach the tour operator had laid on to take us to our hotel along with lots of others. Crisscrossing Cairo during rush hour is a feat all on its own, the cars were one chaotic mess, hooters honked every second and how we didn't have an accident begs belief. The coach didn't tale a direct route but passed along narrow streets, we did get a glimpse of the mighty Nile as we crossed over a bridge, it majestically moves past all the chaos as it winds down into the plains on its way down to Luxor. We stopped several times to off load baggage and people at hotels and finally during the late afternoon we were outside our hotel just opposite the Pyramids of Giza.

What a sight the pyramids are, we could see them long before we arrived at the hotel. It was hard to believe we were actually here in Cairo. The hotel bedroom was more than we could have hoped for and we felt truly blessed, from the window we could see the great pyramids, what a view. The hotel had two pools and as we stretched out in the sun under the shade of an umbrella we could see the pyramids. Its strange how being in the midst of a modern hotel I could only begin to imagine all the things the pyramids had seen over the centuries. Modern day Cairo is a mass of cars and at first I found it difficult to sleep after living so long in the quite of Clarens and now being exposed to all the traffic, even at night it doesn't let up. The honking of the cars can still be heard quite clearly through the windows of the hotel bedroom.

We wasted no time in booking two tours as that would be all we had time for as we only had two days in Cairo. The first would be to the Pyramids an obvious choice. It was extremely hot when we got there, we paid our entrance fee and immediately Peter had the camera ready to take photos. The pyramids are much larger close up than I had imagined, the bricks stand up to my shoulder and above us were hundreds of rows of blocks. The guide told us that originally each of the pyramids would have had an outer coat of marble but time had eroded the outer covering. They must have been a sight shining in the sun; only the very top of one of the pyramids had a partial coating of marble on it now. We were not able to go inside the pyramid as the guide told us the stairs were very steep and just led to a single chamber with nothing inside, the air was difficult to breath and he recommended we didn't go in and we took his advice. He took our photo as we sat on the pyramids huge blocks, I was a bit disappointed at having come so far and not be able to go inside and also disappointed because I had imagined being able to see a tomb in all its splendour. They had taken all the artefacts out of the pyramid years ago and they now lay in the Egyptian museum.

We went to the museum the following day with another guide. Outside the building which now houses the artefacts is a long pond. It is planted with lilies and papyrus symbolizing Upper Egypt and

Lower Egypt. I could have spent a couple of days walking around the museum as it was fascinating. We did see the sarcophagus of the kings and lots of mummies, there were so many beautiful things it would take a full chapter to tell you about them all, but suffice to say we had the most wonderful time.

The following morning we flew down to Sharm and stayed at a wonderful hotel on the Gulf of Aqaba. Our hotel was about ten minutes' walk from the beach were we spent time just relaxing. There was a shuttle bus from our hotel even though it wasn't far to walk and we had one evening just missed the last bus for the evening, we decided to walk but just as we started Peter had bad chest pains, I don't know how we made it back to the hotel and I was very concerned. The following day we chose to walk down to the beach and called in at a sister hotel just across the street to see how the other half live as you do. We had a look around but Peter had forgotten the sun tan lotion but felt so ill he couldn't make it back to the hotel. I sat him in the reception area while I went back for it. Again later that afternoon he was struggling and I called the Hotel doctor to see him.

The doctor checked him out but to be on the safe side called an ambulance to take him to the hospital to do further tests. Well it's not the nicest thing to do on your holiday and especially not in a foreign country to have to go to hospital. We had to go with an interpreter and just like the roads around Cairo the hospital was just as busy only this time we didn't understand what was going on. They admitted Peter for the night and as I said goodnight to him up in his private room I could feel his fright and anxiety, I didn't really want to leave him as there seemed to be nobody around but I had to get back and update the insurance company that he had been taken into hospital and sort out the implications of that. We were supposed to be going home the following day and I wondered if we would be on the flight home the following day or not.

As I left the hospital it was just after midnight and Cairo isn't the place for a lone woman on her own. The gate keeper called me a taxi, all I could tell him was the name of my hotel and hope he understood me, it was very scary as we travelled through the streets until I started to recognize some of the land marks and knew we were close to my hotel. I had no money on me as we had left in a hurry and had to go to a bank that was still open and just hope I could get some money out to pay the taxi driver. Back at the hotel the staff were wonderful and asked how Peter was doing. Even though the hour was late they sent me some sandwiches and fruit to the room. I got hold of the medical people who insured us and brought them up to date. They were even making plans for me to have an extended stay if it was required and put a counter measure in place in case Peter needed to be air lifted to a specialist hospital later. I was exhausted, frightened and alone but remembered God never leaves us or forsakes us. I prayed earnestly that night for God to be with Peter and to keep him safe. I knew he must have been scared whit less and although I felt at ease after praying he was in no shape to pray for himself.

The following day as I got there early they were releasing him, they said he had an angina attack but was able to travel; we were so relieved I could have kissed the ground. When we arrived back in South Africa it was very late when we got home. I had driven all the way back from the airport which is about a five hour journey with a break but was pleased to get home. Peter still didn't feel well and had another bleed as we got indoors. I phoned Dr McAlpine and he told me to bring him straight in the following morning.

They did anther scope on Peter and kept him in during which time they took a biopsy and found cancer of the stomach. It was now early August and the year had been one hospital after another and I wondered where it would all end. Dr McAlpine told us he would have to take away the whole stomach, it would be a bad operation but after Peter would be able to live with no stomach as the intestine over time would act as his stomach. It would mean starting from scratch with liquids and building up to solid food but it was the only option open to us and he agreed to have it done. Peter was sent down to Bloemfontein to have two stents put into his heart so that he would withstand the operation. But because they had given him blood thinners he wasn't able to have the operation until the medication had worn off, otherwise he would bleed to death literally on the operating table. We used the time to have chemotherapy to shrink the cancer which we were told was contained in his stomach. If the cancer had spread his chances of survival were none at all but because it was contained he stood a very good chance of making it.

The news came as a real shock and when the doctor had left us that day in the ward Peter and I just held each other tight and cried openly. I felt so helpless and Peter was frightened. As Christians many people feel we should put our faith in God and have no fear, we had put our faith in God but we are human and I have to tell you the fear was real and palpable.

The rounds of Chemotherapy went well and Peter suffered very few side effects. I was waiting for the nausea and hair loss but it didn't come and during the course of his treatment talking to the nurses I realized that not all treatments led down this path. The nurses were great and one nurse in particular was very sweet, she was a born again Christian and prayed with me, it was a great comfort knowing that even here in the midst of despair God had place strategic people who really cared enough to sit and pray with you, what a blessing.

As soon as the Chemotherapy was over we had a couple of weeks to allow its effects to subside before they began surgery. Peter had done really well and it was a time we appreciated each other more and God more. He was able to continue his regime of walking the dogs and we would often walk up to town, with Ben and Gus our collie and Labrador dogs. We would stop for coffee by the square and then make our way home. Because of the two stents Peter had never felt so good and all the tiredness of the past had gone. It was the day before his operation as we sat he said to me "did I think he should have the operation or should he leave it up to God to heal him". I think he was scared of the obtrusive nature of this operation, he still had memories from when he had a part of his stomach taken when he was in his twenties and I knew he was scared.

All the while there is hope we soldier on and Peter's chances were looking really good, it would be a huge operation and I had looked it up on the net and seen that it took around two years for people to feel as though they are back to normal but what option did we have really.

The operation was to be at Bloemfontein in early November and with trepidation we set off early in the morning, Peter didn't have to book in until later that day. The operation followed a few days later, it went very well and the specialist was pleased with it. Peter was in an isolation room in ICU but they allowed me to visit whenever I felt like it. God had been with Peter and he was totally at ease although hooked up to everything barring the kitchen sink.

After a few days he sat in a chair at the side of the bed but still felt disorientated due to the morphine. He said there had been tanks in the ward and that he had seen Prince William who he pointed out to me, it was one of the nurses, I realized it was a side effect and didn't worry about it; it would pass and was just one of the phases he would have to pass through. On about the fourth or fifth day it was clear something was wrong and the doctor took Peter down to theatre again, they found an abscess on his colon. More surgery followed, I was joined by Karen and we kept vigil outside the ICU waiting for him to come up from surgery, it had been over four hours and still no news.

The specialist came and found us sitting outside in the waiting area and told us he had cleaned the site and it was still weeping, he had left the stomach open as it would take many more operations cleaning it until the wound healed and they were able to close Peter up. They were keeping him under close observation and he was in a semi-comatose state which meant he was unconscious and unable to communicate.

During this time I don't know what went through my mind, I felt numb, it was like falling from a building into a never ending pit and I couldn't see the ground at all. Jo arrived from Ireland as she didn't know what was going to happen so I felt it best she came to be near her dad. Every two days Peter would go down to surgery again to have the cavity washed out. Every day we sat around waiting for news, each operation was at least three hours, sheer purgatory waiting for news. We were staying with church friends of friends, they were so gracious and kind. All we did in those days was to get up have breakfast and go to the hospital, it was a continual round of waiting to see if he had come through.

God was my strength at that time, I don't know what I would have done without my faith, I think I may have given in under the strain if it wasn't for my faith in God.

Jo had to go home after a week, Peter still was on an incubator to help with his breathing which made it impossible to speak but he appeared to know Jo was there. David our Grandchild was just outside in the waiting area and we took it in turns to take him as he wasn't allowed into the ICU. The shame was that a day after Jo went back to Ireland Peter received a Tracie that allowed him to talk, his voice was very weak at first but grew stronger every day but poor Jo had missed that. It would have meant so much for her to hear her Dad speak to her, instead she just held his hand while he was in a coma willing and praying for him to get through this ordeal.

Just a couple of days before Christmas Peter was transferred to Bethlehem back to the hospital he had first been diagnosed as having cancer in. It was a major step forward and it was a great Christmas present. At first he was in the ICU but as he grew more stable they moved him to the wards. It was a great relief to see him back in the ward making progress but just as he began to make progress and was able to get out of bed and walk to the nurses' station he was again hit with another abscess. This time the abscess was on the stomach wall and they were able to drain it from outside which was a relief. He was still being fed directly into his stomach through a drip so had not made the transition to soft food but they kept trying him on soft foods but he was too weak now to take anything. Each day the physiotherapist would arrive only to find Peter wasn't up to walking.

The doctor thought it best that they either sent him home or sent him across the road to a rehabilitation centre to make his recovery. I wasn't sure what to do but took advice from two friends who were doctors and the two nurses I knew. One doctor said it best we take Peter home and the others were all of the opinion he should go to the rehab centre to recover. He still had a tube in for feeding, the abscess was draining and his original wound needed sterile dressings and quite honestly I didn't feel up to the job, the whole year had been pretty traumatic and taken its toll, normally I think

I would have taken Peter home but it was too much for me at the time.

Peter was moved over to the rehab centre the following morning. The centre was bright and cheerful, it had its own dietician and physiotherapist so I was happy for Peter to be there and felt it was the right decision. One evening Peter told me he didn't think he would ever make it out of the hospital to go home. I told him it was nonsense, but he felt looking at his body and all the tubes it was impossible for him to come to terms with it all. It worried me greatly his defeatist attitude. I prayed with him and we cried together. A few days later he told me he loved me and the look that came over his face I recognize now was defeat, a look that said I hope you will be alright without me but I have to go. At the time I didn't know what to make of it, I just hugged him and told him I loved him too and laid my head against his chest as it was the only place free of tubes. Looking back I can still see his face that morning, his eyes looked so different, sad and questioning.

I was so troubled by what I had felt the next day I went across the road before going into see Peter to see his Doctor. I made arrangements for Peter to come home as he didn't appear to be making any progress where he was and home would be the best place for him. I felt almost cowardly for not having him at home before. The doctor agreed with me and it was settled he would be home by Wednesday. He asked as soon as I arrived had the farm been sold, I could not tell him any good news on that score but was bursting to tell him he was coming home. It didn't get the reaction I was expecting, he just said Wednesday would be too late, I still didn't fall in as to what he had just said but just confirmed that he would be going home on Wednesday and wasn't that great?

Peter asked if he could go into the garden which we had done through the use of a wheel chair a couple of days before and I knew he had enjoyed it so much. It must have been wonderful to feel the wind on his face as it had been over two months since he had been outside and the hospital atmosphere must be so insular. I arranged a wheel chair for him and we undid all the drips and transferred him to a chair. Immediately his eyes rolled back in his head and he fainted. The nurse got him back into bed with my help and called another sister to help. Together after about twenty minutes of trying they were unable to get a line into Peter who had now come around but looked deathly pale. Looking at Peter I couldn't stay in the room and said I was going to get some air. I think at those times God gives you a sense of what is happening. I had only minutes before said goodbye to my friend, who had visited Peter, she had left to go and get some provisions but as I stood outside smoking with shaky hands I phoned her. I asked her to come back to the hospital as things didn't look good, as I said it I still didn't realize the implications of what I had said, there was no urgency in my voice more an acceptance.

As Amanda my dear friend was dropped off by her colleague the nurse who had been with Peter was approaching me. She said softly that Peter was slipping away and I should come immediately. Peter passed away ten minutes later in my arms...... At that moment my Pastor Gavin Northcote pocked his head around the door but I wasn't taking anything in. Later that night as I ran on auto pilot things just happened around me, I couldn't sleep but went to bed, I think more to be on my own with my own thoughts. As I curled up in bed with Peters favourite blue shirt which matched his eyes held in my hands my heart broke. Tears came freely and just kept coming. It had taken two failed marriages and a long road to find this Godly gentle man and now he was gone to be with God. We had just eight brief years but what happy years, joining two families together as one and traveling across continents to finally find what God's purpose for us was. I will never regret those years; God brought us together and placed us in Africa helping the sick and the dying. Peter had his wish, he did what few people do in their lifetimes, and he finished well, what more could you ask.

I pray I finish well too, I don't know what the future holds, I won't pretend that I have not struggled, I miss him every day, we had the funeral and all the children except my son came out to Africa, he was unable to come due to finances and work but I know he was here in spirit. I had another memorial service in the UK for all the family who couldn't make it out to Africa and was able through Gods strength to give a testimony of Peter's life. He had been an alcoholic but God had done wonders in his life and turned him around. At his time in life he never imagined he would again find happiness but God had it all in place before the beginning of time. Peter gave freely of himself in helping the poor and the sick and poured himself out, hours spent taking people backwards and forwards to hospital, sitting with them and praying for them. I was blessed not only with a gentle husband but a husband who didn't mind having sick people dropped on him staying in our house. He wasn't afraid to take chances and pioneer things and was a fabulous blessing to me and to his family and the community. He will be sorely missed as he touched thousands of lives here in Clarens and around the world.

For those of you who are struggling with bereavement I have to say the road is a long one. If I have learnt anything through the death of loved ones which I have had my share it would be that God is ever present, he is faithful and has been my rock during this time of mourning. His church is like a mighty army all across the face of the earth. During the period after Peter's death and just before he died I travelled to many places due to hospitals and funerals, seeing family etc. The one constant thing was always Gods church. They housed me and fed me and encouraged me. Often church members would encourage me with bible passages, some had pictures which I think of fondly and have helped me through the tuff times. My faith is a constant too, I am rooted in the belief that one day I will meet Rafilowe and Peter again and we will be reunited once more in the presence of God. Peter has no more pain and is not suffering anymore but rejoicing with God.

Shortly after his death I read a book on bereavement, I had all the classic symptoms, forgetfulness, pain anger on some occasions, I couldn't come to terms with the fact he had undergone eleven operations successfully but had still succumbed to death in the end. I was angry with God, the surgeons, just about everyone but then I realized God gave us free will and through Peter's life he had made choices of free will. He had given into drink which in turn made him a diabetic and had a lot to do with his ulcers. This may sound harsh coming from his wife but I know in the end Peter gave his life totally to God and was a forgiven man. Jesus died on the cross a painful horrific death so that Peter could have salvation. He took that salvation and gave the remainder of his life over to God as I have done as well. I won't ever know all the answers this side of heaven but by faith I take each day at a time and walk in Gods glory and all that he has purposed for me. I do hope you too find your way to knowing God, it has been a real privilege to serve God and every day he has challenged me. I'm still seeking his ways and it is not always sunshine and roses but I have never felt so fulfilled in all my life as I do now. I am not perfect by any manner of means and I am not anything out of the ordinary except for one thing, I am an heir to Gods throne, a daughter of the most high and confident in it.

I hope you have found my story inspiring and you have come a little closer to knowing my God. If you want to know more, contact your local church and get hold of a good bible or look for an Alpha course or just looking course, you will never regret finding out the truth for yourself.

ANALOGY

Psalm 68 v 4-5

Sing to God, sing praises to his name, extol him who
rides on clouds his name is Lord and rejoice before him.
A father to the fatherless, a defender of widows is
God in his holy dwelling.

I have always been interested in swimming and wanted to use an
analogy of swimming to help those looking for what is missing in
their lives as I was, I hope it helps you.

When I set myself the task of swimming the Channel the first
thing I did was to find out if there was an organization that headed
up all the training and who would be willing to help me.

If you are searching to find out more about becoming a Christian,
I suggest it is not dissimilar. Seek out courses in your location, see
if they do a Just Looking course or an Alpha course. If however
you are looking for a church, I suggest first doing your homework.
Find out what the church you are looking at believes in, does it
follow scripture, but more than that, are they outward looking or
only interested in helping themselves. A good church will have
some projects in the community, they will encourage the youth
with some form of outreach to them. What are they doing amongst
the poor? The bible says in James 1 v 27: Religion that God our
Father accepts as pure and faultless is this: to look after orphans
and widows in their distress, so they should be helping the poor of
the community.

Before I even began to train I needed to know what was involved.

. I needed to know how to achieve my goals and what to do. In my case the Channel Swimming Association had a book, which I bought telling me all the rules and how to train, it told me of all the things I needed to know to achieve my objective. Wave conditions and currents, what to wear and how to protect myself, without this information I would not have been prepared for the trial that lay ahead. It is no different in the Christian world; you will need a good bible. Reading your bible is essential to understand where we are going and how to achieve our final destination.

The second thing is a lot to do with training; if I wanted to succeed I knew I needed to train hard.

I would have been very naïve if I thought that I would just be able to jump in and swim across the Channel. I began training the year before in a pool environment; this was in preparation for joining the other Channel swimmers at Dover to begin my training in earnest. Working in the pool made me fit enough to join the other Channel swimmers but didn't make me a Channel swimmer. At Dover with the other Channel swimmers, week after week we added to our skills and endurance getting used to all kinds of conditions. Sometimes the water was very calm and sometimes it was rough. I had to get used to all the different conditions. The same is true when we become a Christian, we need to train ourselves and be disciplined, not to make life hard but to make it easier when problems arise. If life was all smooth sailing it would be a breeze but we face many challenges and mountainous seas and we need to know how to face the waves ahead. It is a long road which will take until we leave this mortal earth and join our Father in heaven, so we will need endurance. We need to press in and train hard.

How do we do that? The bible talks about putting on our armour. Ephesians 6v11 says Put on the full amour of God so that you can take your stand against the devil's schemes. And in verse 14 onwards it tells us what they are. The belt of truth, the breastplate of righteousness, and with your feet fitted with the readiness that comes from the gospel of peace. In addition to all this, take up the shield of faith, the helmet of salvation and the sword of the spirit.

So we need to be disciplined and truthful, righteous, which means to lead a holy life following the scriptures. We need to be peaceful, slow to anger and quick in love. We have to have faith in God, without this we will sink at the first wave. We have to understand that Jesus brought us salvation, he saved us, by dying on the cross for our sins, and he has made a way for us to come to God the Father as pure and blameless. If we have faith to believe this about Jesus, then we have been saved and have our salvation.

When talking of the sword of the spirit, it is another way of saying Gods word or his bible. If we read and fill our minds with his words we will live the life I am talking about.

I got myself a good trainer; it wasn't good enough to do it on my own.

A good trainer is also essential; a trainer will be able to get rid of some of the bad habits which hold up our progress. As we listened to our trainer our strokes became more effective and we covered more ground. A trainer can be someone in the church who is a leader, maybe the person who you respect who holds a position of leadership within the church and is willing to disciple you. Look around and keep your eyes open for such a person.

Channel swimmers need to be around other Channel swimmers.

It is no good going and training with people who don't push you , I needed to be around like minded people, people with the same objectives as myself who were going to take the training seriously and not hamper my progress. The church is like a training ground with likeminded Christians who will encourage you in your journey. Some are new Christians and others mature Christians who will stand beside you when things get rough in life's stormy seas and show you the right way to go, not only through encouragement, they also give practical help as well as advice.

Attitude and thinking as well as speech play a huge part in reaching my goal.

If I told myself that I was too weak, or the training was too hard for me then I don't think I would have a chance to reach my objective of crossing the Channel. I would have talked myself out of it before I had even begun to train. Have you ever heard the expression "be careful what comes out of your mouth". Ephesians 4v29 says this: Do not let unwholesome talk come out of your mouth. It is a good reminder that what starts in the brain as a thought often gets translated into deed or word. All of our actions always without exception start by what we think first. It begins with thought, then word and finally the deeds. We never complete and action without first thinking about it. So if our thinking is wrong we will more than likely do the wrong thing. We are however able to stop it at this stage, before we action it, either through speech or deed. Our attitude is always led by our thoughts, so we must change our thoughts, from a "cannot do" attitude to a "can do" attitude. The second part of that verse in Ephesians says, "But only what is helpful for building others up according to their needs, that it will benefit those who listen". If we get this right for ourselves, we can also use our speech to encourage others to do likewise.

Before setting out on my journey across the Channel I needed to engage a pilot and boat to accompany me.

A good pilot is worth his weight in Gold, he plots the course needed to take me across the Channel and takes into account the currents and weather, and he matches the course carefully with my stroke rate and knows whereabouts he wants me to end my swim. I also need a boat which is reliable, it has shelter against the weather and a galley to prepare my food for the journey I also needed to have an observer to watch my progress. The boat holds the crew which is not unlike the church. You see a church is not the structure but the people, just like the boat crew they will encourage you during your swim in life's oceans, and they will feed you on God's word. Keeping close to the boat or in this case the church will help you from getting lost amongst the waves of life. I would never dream of going without a boat and taking my own course, I would probably end up going round in circles and it is impossible to see the opposite land fall from the water but those on the boat have a good view ahead. The church has been around for centuries and has a clear vision of life and where it needs to go. We need to be in church and be fed the word of God constantly. If when I am swimming the Channel and I get tired or get into trouble the crew are able to throw a life line. The church threw me a life line when I first became a Christian, my life took on new meaning. I was changed for ever and God was right beside me every stroke of the way.

I engaged an observer to be on my boat, Channel swimming regulations require me to have an observer.

The observer is there to ensure I had the right kind of costume and that I didn't use buoyancy aids. He also checked what grease I used and if I took any medication that was not permitted under the associations rules. My observer was also very encouraging and just at the right times came out on deck to encourage me just as my courage was leaving me. The observer makes us accountable for our actions. The church acts as our observer who watches over our progress, the church helps us to stay accountable to one and other and encourage us on our way.

I had to choose a pilot who was skilled and knew the Channel well enough to get me across.

There are many pilots to choose from but when I was arranging my swim I considered very carefully which to choose as I needed him to lead me safely. In life there are many pilots to choose from. If we look at Jesus being our pilot, then we have chosen well, he has been in this world and knows pain and suffering because he experienced pain and suffering himself on the cross and there can be no other pilot like him. He knows the course of our lives; he knows at what pace we are going and adjusts the speed accordingly to keep pace with us. Some of us are slower than others and some are faster but no matter what your pace Jesus knows just where you are. Don't let money, fame or career become your pilot and lead you through life, on our own we get lost in the ocean of life.

If you want to know more on how to become a Christian remember to find a good church, or attend an 'Alpha' or 'Just looking' course available near where you live.